The New Politics of Experience
and
The Bitter Herbs

Theodor Itten & Ron Roberts

PCCS Books
Monmouth

First published 2014

PCCS BOOKS Ltd
Wyastone Business Park
Wyastone Leys
Monmouth
NP25 3SR
UK
Tel +44 (0)1600 891 509
www.pccs-books.co.uk

The New Politics of Experience and The Bitter Herbs

A CIP catalogue record for this book is available from the British Library

ISBN 978 1 906254 74 2

Cover designed in the UK by Old Dog Graphics
Cover art: Comet (2005) by Tom Cramer is taken from his body of work entitled *The
Politics of Experience*. The collection was inspired by the artist's rereading of literature
from the 1960s, taking its name from R.D. Laing's book published in 1967. To find out
more about Tom Cramer visit http://tomcramer-art.info

Typeset in the UK by Raven Books
Printed in the UK by 4edge, Hockley, Essex

There is no passion to be found by playing small – in settling for a life that is less than the one you are capable of living.
Nelson Mandela

When the people are not awed by authority,
then great authority is attained.
Their homes are not small to them,
their livelihood not tiresome.
Just because they do not tire of it,
it is not tiresome to them.
Chuang Tzu

For Evelyne (TI)
and
Merry, Wandia, Subi and Marina (RR)

The Authors

Ron Roberts is a Senior Lecturer in Psychology, Criminology and Sociology at Kingston University, London. He has also held posts at the Institute of Psychiatry, University of Westminster, King's College Medical School, University College London, St Bartholomew's Medical School and the Tavistock Institute. He was introduced to psychology by a friend via Richard Gregory's ground-breaking book, *Eye and Brain: The psychology of seeing*, a bit of psychoanalysis and R.D. Laing. Laing made a great impression and kept him interested in the human side of the discipline through a tortured three years of a psychology degree that treated people as little more than machines. After graduation he continued to seek out alternative voices and views from 'the other side' – ones omitted from official accounts of 'reality'. Eventually he had the good fortune to do a PhD on Dreams at Leicester with Kevin Howells. Various post-doctoral jobs followed which brought him into contact with the radical end of science – joining the British Society for Social Responsibility in Science (BSSRS) and writing for, and editing, their magazine *Science for People*. He has also researched in the field of public health/epidemiology, chiefly on social class differences in health. This is his fifth book. He edited *Just War: Psychology and terrorism* (2007) and is the author of *Real to Reel: Psychiatry at the cinema* (2011), both from PCCS Books.

Theodor Itten is a psychotherapist (UKCP) and clinical psychologist (MBPsS) in private practice. He was an apprentice of psychoanalyst R.D. Laing and a student of social anthropologist Francis Huxley. Between 1972 and 1981 he studied Social Science, Psychology, Anthropology and Philosophy in the UK (Middlesex University and City University) and trained in psychoanalytical psychotherapy with the Philadelphia Association, London. He is a past President of the Swiss Psychotherapeutic Association and presently Executive Editor of the *International Journal of Psychotherapy*. He is co-editor of *R.D. Laing: 50 years since* The Divided Self (PCCS Books, 2012) and author of *RAGE: Managing an explosive emotion* (Trans. Ruth Martin, Libri Publishing, 2011), *Jähzorn* (2007) and *Jack Lee Rosenberg* (2002). He currently lives in Hamburg and St. Gallen. Visit his website at http://www.ittentheodor.ch.

Contents

Preface

Modern academic and experimental psychology is to a large extent a science dealing with alienated man, studied by alienated investigators with alienated and alienating methods.

(Fromm, 1973: 69)

I always thought that psychology goes on in the writing. So one of the questions I used to ask myself was how do you write psychology? Well, you must write it so that it touches the soul, or it's not psychology. It has to have that moving quality of experience, and that means it has to have many sorts of metaphors and absurdities and things that go with life. Otherwise you're writing an academic or a scientific description of something but it's no longer psychology.

(Hillman, in Hillman & Shamdasani, 2013: 200)

Experiences are subjective facts. They bind us to the earth and give us a presence amidst the whirlwinds of fate, in which we are all, in one way or another, psychologically complicit. A lot of what is done in the name of psychotherapy and psychology nowadays is driven by motives which are base, shallow and commercial. Theorising the human condition too often follows the ideological fashions of the day which can so easily be described in an age of 'terror' as biological/corporate fundamentalism. This toxic mixture not only bewitches the general public but also makes epistemological (and increasingly commercial) slaves of professional psychologists.

By common consent psychology is still a young science. One of the presumed characteristics of any science is that new knowledge eventually replaces old, that previous errors of fact and reasoning give way to advances in wisdom, method and agreed fact. Psychology, however, unlike the traditional sciences of physics, chemistry and biology, has failed to develop in this way, since it will never be a natural science. Like economics, its partner in crime in pseudo science, psychology has continued to 'ignore empirical evidence that contradicts mainstream theories in favour of "overly technical nonsense"'[1] and has studiously neglected the insights of past thinkers who have reflected on the human condition. Addicted to the use of quantitative methods and technologies capable of visualising activity in the brain, psychologists have hoped that recourse to these methods will somehow cover up the prevailing bankruptcy of ideas and enhance its reputation as a bona fide science. Despite the interest in consciousness as the great unsolved mystery there is hardly a move to learn from those who have given considered attention to the nature of human experience. As Fromm (1973: 82) argues, Marx attacked 'the prevalent opinion that consciousness is the ultimate datum and the quality of all psychic life'. Marx's view, that consciousness is the product of a social life tied to a particular system of socio-economic relations, has gained increasing credence among critical social psychologists but remains utterly ignored by the majority who cling to the desiccated fruits of positivism. The pretence that psychology is just like any other natural science can only be maintained by repressing knowledge such as this.

In this book we explore how this state of affairs – the covert politicisation of experience and selling knowledge to the highest bidder – has arisen, how it continues unabated, and in whose interests it does so. One of its consequences is that the very voice we employ to articulate our understanding of the human condition, whether in the midst of the therapeutic encounter, reflecting on the therapeutic encounter or theorising it, has become infected with psychology's hunger for status, power and control all masked by an ill-judged pretence of neutrality and objectivity. This has made the relationship between the practical and academic sides of psychology deeply problematic. Rarely, if at all, do they speak to one another in a common and human frame of reference and rarely is this problem even acknowledged. For all clinical psychology's aspirations to produce scientific practitioners, the audiences for psychotherapeutic and academic discourse remain largely distinct. The approach we have chosen to take in unravelling this is analytic, historical, personal and experiential. In our attempt to bridge this gap we seek to return to a fresh and new *Politics of Experience*. This must begin we believe from our own experiences – both in the lived worlds we inhabit and in our respective professional domains of psychotherapeutic and academic practice. One of our purposes here is to bring not only these two distinct discourses together but to conjoin our professional lives to our personal ones. From there we can move out on a practical and theoretical journey which privileges experience. Herein lies the hope that psychology may one day be free of the alienation that has bedevilled it. From this personal (and interpersonal) bedrock, informed by our fieldwork we examine movements to empower people in the mental health and education systems, looking at the cultivation of resilience, intellectual and emotional self-defence. What is it that helps people, in and out of psychotherapy, to help themselves and marshal a continuous practice of awareness and wellbeing? At the same time we continually reflect on the wellbeing and health of our own professions. What is the promise of a thorough and ruthless re-visioning of psychotherapy and psychology in our day and age?

So what exactly are you about to read? In the opening chapters, we reflect on our own origins and visions and the fundamental assumptions which have driven the disciplines of psychology and psychotherapy. From our respective existential and professional origins each of us brings a set of experiences, ideas and visions to be coupled with (or decoupled from) the professional traditions in which we operate. Thus we come to examine how apprenticeship training and self-experiential exercises inform the stances taken in professional work and presence. As persons engaged in professions we both enjoy and cherish, we ask how the personal inspires our professional habits and vice versa. Starting from the position that experience is the basis of any theory, we look to expose the core experiences, practices and assumptions which inform the variety of our approaches as psychologists and psychotherapists. By looking at what we actually do and have done we are concerned to provide an in-depth picture of how reflexivity actually operates in practice as opposed to a sanitised academic presentation of it. This necessarily entails that we must speak with (at least) two voices and on occasion different styles and idioms. This is unavoidable as we traverse the multiple gaps between theory, method, practice and experience. As we dance between description and analysis, experience and reflection, the levels of harmony and disharmony between practice and theory will move in and out of play. Sometimes the traumas of life lead us to speak with what sounds like different voices, embodying different plans, life histories and goals. Such multiplicity is not always a 'bad' thing. Unlike a lot of what passes for psychology, we do not wish to lie, fabricate, or mislead. What you will presently find in these pages is what we honestly believe and know is there. It is a conversation between us as much as with you the reader. Laing was never able to satisfactorily resolve the question of how psychological practice and theory could remain fully human and avoid depersonalising, alienating or mystifying its subject. This book is our attempt to see how much further we can push the argument. Throughout this, the subject matter is and will always remain the human 'us'.

In the centre of the book we turn to Laing's work. A specific area in which the fruits of Marx's insights were applied to psychological life was Laing and Esterson's studies of family life. First of all we examine its relevance for understanding forms of social and collective memory. This calls attention to the intergenerational passage of a wider social form of memory in which our collective behavioural past is recalled, relived and re-presented from one generation to the next. Bringing psychoanalytic insight to historical legacy, this chapter lays bare the nature of our fragmented subjective reality in the early twenty-first century. We continue by reflecting on Laing and Esterson's masterly study of thirteen women in the midst of psychiatric and familial mayhem (they initially studied over one hundred families and presented these selections). This chapter provides a critical reading of the dynamics of female power revealed in the original study.

'Therapeutic compassion' is based on Theodor Itten's experiences discussing the role of intuition and science in psychotherapy informed by the unfinished work of R.D. Laing and over thirty years of the author's professional experience. In this exploration deeper issues of the 'Self and Others' are illuminated. Chapter 8 'The politics of memory: Field notes from an urban anthropologist' is a collection of strange tales compiled by Ron Roberts from the urban academic jungle. Spanning murder, corruption, politics and thought control in the ivory towers, these stories reveal not just how truth can be stranger than fiction but why 'fiction' as such has an essential place in understanding the facts of our lives, how it has come to constitute an inseparable part of the real. It is a reminder to our readers that countless stories from our lived real lives find outlets in our professional productions, and we would hope consciously so.

Formerly envisaged as a book with Laing, 'The politics of truth in psychotherapy' is now the title of Chapter 9, where Theodor Itten reflects on the curative and emancipatory aspects of psychotherapy as the two sides of any truth in the process and praxis of healing. The aim here is to extend Laing's work on the politics of the family, synthesising research knowledge on the science and experience of psychotherapy and in so doing to cultivate yet further variations on the ever-present problematic of how professional stories address the lives of others.[2]

As befitting the one of us who is engaged in a university, Chapter 10, 'Psychology: Individuals, morality and ideology' is a thorough critique of the politics and limits of methodological individualism in psychology. We are not the first to have misgivings about the elevation of the individual to semi-divine status in our discipline. Thropp (2009), for example, presents a provocative research study on North American culture which she feels is dominated by the language of psychotherapy and a colonial commitment to hyper-individualism, in which psychotherapy and its language game are being employed as panaceas for social problems. The battle between the personal and social in psychology and its relationship to state interests forms the heart of this chapter.

In bringing our insights together in Chapter 11, we resume with an overview of 'The new politics of experience'. Here we ask a series of searching questions about the nature of psychological and psychotherapeutic practice. If we have advanced so far in our understanding of the human condition shouldn't we all be getting well by now? How does contemporary work by professionals match with the experience of patients and mental health service users? What explains the continuous need of professionals to create new approaches and fresh techniques and does this reflect an inner critique of one's own professional competencies? The present trend for diverse movements in empowerment, resilience and wellbeing for both patients and professionals are critically examined. Here we treat subjective experience as evidence based and reflect on just what has been learnt.

We present this book as a cordial challenge to our colleagues in the therapy rooms and ivory towers, to come clean and participate in rejuvenating what is, and continues to be, a search for truth – both in formal knowledge and the nature of human experience. This search is, in our view, a journey which takes us both inside and outside the workings of our selves. Some have called this path 'soul-making', others 'calling and listening to the shade system' (our elders' notion of the unconscious and the collective unconscious). We call this the 'New politics of experience' – a taboo-free journey, as much as that is possible, into the professional, personal and collective unconscious by way of contrast to the regular diet of nonsense, clothed in academic jargon, which behavioural science journals spew out in the interests of the late-super-capitalist monster. Psychology and psychotherapy are two independent yet related human sciences. It appears, to us at least, that the 'psy' professions, as they garner ever greater public adoration and corporate support, have become entangled in a net of smug self-satisfaction. This is a dangerous moment for us all. Our clarion call here is to disturb that equilibrium – to disturb, unsettle, educate, inform and perhaps also to annoy – in order to create a fresh voice on our experience in the world. This is an adventure to visit unexplored professional territory and return to the lost subject of the soul. Where academic angels fear to tread, novelists have created a world from and for our emotions. We invite you to join the 'resistance movement against the destruction of love in social reality' (P. Tillich, cited in Fromm, 2011: 59).

Your thoughts and reflections are very welcome.

Theodor Itten and Ron Roberts
St Gallen & London
New Year's Day 2014

Endnotes

1. Adam Posen head of the Peterson Institute, a Washington-based think tank (cited in Inman, 2013).

2. See Hillman (1998) for a discussion of the case story as a means of creating healing fictions.

Acknowledgements

Ron

Without the ongoing support of my great and best friend Merry, I probably would never have made a go of it in this profession. She is everything a friend should be – encouraging, supportive, critical and honest – as well as being a tireless campaigner for justice. I consider myself incredibly fortunate to know her. Likewise her daughters Wandia and Subira have made a huge positive difference to my life. They have taught me much and are a great joy. Chris Hewer, Ana Nikcevic and Anthony Esgate have also given me many necessary laughs and contributed to my survival in the Kafkaesque world of contemporary higher education. An honorary mention must also go to Alice Comi for her contribution to 'Academics Anonymous' and for reminding me how important it is that we academics are treated well. I would also like to appreciate all the mavericks – both intellectual and non-intellectual I have encountered, either in person or in writing, over the years – who have communicated to me in any shape or form that it is OK to be different. Finally I would like to give thanks to my friend Marina, a lovely soul, who has brightened up, without measure, the last days of finishing this book.

Theodor

My first and deepest thank you goes to Evelyne Gottwalz-Itten, my beloved wife, for her love, her tremendous inspiration, dedication and encouragement, as well as insights, emotional and intellectual support. My heartfelt gratitude goes to my long-time friends, who often lend me their ears, critical thoughts, endless encouragement as well as their wisdom of the heart. Their insights into my profession of the healing arts and our various practices to live and sustain an authentic, good and wise life have been very important and invaluable to me: Michael Albers, Deirdre Bair, Klaus Beeler, Brian Evans, Hans Feurer, Ada Holl, Francis Huxley, Jürg Gassmann, the late Hazel Nash, Kurt Roth, Urs Ruckstuhl, Bernhard Schär, Rupert Sheldrake,

Peter Schulthess, Rolf Vetterli, Birgit Voss and Karin Wallenczus. For their inexplicable good humour, lively, loving and thoroughly modern minds, a very warm thank you to my adult sons, Dimitrij, Anatol and Raphael.

We Two

A big thank you to our editorial peer reviewers – Merry Cross in London, and Thomas Redl in Vienna, who read our manuscript with great care and made important suggestions for improving the text. Our thanks go to Paul Jarvis, the managing director of Libri Publishing, who wished this book from us, after publishing Theodor's *Rage* in 2011. He kindly allowed us to stroll on to a more psychologically oriented publishing house. Lastly we greatly appreciate the unbridled enthusiasm of Heather Allan at PCCS Books – a bit of a star. We thank her and the rest of the team at PCCS Books in particular Kate Morris and Sandy Green for not only seeing our manuscript through to a fine book but for maintaining and nurturing a truly radical spirit in our discipline. In the present age of intellectual as well as financial austerity that is no mean achievement.

Part One
Experience

truthfully, forcefully and taking issue with power must be part of the new politics of daily experience.

None of this can be accomplished with ease. We all know from personal experience how frightful living can be, especially when the feeling is one of losing your bearings and any sense of control over your emotional life and habits. To be delivered into a hopeless, even at times helpless, predicament – where we are at the mercy of others is an inevitable and unenviable part of life. These moments can be resisted, fought, endured or absorbed. Not always, but usually one survives. This is worth remembering. Faith in one's survival and self-belief are important strategies to fortify one's resilience. Nietzsche famously believed that one was psychologically strengthened by adversity – a belief with some empirical support (Li & Fung, 2013; Seery, 2011; Seery et al., 2013), though it is perhaps equally true, as *The Joker* in Christopher Nolan's (2008) *The Dark Knight* maintained, that whatever doesn't kill you also makes you stranger, and the less support one has from astute others, the stranger it will make you. To deal with life well, other people are essential. These are not some optional 'extra' to be factored into a psychology of resistance however. The history of one's relations with others, for good or ill, effective or counterproductive, are carried around with us – we are in actuality the history of our relationships with others. How a singular person responds to adversity is always a matter of social psychology. The issues are relational in their origins and also how they are responded to.

Following any road to the Kafkaesque Castle of our dreams means that one will tread a path laden with pot holes, as well as oft paved with lies – banana skins masked as definitive scientific, holy or national truths. These depend on us for their power – our own unquestioning belief in both the inherent goodness of those who wield power and their right to guide us, aided and abetted by our continuing projections, no doubt of childhood origin, that their actions are forevermore laced with benign intent. Thus we hypnotise ourselves and permit them to hypnotise us – to believe that everything will get better, that no other group of people is better than us, that nothing we do to challenge them is good enough, that God is on our side, and that more research and analysis are always needed – an eternal, meaningless mantra. No wonder sections of the populace, insufficiently hexed, don't trust a word of it – witness the refusal of many parents (in the UK at least) to have their children receive the MMR (measles, mumps and rubella) vaccination – even when what is said (in this case the safety of the vaccination) is true. Despite the soothing lexis of the proselytisers of the word and statistics, not all science is equal – some is, as Orwell might have proclaimed had he been acquainted with the politics of science, more equal than others.

The possibility that 'our' institutions may drive people to distraction and at worst to psychological breakdown – institutionally induced insanity let us call it – is virtually a taboo, seldom, if at all, admitted by professionals. 'Stress at work' is the nearest we come to discussing it – but even there, where it is barely acknowledged, it is seen as a failure of coping on the part of the luckless individual. Institutions waging war against citizens, and doing so with impunity, has a long history. The celebrated respondent acts of cursing, noted in the writings of Kafka, Philip K. Dick, and other novelists and poets, testify to the works of frightened people. The fright of those who woke up first is further testament as to why we must learn to conquer it. Kafka (1976) showed us, did he not, the disconcerting realism of the Castle's metaphoric door. In his novel *The Trial* (1914–15) the doorkeeper refuses sternly to open the door for K – a door we learn which has been specially made for K to be kept closed. Just as K is never given the key to the door, the key to the story is itself uncertain. Kafka depicts the bureaucratic nightmare we are now all painfully familiar with – not least the disabled people of the UK deemed too ill or disabled to work by one organ of the state and not 'ill' enough to avoid work by another and thereby robbed of welfare support.[5] We stand collectively, like K, before the doorkeeper. Collectively we appear to have lost the plot as well as the key to resolve it. The stranglehold of the all encompassing bureaucracies which run through the governance of virtually every activity whereby a human being must interact with an institution now resembles an authorless story. Are we aware we are trapped? Are we trapped? If we are, is there a way out? If we aren't, are we trapped into thinking there is? How can we escape whether we are trapped or not? Laing, in *Knots*, had this to say:

> some are of the opinion that there is no gate
> that is their opinion
> there is no way of knowing except to go
> through it. (Laing, 1970: 86)

Generation after generation in our particular field of psychology and psychotherapy feel there is a way out from the impasse of *this* stultified existence, are prepared to dance with their hopes and fears. They feel a pull towards the door and leaning towards it encounter an army of self-styled gurus and prophets circling about their wisdom, their madness and their folly, who claim to have actually stolen the key, which is now safely entombed, they say, in their pockets of theory and esoteric knowledge. Shamans and tricksters alike make a tidy living feeding and soothing our longings – to see beyond the door, past the refractive surfaces of appearance and grasp head-on the real.

What do we discover behind the mask of the Darwinian riddle of nature? Is it not the smiling face of authority? In the West we all now 'know', having been suitably educated in the pedagogical laboratories of capitalism, how dynastic traditions all over the globe, driven by a hidden natural impulse, have moved, and as we speak are moving still, inexorably slowly in some cases, to a future, modernised, enlightened political paradise. We call this end point after the Greek model – democracy. This, we are told, is the highest expression of humanity's collective calling – to vote, buy, sell and exchange in bliss. Our coming into the world sees us cast into the free-market void; home is a trans-generational residency situated amongst a primary collective of mostly mother, father, siblings, family, tribe, and clan. We experience authority as parents, teachers (from primary school up and onwards to university), doctors and then politicians with the might of the police and military at their fingertips. It is the 'big other' of power – the amoral core at the heart of our civilisation. In psychology the sole permitted reference to this reality occurs under the lamentable guise of measurable attitudes. Heaven forbid we should ever act on them, should they depart too many standard deviations from the mean of normality – the zone of quiescence. The power of authority is based on emptiness, a glossy shopfront, backed up by uniforms, privileges and threats which produces a transference in which we donate to others the right to define what is the case, what is done, in whose name it is done, when and how; all this, in the service of what? Duty? Fashion? Tradition? Repressed fear?

Given this, who is prepared to follow the vanity of prearranged sanctioned truth or to rebel against it? The megalomaniacal drive, situated all around us, is global, a geopolitical system of considerable operational complexity but strategic simplicity. The aim is to maintain and entrench power. The means to ensure this are brute force and the controlled obliteration of the truth via advertising, public relations and subservient intellectual con artists. The powerful profess always to know what is best for us, and we must happily collude in the lie that they do – which naturally enough requires us to pay no attention to the amalgam of theoretical and empirical cover-ups of what is really going on. Psychology, like psychiatry has an ignoble history and cast of characters – the hoards who have taken their degrees and signed on to be handmaidens of the security-military-industrial complex – whether with the Stasi in the former German Democratic Republic (DDR), the Behavioral Science Consultation Teams serving the US invaders in Iraq or the legions of psychologists helping employers to screw the last ounce of juice out of employees. None of this features in the standard curriculum, the purpose of which now is to prepare students for a word of compliant work rather than to think independently and challenge the structural violence and abundant nonsense which surrounds them. That is to be made invisible – easily done when the universities of today are staffed to the brim with those who have already lost the will to see, let alone to think.

The possibilities of belonging, of being secure, of being good enough and a worthy self-agent embedded in a caring community, to eat and drink, digest, rest, sleep and shelter, with warmed body and soul, are the basic needs of our species. Over millennia we have constructed grand human settlements, cultivated language, generated grand stories of our origins and purposes – myths to instil in us the hope and belief that in a frightening and unpredictable world there is at least someone, sometime, and someplace who knows where the key lays hidden, can tell us what is going on. The realisation that death eventually claims all of us – that all things that rise, in time also fade, strikes terror into the average Western man or woman. This is no accident. We are supposed to believe like Voltaire's Doctor Pangloss that *this* is the best of all possible worlds, that there are no other truths greater than the one truth – that there is no alternative to capitalism. Ergo all manner of institutions and organisations must promulgate systematic lies. Our professions play a pivotal role in this. In psychology the gap between the theoretical maps of human beings and the maps we use of ourselves in our daily encounters grows ever wider. Many who service the structural deluge of misinformation usually do so with little or no conscious, explicit awareness of the functional role they occupy. Many however also do, and nurture private unease at their seeming inability to do anything but comply and concoct further alienation. Then there are those who have been granted the privilege of seeing through the game of mystification, confusion and conflict. The question for all of us, no matter which category we belong to, or think we belong to, is what do we do next? How do we step across the bridge from our own alienation? We must also pose the selfsame questions to you, the reader.

We two belong to the post war (World War Two) generation of the early 1950s – probably in the Western world the most fortunate time in human history. Like many of our contemporaries we felt called upon to open the doors of perception in the twin decades of the 1960s and 1970s – doors framed by the humanist passions of the time, the speed of jazz, the jazz of speed, the rolling waves of lust that swim perennially over the stones of desire. This, in the dawn of space travel, the moon landings, the Vietnam War, the civil rights movement, Timothy Leary, the Beatles, the professed era of peace and love and the grand phantasy of purity and fulfillment. Here we are. We aimed to become who we were and are, more or less. We have danced to the literary tunes of Hesse, Marcuse, Mao, Nietzsche, de Beauvoir, Sartre, Sagan and more. Many a theoretician, politician, religious seer and anarchistic jester have laid out their traps. Who is to say who fell into what? After all is said and done, the bifurcation of reality into a dance between self and other is the gentle price we seem to pay to live on earth amidst a life of riddles.

Research has given rise to competing claims about what works and does not work in the applied fields of psychology – clinical, health, educational, occupational and counselling – and psychotherapy. These claims are rooted in basic assumptions which together have come to comprise the centre of orientation – the common sense of the discipline for one generation after another. One of our self-appointed tasks in these pages is to take issue with a range of these. Centres of orientation are important to consider – they are usually the bedrock of one's belief system and the last part of it to remain when challenged. In Moscovici's theory of social representations (Moscovici & Duveen, 2000) – formulated to provide a social psychology of common sense – theorists have come to distinguish between core and peripheral elements of representations in order to explain the stability (or lack of stability) of certain beliefs (Abric, 1994). The centre of orientation in a person considered disturbed is what we mean by their madness. What is ours? As we assess the boundary and limits of civilisation, as it presents itself to us, in these strange European days, we are often shocked by its thinness; the 'normality', of racism, religious fundamentalism, disregard for the young, deference to royalty and political despots – and a range of other deadly sins are all too apparent in our everyday living – but more so to the people ostracised to the margins by our normality. Like ancient barbarians, we can still witness stigmatisation, intimidation, ostracism, torture, and drudgery to stir up anxiety and frighten folks to toe the line as defined and proclaimed by the lawmakers of the land we happen to live in. How do you feel about this daily parade of others' discomfort? Do you find the pretext for it flimsy? How disturbing is it exactly? If human psychology is not an attempt at speaking truthfully from at least one person to another what is it? How does this reality imprint itself in us in our theorising – official and unofficial, about the world and the other? How does it structure our grammar of living? How is all this etched into the recesses of our mind, to forge the unconscious 'design' that is to be found and deconstructed from the self-forgetful works of artists and scientists?

The immense energy and publicationary zeal of our fellow psychologists and psychotherapists is beyond our individual ability to keep up with. We would like to be informed, to know the latest operational definitions in psychology, the relevant findings and criticisms pertinent to joy and suffering. Sometimes it seems to us that the enterprise is so flimsy that its entire point may be simply to keep us busy, to avoid a fundamental critique of what is going on around us while conveniently destabilising the centres of social awareness in the population at large – to give them a psychologised simulacrum of reality. As young students we had to learn a new language, wherein we developed an odd form of rhetoric possessed of an illusionary analytic precision, forcing us to step outside of the ordinary simplicity of language, and leading one more into darkness than insightful light. Having conquered the supposed intelligentsia this language is now making its way out into the broader social sphere. The presumptions, assumptions, hypotheses and theories have given rise to a verbosity and jargon, which serve to keep the masses at bay rather than serve the enchantment of the soul. We see these present undercurrents of our dear science as a protective reaction by its agents, to cope with the complexities of a natural and social world which they find fearful. They offer no viable blueprint for action. Do we not need to pause, before we attempt to digest any more of this indigestible stuff?

'The universe is not only queerer than we suppose, but queerer than we *can* suppose' (Haldane, 1927/1977: 286). This quote of J.B.S. Haldane warrants reflection. It perhaps ought to be the starting point for any study of the human organism. Mindful of what he sees as a crisis in the profession, Jerome Kagan (2012: 339) reflected, 'if more psychologists recite this quote as mantras after their morning coffee, they might archive some of the deep insights that they, their mentors, and their mentors' mentors have sought for a very long time'. As an elder, now free from the shackles of university alliance, he can now admit that in our field, experience is the core. 'I noted that personal interpretations of *experience* are as basic in psychological theory as cells are in biology' (ibid: 336). So we must return to experience. That is what we wish for and for this book to provide some food for thought along the way and for the reader to note that it is not just the universe that is queerer than we can imagine – so too is the discipline of psychology.

So what do we offer? Naturally we wish you to be free from conditioned preconceptions and to find your own perspective in this fragile divinatory endeavour called psychology. We invite you to suspend judgement for now on your existing view of whatever is the best way to 'do' psychology. In this book we explore the influences and traditions of psychotherapy and psychology that we have grown up with (and out of) and critically assess the present state of affairs in the art of human science. Our approach, in keeping with our stress on the primacy of experience, is to anchor this critique within the personal, historical and sociocultural contexts we happen to have lived through. The aim of this book is to make visible from the inside of our profession, what it means to practise what we know and believe in as well as to elaborate in detail the interplay of practice with theory growing out of everyday experience. As will become apparent if it isn't already so, to be authentic in a profession professing to be concerned with honesty and truth, but so appallingly permeated with hypocrisy, is far from easy and is not without risk. This is our first pass through the malaise gripping our disciplines. Now we must for a short while turn back to us – to trace through our own experience how we came to arrive at this point. Biography and autobiography are both vital and neglected research tools in fathoming not only the human heart and mind but the state of the 'psy' professions.[6] So the following chapter in which we lay out some details from our own lives forms an essential part of the psycho-logic by which we have developed and brought our thoughts to the present moment.

Endnotes

1. See Rose and Rose (2001) for an expansion of this argument.

2. See http://en.wikipedia.org/wiki/History_of_statistics. Last accessed 28 April 2014.

3. Buddhist practitioners speak of pre-conceptual experience. One of the products of 'successful' meditation practice is to distinguish this from the distorted picture of reality we get when habitually relying on our customary cognitive habits of perception (see Hagen, 1999, 2012).

4. Kurt Lewin first developed a field theory of psychology in the 1940s. It remains undeveloped and largely abandoned (see Deutsch, 1968).

5. See Cross (2013) for a more complete rundown of *The Trial* inflicted on disabled people by the UK government. 'One need not consider everything true', Kafka's priest intones, 'one must only consider it necessary' (Kafka, 1946: 264). The current treatment of disabled people (and others) is not necessary but sadly true.

6. See Parker (2013) for further evidence of this.

Chapter 2

Where do we come from? Origins and visions

> Something undifferentiated was born before heaven and earth;
> still and silent, standing alone and unchanging,
> going through cycles unending,
> able to be mother to the world. I do not know its name;
> I label it the Way.
>
> (Verse 25: *The Essential Tao*)

Theodor Itten

Das Unbewusste, Sigmund Freud's (1915/1972) essay on *The Unconscious,* was the first of his works I took it upon myself to read. There is only one chance to make a first impression. *The Unconscious* was confusingly important. I didn't get it. The wording was to me, then just 19 years old, as strange as Chinese. This was my first psychology book. The next was to be *Memory, Dreams, Reflections* by C.G. Jung (1965)[1] which I began reading upon arriving in London in the autumn of 1972. I did not know that this Swiss depth psychologist and psychiatrist had lived in Bern until I left there for London, where I was to live, study and do my nine-year apprenticeship in psychotherapy. Still, in Bern I had had my one and only consultation with a Freudian psychoanalyst. So how was it that I came to enter the field of psychology, depth psychology and psychotherapy, and not, for example, become as R.D. Laing once remarked 'a meta-peasant'? There is of course, more than one way to tell a tale, so the present one should be considered as a limited edition rather than a unique rendition.

Presently I am remembering a recurring childhood dream of mine, around the age of five or six. At that time I was living with my two older sisters (a surviving twin of eight years – her co-twin having been burned to death at seven days from a leak in a hot water bottle during a freezing January in Honyen – and her sister eleven months older than me), as a so-called missionary orphan, on the land of my grandmother, Flückiger land. With the party was also Martin, her second youngest son of eight children, of which my mother, Rosmarie (1923–2001) was the eldest. On the wall over the corner dinner table, where one could see the river Aare, hung a picture – rather high up for me then – of my uncle Theodor Scheurer, who passed away in 1946, as a 17-year-old teacher training student. He was called 'Teddy', and so was I, like the teddy bear I played with in my arms.

In the dream, from which I would wake up screaming, was a snake[2] which was following me everywhere, just a few centimetres behind my left heel. She quietly snapped at me, always, thanks to the *mise-en-scène* of dream production, not quite biting the running me. Waking to a dimly lit sibling shared bedroom, my granny would sit down on the edge of the bed, stroke my dark blonde hair and hum a soothing tune. Only years later did I begin to know, trust and appreciate the animals[3] in me. They are often faster and more intuitive than my conscious reasoning. She, Rosalie (1893–1971) was in her time a midwife, practising her skills in Sin Fung and Honyen in the provincial area of Guangdong, together with my grandfather Hans Scheurer (1883–1946), who was a Basle missionary to the Hakka[4] – he married Rosalie Flückiger in Hong Kong in 1921. Both of them later published short stories and books about their experience in China, aiming above all to bring the word of the gospel to these Asians.[5] In 1928 they returned with their family of eight (two daughters and six sons) to Aarau, Switzerland. My mother, five years old at that time, being a Chinese-speaking Swiss, found herself located in a psycho geographic field which was alien and linguistically strange to her. She would eventually leave for China again in 1947, to meet up with her 27-year-old fiancé, Ernst Itten (1920). In those days, as was usual among missionary task groups, this was an arranged marriage, with a loving cover story (at least for some time for us children). In January 1948, like her mother before her, she married in Hong Kong. So much for starters then!

When Mao Zedong (1893–1976) came to power in 1949, all missionaries had to leave the Chinese mainland and, if they wished to, move to Hong Kong, then a protectorate of Great Britain. So my future parents settled there, together with Ruth (1949–88) and Verena (05.01.1949–13.01.1949) for another two years, before taking a sabbatical in the spring of 1951. My mother was then already pregnant with her third daughter, Ursula, born in April 1951. Two months later, I was conceived and called Theodor, after my mother's deceased brother.

I remember one particular story that went as follows: my granny Scheurer-Flückiger was quite angry at her daughter for being so broody (she herself had five children in five years!). Anyhow, clever as my mother was, she scored two points at once with the Greek name 'theos-doros', for one, it is literally a gift of God and two, here you have a substitute child for your lost one. After living together with my parents and two sisters in a wee hamlet called Weissenried – white reedy marsh – near the small city of Langenthal (where I was born on the 5 March 1952) we started visiting our granny in Wangen a.A, about 15 km to the north, in her new cottage, on the land of her and thus our ancestors. One of her brothers was labouring on the farm and became a close confidante, since she had lost her husband six years previously from an infectious illness. Little did I know of my parents' intention to return to Hong Kong. My father went back to the University of Bern, doing a master's degree in theology, while my mother, who, like three of her brothers, was a school teacher, helped out on one of the hamlet's three farms, to bolster the student family's income. But then, suddenly, I was to experience my first wrench from paradise. Somehow half-consciously I was aware that we had changed our location. In hindsight somewhat luckily I ended up in a village where there was quite a sustaining extended Flückiger family scene, running three farms, spread on different edges around this village with about 500 inhabitants, mostly peasants, artisans and shop keepers. We moved there in late 1955. We three young children were to be left behind while our parents went to London from January to August 1956, staying at the Foreign Mission Club at 20–26 Aberdeen Park in Highbury. For a few months they came back, only to leave in the dead of night for Hong Kong on Christmas Eve 1956. I just could not believe it. It was a tragic and dramatic turn of events for my soul.

How long, I would ask my Granny during the following Christmases, till they return? Well, she would whisper under her tears, sitting with us three, all wet eyes, on the floor beside the candlelit tree, in four years, then in three years and so on, all totally beyond my comprehension of time. They would be gone for longer than I had already lived. Thus, in felt reality I became a missionary orphan. When my parents returned in June 1961, my sister and I, accompanied by Granny, were the welcome party to strangers, who only lived within me as 'internal parents'. The early bond was torn five years previously.[6] Maybe this was one of the factors which propelled me on an inward journey. Paul Brunton (1898–1981) born in London as Raphael Hurst, lost his mother too in early childhood. He became an esoteric philosopher and author of mystical books. Two of his books were on my bedside table, in easy reach for a 17-year-old to read last thing at night. *Der Weg nach Innen* and *Entdecke Dich Selbst*.[7] This melange of Hindu-Buddhist yoga thinking helped to wean me just a wee bit from the luring Judeo-Christian milieu I happened to find myself in.

As was usual at that time, children of Basel Missionaries, when born in Switzerland, neither joined their parents, nor were brought back on sabbatical, because it was considered they could encumber their parents' duty and be a nuisance in absorbing their attention, which was given to spread the word of 'our Saviour, Jeschu'. The Basel Mission ran their own children's homes. Lucky for us three, there were not three places in one home. So the plan was to place Ruth, she being the oldest, in Basel, and the other two in Hasliberg, in the Bernese Alps. My granny put her foot down and said 'no way!' What then? She took it upon herself to look after us, grandmotherly mother that she was, all assembled round her table in the new cottage. We lived there till my parents came back for yet another planned one-year rest in Europe during 1961–2. Then they wanted to go off again leaving us where we were, and taking with them the daughter born in Hong Kong in 1958, and the *in utero* brother-to-be in 1962. They did not reckon with us, through our spokesperson, 12-year-old Ruth. We were absolutely adamant. Either/Or[8] – we all go to Hong Kong or we all stay in Switzerland. Once I discovered that my granny, like my grandfather, who had died six years before I came into the world, had written a book and a series of short stories about China, I developed the inner courage to bring feelings and thoughts, experience and dreams onto paper.

The first time I visited Hong Kong was in the mid-1990s (1995–6). I was the last of our family to do that. Don't ask me why, maybe it was because of my outsider status, the black sheep position which I shared with my sister Ursula. With heavy hearts my parents decided to move into a vicarage eight miles south of our then home. There I grew into an angry, rebellious, often seriously sad young man. At that time, before leaving comprehensive school, I would have been ever so happy to have had the opportunity to talk with a psychotherapist, who would walk alongside me, on the edge of the threshold between home and school. Now I have been doing that for thirty years. I lived in my two families – the elder children were one, and the younger children and their (our) parents were one, in Herzogenbuchsee, 30 minutes to the east of Bern, the city where my great-grandfather, great-grandmother and the rest of my father's (the Itten) family lived. Eight years later, after reading books by Karl May (1842–1912), Franz Kafka (1883–1924) and Hermann Hesse (1877–1961), to oil my puberty, I had an additional linguistic repertoire to bring to my inner fire and rage;[9] to be followed by various poets like Wolfgang Borchert (1921–47), von Droste-Hülshoff (1797–1848) and Else Lasker-Schüler (1869–1945) with their romantic dreams; there came the time for the book of Max Frisch (1911–91) and my absolute favourite playwright, Friedrich Dürrenmatt (1921–90). Only thereafter, egged on by my long-time friend Kurt Roth (1953) (and Iris Bieri (1954), my then girlfriend), did I finally pick up Freud.

The cover of *Das Unbewusste* was held in a deep blue with white lettering. Magic! The first essay I had to put down after a few pages, because the language with its depth psychological concepts gave me the creeps. I allowed myself to hop to essays like: *Beiträge zur Psychologie des Liebeslebens; Warum Krieg?; Die Zukunft einer Illusion*; ending with *Das Unbehagen in der Kultur*.[10] The next psychoanalytic book I held in my hand, in London during the spring of 1972, was Charles Rycroft's *A Critical Dictionary of Psychoanalysis* (1972) – a slender Penguin edition. It was in there that I read the name of R.D. Laing for the first time, fully unaware of what was to come.

Coming to London meant to get into a new language, and to be in the place where my parents were when they first left me behind. I was doing a kind of catching up, albeit unconsciously at that time. After three months of language school in Forest Hill, south of the Thames, I moved north to Crouch End, where I would remain for about the next eight years. Being in a placement as a youth worker for a whole year with the Swiss Churches in London (exploiting the old parents' network) my work was in Eglise Suisse, 79 Endell Street, WC2 and John Southworth Youth Centre down by Victoria Station. There I began to meet not only young Swiss language students and au pairs, but also lots of young West Indians, who partly used the Centre as their youth centre. The whole team of priests, pastors and youth workers met in a fortnightly sensitivity group at Vera von der Heydt's Kensington consulting room. When I first met her she was 74 years old. Having read Bertrand Russell's *Why I Am Not a Christian*

(1967) and Søren Kierkegaard's *Practice in Christianity*[11] I so much hoped to get away from religion, and now I was walking into a depth psychology founded by another son of a preacher.

In the beginning, being in therapy was like a confessional. As Vera von der Heydt was like a grandmother, I was hoping she would soon die, taking my inner secrets and reports of bad behaviour with her. We would meet however through the years, after I stopped seeing her as an analyst, maintaining a friendship, corresponding, and even introducing my three sons to her on our last meeting in London in 1994. In her talk on 'A Session with Jung' she shared her profound experience, as Jung brought her back into her body and into her senses.

> Sensation is my superior function, but for years I had attempted to replace it by thinking. I did not want to see or hear or taste, nor be aware of the senses in any another way, but Jung, so I felt, had accepted the language of my senses and of my body; he had taken my hurt, my wounds seriously and helped me dwell on them and to recognise them as belonging to my life and to my totality. And my mystical experience he had given supreme value by not discussing it. I felt healed in the deepest sense of the word; for the first time I really understood that healing is a process that is a constant transformation when one is sufficiently awake to remember all parts of one's being. (Heydt, 1983: 24)[12]

She encouraged me to study social and abnormal psychology (as clinical psychology was then still called) and to trust my free and natural way of feeling. She herself grew into analytical psychology, going to Edinburgh, where she learnt on the job in the Davidson Clinic, which brought Tavistock-style family therapy to the community. Her master was Winifred Rushforth (1885–1983) with her radical approach to psychotherapy (Rushforth, 1981, 1984). Heydt has been in love and analysis with John Layard (1891–1974) then in Oxford, who treated her with consideration and generosity; we will meet both of them in later chapters. They are important background influences in the way I practise as a psychologist and psychotherapist. Rushforth invited Laing a few times for talks in her clinic and Layard was for a time in the late 1960s in therapy with Laing. Vera taught me to listen to the inner world, to flirt with the sense emanating from the dream world, and to recognise the healing which came from total acceptance of my own individuation. She quoted Jung: 'Sie müssen es ihnen vormachen. You have to show them what it is about' (Heydt, 1988: 6). By trusting her as my soul's guide, I came to trust myself. Freud himself once said

> ... we cultivate between ourselves what we feel is decent
> and genuine ... we are certainly involved in something to do with
> suffering, and suffering, allowing experience to happen. The
> metaphor there for me is the Heart ...
> ... we do our best within the limits of what is allowable or
> permissible. And we live then with the belief that if man gets away
> with the crucifixion, the resurrection is out of our control. (Laing,
> 1975: 1–22)

Our everyday reality in the here and now is often helped along by our imagination. When dream images are seen through, rather than merely looked at and mirrored, the ideal becomes real. We humans are a bundle of habits and peculiarities that have come together without the aid of a central organising force. Structural anthropology has been pondering this issue of the habit of a true and a false self for quite a while. If we are in our true selves, are we actually mentally healthier? Yes. We can choose if we want to, but don't have to, as we are always on both sides of our animal nature. On the one side, we are highly developed and cultivated primates. On the other side, the human beings that we became have developed the ability to reflect on the culture of our own nature. 'Suppose', said Laing (1977), 'you do not want to be jolted out of it, but believe that this is something you want to go through. Who will *allow* you to go through it? Where will you be allowed to plumb the depth of your agony, despair, bewilderment, confusion, perplexity, until new beginning dawns?' Where indeed?

With Laing and within the PA, there were folks who would listen to me, who respected me, took me seriously, and understood my weird experiences, language and gestures. I found human warmth, camaraderie, tolerance, forbearance, a refreshing and new consistency in bonding to my emerging vulnerable true self. Remember the dictum: 'To do good and to do no harm'[22] (Hippocrates of Kos, 460–370 BCE), to see no injury was done to the patient in the name of his or her treatment. A very important principle, if we want our places of support for other people to be experienced as asylums. I lived in a therapeutic household, the Archway Community, part of the Philadelphia Association London, from autumn 1976 to the summer of 1977. The houses I lived in were 27 Shaftsbury Road, and 132 Tollington Park Road, North London. In February 1981, four years after leaving the households, I graduated, and I was elected an Associate member of the PA in the spring of 1981. Ronnie Laing and

I remained friends until his early death, at the age of 61. Presently I am 61 years old and still an ordinary Member of the PA.

Ron Roberts

Properly speaking, I suppose, my psychology career properly began with a copy of *The Divided Self*, lent to me by my friend Merry while I was studying for my A-levels. Supplemented by other reading – Gregory's (1997) *Eye and Brain* and an introduction to Freud, I was hooked – this was what I wanted to study. My parents were not best pleased, I think they had harboured hopes I was going to opt for medicine – perish the thought – and the possibility of me undertaking systematic enquiry into the depths of the mind never really sat easily with my mum's Catholic beliefs. My interest in the problems of existence and consciousness however had surfaced some years earlier. Even before I had left junior school I was absolutely fascinated by the sheer fact of existence and its accompanying mystery of conscious awareness. I remember staring at the end of my index finger and wondering at what point it ended and the rest of the world began.

In those days I looked to the night sky to try and find answers. The dark depths of space called out to me to find my place here. After two years of saving from my pocket money I had my first telescope through which new stars were revealed, the planets brought a little closer and my enchantment with the night sky magnified along with everything else. In retrospect I have considered how, along with its intrinsic majesty and inexplicability the heavens offered a refuge from things nearer to Earth. By this I mean the other great conundrum in my life – the madness, wildness, volatility and violence which surrounded me. I was born in Liverpool in Mill Road Hospital,[23] the very same one where John Lennon made his entry into the world. My first five years were spent in Speke Road in Garston, the ground floor flat a stone's throw from a pub adorned with the smiling face of the Laughing Cavalier. I recall that there wasn't too much laughter there and by the time I was five the family had moved several miles just outside the city boundaries to Kirkby, a new industrial area built to house the burgeoning population of Liverpool – then around three-quarters of a million. I had two brothers, Russ and Mike, both of whom had experienced something of a Catholic education before the move. The Catholic Church in its own way exerted a profound effect on my life – not to mention the lives of others. When we got to Kirkby lyrical about the beauty of computers I put pen to paper about the merits of *The Divided Self*. It did not seem to be appreciated.

I was one of 14 students there studying psychology as a science, which meant, besides additional study of zoology, chemistry and physiology as subsidiary subjects, that we were not permitted to sit the university exams in philosophical issues or clinical psychology – the two areas of the discipline in which I was (and still am) most interested. This ludicrous elevation of 'scientific' psychology above all else is alas still with us. Sheffield psychology department was peopled by all manner of oddballs, as I suppose any psychology department is, but the students sensed, correctly in my opinion, that there was something not quite right there. The members of staff were also, with few exceptions, cold. When my dad died midway through my second year, I was told on my return simply to catch up with the work (three weeks) that I had missed, no commiserations or expressions of sympathy. I mulled my way through the year somewhat in a state of shock. It was also a course which was intellectually narrow-minded, everything was to be cognitivised or reduced to biology. My areas of interest were dismissed by the staff. On occasion I was told what mark I would receive for a piece of work before I had even submitted it in an attempt, no doubt, to dissuade me from doing something in which they were not interested. What they were not interested in, but which I was, encompassed animal behaviour, philosophical issues in mental health and parapsychology.

I survived the boring rigours of computational models of everything at Sheffield and moved to London in the autumn of 1978 to study for an MSc in human communication at Guy's Hospital Medical School, then of the University of London. Here, academically speaking, I landed on my feet. Not only did I meet another student, a Scottish guy Harry, who was an avid fan of Laing, but the lecturing staff were altogether more geared to a humanistic approach. I encountered Fay Fransella who introduced me to the delights of Kelly's (1955) Personal Construct Theory (PCT). Fay would go on to supervise and assess my dissertation, detailing a personal construct approach to dreams which was my entry ticket to later doctoral study. At the time I was immersed in reading a variety of stuff on language, including Chomsky. I attended Jean Aitchison's course on transformational grammar which was a joy, but was also exploring Freud – doing a careful reading of *The Interpretation of Dreams* which I found riveting. With Fay enlightening us to the subtlety and depth of PCT, the idea to put all this together came to me in a dream. In this I was standing by the seaside at night, watching a multitude of stars fall from the sky. I awoke with the idea that all these stars represented various aspects of the self, all of which were involved in knitting together the products of one's night-time thoughts. I sketched out the ideas on a blue airmail envelope I had to hand – and my thesis on the personal construction of dreams was born.

Being at Guy's also meant one was privy to events in the medical school. Laing was invited to speak there in 1978, I think. I went with Merry and we both sat entranced by the anecdotes and tales which Laing passed on to the small but packed-out lecture theatre. Clearly and surprisingly to me, he appeared to be quite ill at ease in the midst of an audience. I saw him speak once again at a much larger venue (the Middlesex Medical School perhaps?) in the company of an altogether more hostile group of medics about the inhumanities of the medical approach to childbirth. Anyway, my dissertation secured a distinction and led to a first published article (Roberts, 1981). This stood me in good stead when I came to apply for PhD study, but this too was tinged with a hint of good fortune. I hadn't initially thought of doing further research and when wondering what to do after my Masters, had applied for a post with the mass communications department at Leicester. As luck would have it, the application form they sent me was a general one with provision on it to apply for doctoral research. I bit the bullet and decide to do this. I was invited down to Leicester where I was interviewed by Kevin Howells. Kevin, a friend to this day and someone who appreciates a different take on things, saw something in me and offered me the funded SERC[24] place. Leicester was a great psychology department, full of friendly characters, a model academic institution I continue to remember fondly. The head of department, Professor Wladek Sluckin, a Polish Jew, was a reserved but dignified man, who took an interest in what all the postgrad students were doing and let the place run itself. No doubt he would turn in his grave if he could see what has happened to academic life. I confess to being the author of a rumour, aided and abetted by Kevin, that Wladek was a devotee of the martial arts and would practise kung fu routines in the department in the evening, once all the students had gone home.

A few years later I was out in the world with a PhD on dreaming under my belt. I've always considered it pleasantly interesting how my initial fascination with science and astronomy, cultivated by endless hours of stargazing, led me to a PhD study which involved investigation of the other great mystery of the night – the conscious (and unconscious) secrets of the mind as revealed in dreams. Similarly the work I now do on social and collective memory I also think has echoes with the other great enigma of space, that of time. So in a way I see significant parts of my intellectual life have been dealing with the psychological counterparts to the key dimensions of physics. But in that I am probably far from alone, though the connections to it may not be typical.

Completion of the doctorate however was not before I had to endure a bruising viva with Melissa Greene [not her real name], then in the inner sanctum of construct theorists, whom I had considered would be sympathetic. Having ditched construct theory halfway through the thesis though, she wasn't. Her view enunciated with clenched teethed hostility was that science was about sticking to one theoretical perspective even if that perspective didn't work. I thought reality should take precedence, she begged to differ, a view I personally still find ridiculous. I was forced to rewrite. I consider the original version, which I no longer have, to be the better piece of work. Despite her reputation as a humanistic and good-natured 'radical' psychologist, I found her to be something of a bully and in my eyes the encounter between us that day owed much to the legacies, structures and parameters of the English class system. She had the tightly controlled diction of the English upper middle class and, I thought, was used to getting her own way. She admitted that I had defended the thesis well but still insisted on a rewrite. If I think back to the three-hour grilling I received, what stands out is a curious period where she proceeded to ask me the identical question (something about Freud's approach to dreams) three times in succession – each time as if she hadn't heard a word of the preceding thoughts I had offered. It was a strange afternoon. Feeling very discouraged I didn't bother to do the rewrite for another six months or so and owe some thanks to Graham Beaumont at Leicester – he of the double brain fame (Dimond & Beaumont, 1974) – for easing my way through the university bureaucracy. The experience with Greene reverberated with a host of earlier experiences from school, in which not truth but conformity and obeisance to authority were seen as paramount. The lesson was understood if not well taken.

The best of my teachers have provided me with a model for how to conduct myself. Paul Hope, my biology teacher for A-levels and Johnny Day, my maths teacher who would regale us all with tales of how he had taught two of the Beatles in his days at the Liverpool Institute, were wonderful examples of how to instruct while appreciating the individuality and creativity necessary to be brought to the deepest learning. Kevin was another example and so was Stan Newman who taught us statistics at Guy's. Stan taught from the position that anyone could master statistics no matter what their fears were as long as they put the effort in. Perseverance through potential adversity was essential. I learnt a lot from these people. From those various teachers, lecturers and colleagues I have come across who sought only to impose their will through sanctions and threats, coupled with a complete absence of respect and lack of confidence in oneself, I learned only how to avoid their example and how to stand up to them.

I also perhaps owe something to a teacher, a Mrs Leamond I think her name was, an Asian teacher I had in my primary school when I was about nine. 'Do not send this boy out to work', she told my proud mum, 'Ronnie must go to university.' For my mum, who had left school at 12 because of the war, this really was quite something, not least because nobody else in the neighbourhood that we knew of had ever gone to university. Mrs Leamond also bequeathed another important lesson. She had posed a question to the class one day and I had given the wrong answer. Rather than ignoring it or passing on she made a point of saying what a very good guess she thought I'd made. I don't know whether that made a big difference or not – but I suspect it did, as I've generally never been afraid to be wrong and have always enjoyed debating as a rapid means to check out one's thinking on something and if necessary correct it. Being afraid of being wrong never occurs to me. It is an attitude I try to encourage in others. Furthermore, whatever her faults were, my mother was adamant about one thing, and I thank her to this day for it. 'Always stick up for yourself son', she said. I've done my best to adhere to her advice. My later fieldwork notes (see Chapter 8) contain more variations on this theme.

In the next chapter we will write about how we deal with our work, which encompasses the complexities inherent in the world, and carried from the weight of our own experience. Experience cannot be simplified, and as practitioners we do not simplify it but it is there to be used to hold the horses of the theories which guide us into the world. What we do of course has some bearing on what we think – and similarly of course what we think stands in some relation to what we do. The next two chapters therefore occupy a pivotal place in contextualising the mutual interplay of thought and practice. Each is anchored in the other. As such it is a key part of the argument we are advancing in these pages. We believe there needs to be a whole lot more of this in the so-called behavioural sciences if we are to rescue them from the worst kinds of intellectual dishonesty. It is a truism that the entire history of this discipline cannot be fully understood without recourse to what the legions of contributors were doing when they weren't sat in front of a desk.[25]

Endnotes

1. *Erinnerungen Träume Gedanken* (1962) read in German, just before I was to meet a disciple of Jung's in London, in January 1973, who then became my first analyst, Baroness Vera von der Heydt (1899–1997).

2. James Hillman (1997a: 25ff) has a charming essay on dream animals, 'A Snake is not a Symbol'; where he points out that the snake is a step towards an explanation for the unconscious psyche – an animal of healing propensities.

3. Besides the snake, there are generally horses, tigers, centaurs, dogs, birds, bears, wolves and fish of all sizes, of both genders.

4. The Chinese characters for Hakka (客家) literally mean 'guest families'. The Hakka's ancestors were often said to have arrived centuries ago from what is today's central China and 1,000 years ago from northern China. In a series of migrations, the Hakkas moved, eventually settling in their present locations in southern China (Wikipedia).

5. Scheurer-Flückiger, R (1941, 1944) and Scheurer, H (1940, 1941, 1942).

6. *Are Mothers Really Necessary?* is the title of a book by Bob Mullan (1988) portraying John Bowlby, whose thesis concerned the importance of affectionate mothering, marked by secure attachments and few separations. Bowlby argued that these experiences of maternal (and paternal) care have long-lasting effects on the child's future self.

7. Brunton, P *The Secret Path* (1935/2011), *The Quest of the Overself* (1937/2009).

8. It was ten years later that I came to read Kierkegaard's book with this title.

9. Forty years on I was to publish *Jähzorn* (2007); translated as *Rage* (2011).

10. Respectively; *Contributions to the Psychology of Love; Why War?; The Future of an Illusion* and *Civilisation and Its Discontents*.

11. First published in 1850, Kjöbenhaven, under the pseudonym Anti-Climacus.

12. As Vera von Schwabach, she married, as a 19-year-old rich Hamburg

banker's daughter, Baron Eduard von der Heydt (1882–1964) also from a family of well-heeled bankers. The marriage was described as a 'scenery marriage', since Eduard was homophile and Vera felt neglected; it lasted till 1927 (Illner, 2013).

13. Alexander Newman founded and was first editor of *Winnicot Studies*. He created the *aide memoire* in publishing *Non-compliance in Winnicott's Words* (1995). Together with me and the philosopher Steven Gans, he was in our reading group in 1980–1981, which Ronnie Laing founded.

14. Segal, L (Ed.) (1983) *What Is to Be Done About the Family?* Laing told me that he met her for the first time after the book came out and she had a public discussion with him.

15. Brian Evans wrote up his IQ criticism, which he taught us at Enfield, in his book *IQ and Mental Testing: An unnatural science and its social history* (Evans & Waites, 1980). I am proud that he wrote a unique chapter on 'The impact of the ideas of RD Laing on UK psychology students' for my book on Laing (Evans, in Itten & Young, 2012). Brian Evans, upon reading my first drafted account of the Enfield years (email, 20 August 2013) helped to make this account accurate.

16. L Doyal and I Pennell (1979) helped to sharpen my thinking regarding mental health with a study on the political economy of health, as a growth market.

17. Bernard Burgoyne asked me in the lift going up to his seminar room a few weeks after entering Enfield College, if I had read Herbert Marcuse's *One Dimensional Man*. I said no, only Sarte in French. No no, he corrected ignorant me, he is German. Bernard eventually became professor of psychoanalysis at the Institute for Health and Social Science Research at Middlesex University, and published several books (1996, 2000, 2013).

18. Len Doyal and Roger Harris would finally write up what they taught us, in their introduction to the philosophy of the social sciences: *Empiricism, Explanation and Rationality* (Doyal & Harris, 1986).

19. Jeff Evans, after editing *Demystifying Social Statistics*, blended his work with emotional involvement in *Adults' Mathematical Thinking and Emotions* (Evans, J, 2000).

20. See Laing (1975) for further discussion of the Philadelphia Association.

21. Cohen (1977/2004) has charming and insightful interviews with the likes of Laing, Hudson, Broadbent, and of course Eysenck and Skinner.

22. *Of the Epidemics, Book I The Hippocratic Corpus*, translated by Francis Adams, (1994) MIT Classics Archive. Available at http://classics.mit.edu/Hippocrates/epidemics.html.

23. Some of the hospital's history is detailed here http://liverpoolremembrance.weebly.com/mill-road-hospital.html

24. Science and Engineering Research Council.

25. See also Cohen (1977).

Chapter 3

What do we do in psychotherapy?

> Humour is transcendent when it reflects the unwillingness of the individual to surrender to the impossible conditions of existence and attempts to achieve a measure of liberation from the social, political, economic, and even cosmic forces that remain beyond one's control.
>
> (Elliot Oring, 1992: 119)

I. Setting the scene

The experience of psychotherapy can be described in many colours and metaphors. One of them is to see it as a ritual of involvement, where we meet and contend with life's sadness through laughter and tears, and transform our troubling misery into common acquaintance with one's self. Our soul life, the state of mind (another word for humour) still carries the ancient echo of *psychein*, the Greek naming for our breath of life. As psychotherapists we are a *therapon*, an attendant companion, a potential aide to persons who might turn to us, the purported masters of soul healing through our co-presence in an idiosyncratic relationship. In a variety of discourses of happenings (present, future and past) which patients with a propensity for sentiment are likely to describe as melancholic disasters, we will bear witness to the steady expressive inner voice of experience. As a therapist of the psyche I practise basically the liberation of the breath of life in a human being. Some come to me and say, 'I am empty; I am nothing, in me there is nothing'. These statements can be heard when I ask a patient, after having taken a good few deep breaths, what she (or he) is feeling right now. Body awareness is a means of recognising one's embodied self and communicating it can be a vehicle for expressing tenderness and love to one's '*Self*'. Whatever shows up in the present is accepted as that emotion we recognise, illuminating the unknown – unconscious is located in the body, our direct bios – shared through breath. Psychology is the bringing to words, or into words, of what has been recognised in our inner world, our *interio intimo meo*, where there are no words. Mental health as a practice and journey is nourished from within this sphere.

By so many colleagues, often trained as psychiatrists, mental health is thought of as something to be administered from the outside – a way of thinking one acquires through dogmatic mechanistic theories. The language psychotherapists learn in various colleges of therapy and analysis, both the actual words and how they are used, are without exception prescribed from existing traditions and habits. As a matrix or comfort zone (of the interior) for us professionals, our adherence to school formality (just one of the modalities of theory and practice) functions as a comforting identity kit of established illusions. The liberating function of psychotherapy – the curative and the emancipative – has been recognised for a very long time, certainly longer than I have been in this craft, which by now is over forty years (I began as a patient in 1973).

Research using meta-analysis (Assay & Lambert, 1999; Lambert & Ogles, 2004) tells us that what helps in psychotherapy, in the sense of what 'factors' have an effect in 'treatment', includes the ability and style of the therapist to form a good enough and fitting healing relationship – this counts for about 30 per cent of the variability in outcome. The method and modality of intervention applied accounts for only 15 per cent of the variability, as do expectancy and placebo effects. However, by far the greatest contribution comes from the personal factor of those who seek therapeutic companionship. The so-called 'extra-therapeutic change', taking place in the life setting, for example, economic, relationship, etc., accounts for 40 per cent of outcome variability.

These subjective determinants are within the power and habitual practice of the persons who are our patients (some call them clients). Herein the politics of experience of psychotherapy concerns self-empowerment, resilience exposition (narrative or 'in vivo') and personal (rather than collective) recovery. In the end it is whatever suits us, whatever makes us comfortable in the mastery of a modality in psychotherapy, our technique and method play but a minor part in the proliferation of the intuitive style. In other words, the ability to technically master a musical instrument does not mean that one can truly *play* the music, it is as much the music which plays us – 'who tells the fingers what to do, not the other way round' (Brendel, 2002: 33).

There are always at least two (if not several) solutions and several truths to aid us, when, in the art of healing the soul, we seek a better feel in the world we happen to find ourselves in. Once in a while, even seasoned psychotherapists should ask themselves the question: 'In whose name do I practise? In whose light do I attend to others?' When Francis Huxley, who in his anthropology days had kept company with healers of all sorts – those who practise in the light of the jaguar, bear and love goddess to mention but a few – had posed this question at a grand gathering of psychologists and psychotherapists at the Ojai Foundation in California, he received some disquieting responses. 'In nobody's light' was one and 'in my own light' another. In relation to the first Huxley doubted that he would 'ask counsel from anyone who could say such a thing unless, perhaps, he were a devotee of Zen Buddhism' and regarding the second that if 'that were so I would rather be somewhere else' (Huxley, 1997: vii).

When we come to our limit as psychologists and psychotherapists, what then? Do we just do something in the name of a dogma (like the priests in days of old) or do I dare, as professional competent healer of the soul, allow myself to pause and consider the situation accordingly? What do we do when we don't know what to do? Consider the following:

Rule 1: Distrust all rules including this one.

Rule 2: Those who think they have found the one and only truth are out of touch with reality.

Rule 3: Allow yourself to approach the beginning of troubles from at least two sides, and discover where the two aspects in you meet.

Rule 4: Don't trespass on others and know what you will do and what you won't do before you do anything.

Rule 5: If you can't talk about your highest principle, then live and experience it.

Is the rule that there are no rules? More often than not, there is a confusion and mix up about the three major 'psy' players. They follow different systems of thought – different rules if you like. This need not be. Here are the simple distinctions: Psychology is concerned with *norma*. Counting, assessing, measuring and comparing 'normalities' in any given cultural, economic sociopolitical context. Psychiatry on the other hand is concerned with *nosos*. These are folks trained in basic medicine who acquire a sort of pseudo scientific and diagnostic view, by which she or he labels the phenomenon, which is defined (like *DSM-5*, American Psychiatric Association, 2013) as disturbing and experienced by this professional as dangerous to the soul. Psychotherapy is concerned with *pathos*. We attendants to the breath of life are companions walking along with those who come to us for this service, on their path of *metanoia*, one of change, transformation and conversion. Let me illustrate my position with a vignette. By listening to what the person who looks us up has to say, we get a hunch as to where the garden path in their life leads us too. 'It is the patient who controls what is happening, and the analyst who is a puny, weak figure. Patients go where the hell they please' (Malcolm, 1997: 72).

I, for one, will follow them on their path whether the garden is one of weeds or roses. This to me seems 'the way', a Tao of therapy.[1] On this journey I contemplate dreams and visions, the collective soul, unconscious, shade system,[2] the powers that be, holding both the patient and me in their sway. Then we need to speak up, to let the vision and pictures of our experience in soul making come into language. In terms of giving words to feelings, this is always an approximation only. Thirdly, I visit the other as the other, to see clearly with my own eyes, to view my seeing and to see my point of view as well as her or his, this through the haze of a social situation and existent gender inequality, to be free of transference and countertransference projections. The Chinese sign of Tao[3] represents this clearly: the sign of Tao contains two *schju*, representing feelers on the head, then a line down, the neck connecting the torso. *Dschhog* represents the foot with its various bones in movement. The sign thus represents a head which has received wisdom, knowing about a Way (of going about psychotherapy for example) through his footage. We walk our talk and talk what we walk. This authentic wisdom is a teaching by doing, which can only be passed on by 'being-one-Self-on-the-way' or perhaps by being Self-less. On the way it is tested, on the way it will reveal its proof. Insofar as this truth possesses, yes, contains within itself, a leading function: I am on my way. We are on our way. Everyone is familiar with the emblem of Taoism, the yin/yang, the dark spot in the light, and the light spot in the dark. Lao Tzu probably drew this for the first time in dust, while pausing to express the inexpressible to his companions. Maybe he just wanted to aid his thinking by drawing a model. Lao Tzu was on his way, on this earth sometime between 604–571 BCE. He is reputed to have authored the *Tao Te Ching*, a book about the sense and meaning of life.

One person who understood and lived the Tao of therapy, perhaps second to none, was C.G. Jung. A female patient who suffered from severe depression said of her consultations with him:

> I had nothing to say this day. I took my seat (in the library). He pulled his chair close to mine. I did not want to meet his eyes, so we both stared ahead at the books on the wall. I did not speak, so neither did he. Occasionally he reached out to stroke my arm or pat my hand. The hour passed and I became tranquil. I wish that peace would come with me when I leave, but it disappears without his presence. (Bair, 2003: 381)

In this case, her daughter had taken her own life, after her child had died in an accident at a young age. The daughter had laid all of the blame for her unhappiness in life on her mother. For several years, the patient sat with Jung like this in his library three times a week. Sometimes her gaze drifted away from the books and out of the window, to the waves dancing on Lake Zurich. Jung's presence as a psychotherapist was very effective. Without using many words, he was able to sense how her life experiences had led to her depression, and he succeeded in integrating this heavy darkness into the totality of her life through analysis and psychotherapy. One day, 'she told her diary that "a great cloud has lifted". She left Zürich and spent her remaining decade in prayer, fasting, and meditation; living in relative isolation in another part of the country, sending occasional greetings to tell Jung that she was well. Her friends remembered her as "beatific" and "at peace" until she died' (Bair, 2003: 381). This being in tune with one another in a harmonious dance of communal silence keeps the mind supple. Yet, 'There is no such a thing as silence. Something is always happening that makes a sound. No one can have an idea once he starts really listening' (Cage, 1973: 191).

As wounded healers, we orchestrate the psychotherapy score in and through our wounds. Though we have sought healing through our apprenticeship in the healing arts, be this in a training analysis or training therapy, the injuries to our soul can become a scar on the heart of experience. Our entire recovery is oriented in relation to it. This is a transformation which takes place in and through the unconscious. One of the richest accounts of such a journey where one is a servant to the curative powers of the soul is to be found in Marion Milner's account of an analysis, showing how, as therapists, we can let ourselves be used by the unconscious of the patient (Milner, 1988).

II. See me, hear me and recognise me

Two members of the Philadelphia Association training staff, John Heaton (1968) and Francis Huxley (1990) each wrote a book on *The Eye*. Laing himself was at pains to point out to us that a major part in his theory making was focused on the raw data of the phenomena (that which reveals itself). He tried to depict and then describe the relationship between people's experience (E) and their behaviour (B), and their experience of their behaviour. He commented; 'I want to convey how I see the interconnections between personal interactions and how different ways of seeing may generate different ways of acting and vice versa' (Laing, 1987a: 205). We psychotherapists usually say, 'I see patients'. As a psychotherapist I provide the patient with a freedom to be herself or himself and express their inner longings, fantasies, and wishes, to become who they are. One of the aims of therapy is to no longer be ashamed of who we are. Once I find out what the continuous, compulsive repetition of habits, schemas and patterns of behaviour and experiences wants to show me (the unconscious made conscious) I can become free of it only insofar as I am able to live my habits in a different way and at a different pace. In our idiosyncratic way we accompany patients for a part of their life's journey. Here is a brief reportage from such a stroll.

The young man, let's call him James, was born in 1981. A colleague of mine, who is a friend of his parents, called me up one evening. He described the following: A 21-year-old, first son of his friends, has entered a crisis of meaning after finishing his Matura (A-levels). At present he is not able to lend himself to a daily structure. His inner exhaustion and tiredness is so vast, nothing he does fits properly to the desired vision. This behaviour disturbs both parents, who called my colleague as their friend. Would I be willing to see this chap? OK, said I, he can come and see me in Sankt Gallen, if he so wishes.

For his first consultation he was accompanied by his father. He described the feeling of pressure emanating from his parents for him to achieve something. This produced in him an anxiety about failing which blocks him from doing anything at all. Together with his younger brother he grew up in an easy-going hippy commune.

Both his parents were born in 1955 coming of age in the mid-1970s when everything still seemed up for grabs. Obviously their life story and cultural situation is more complex and diverse than I am able to portray here. Yet, when I took his primary scenario I felt his tension between the 'laissez faire' climate which dominated his hippy growing-up time and the performance expectancy of modern times. Last summer James visited his father's sister in the Ticino,[4] where she conducted seminars on neo-shamanism. The suggestion came from his father who thought this might give him an opportunity for sense making. Now he comes to see me as a young man playing a 'shaman' in earnest, with his anarchistic light worldview, sporting a Rasta hairdo.

In the following few sessions we talk about the other world and shamanic trips to it. It is like travelling without moving. A few days later his aunt calls me up full of concerns. I ask her to please tell me what she teaches with regard to rituals in her seminars. Often I am a wee bit annoyed when it comes to shaman 'light' training, the while knowing how strenuous it is, in traditional shamanic tribes, to become a healer and seer in a profound cosmological sense.

Depending on the continent and ethnicity, the myths and related rituals, songs, herbs and paraphernalia are extraordinarily complex. The apprenticeship, initiation and learning by heart are a long-time affair. My teacher in social anthropology, Francis Huxley, has demanded of his students that they read in depth of what can be learned about this tradition of healers, who are partly our ancestors in healing arts. In his first book, *Affable Savages: An anthropologist among the Urubu Indians of Brazil* (Huxley, 1956), he wrote about ancient shamanic healing traditions. He returned to this subject in 2001, publishing a further collection on the path to knowledge of healing, sorcery, conjuring and tricking, in Shamans through time (Narby & Huxley, 2004). Shamans have practices to be in two worlds simultaneously – the real world and the true world, as their world hypothesis is usually called. They believe what they know and know what they believe.

My patient's firm belief that he has become a shaman overnight is seen by his family as a 'psychotic episode'. We define psychosis as behaviour and experience of a person which cannot be easily placed in our own world of experience. It can also be seen as a denial of reality by paradox. We know it is a lie, yet accept it as an impossible proposition on another logic plane, that of the absurd. This young man would like to train as a clown, magician and pantomime artist and thus his identification by using a shamanic outfit makes sense within his field of intentions. He would like with immediacy to be what he aspires to be, thus he constructs a readymade identity. This is a contemporary, self-made fashionable mode of childhood bluff.

I play along (enter the game) and ask him to lie down on my futon (my Zen version of a Freudian couch); take ten deep breaths in his upper chest and feel the ground holding him, like Mother Earth; concentrate on breathing in and out, being content with what enters and what leaves his lungs; be rooted within. He describes his feelings as a sense of being home. Resting, grounded on the futon, he then tells me stories from his family and friends and his dreams and visions, which he interprets, presenting his insights accordingly as he moves through his narrative. The true self he is looking for is a somatic experience. In his psychotherapy with me he is given enough visionary and actual space for him to transform his life in a way that is a positive and liberating experience. For some of us, for some of the time, the knowledge that as adults, we can do what we want, however we want to do it, is most frightening. His own mind required movement and breath. In our physical selves, breath fills and invigorates our chest cavity, and with it our minds. Following his breath, paying attention to his gestures – the unconscious also (but not only) communicates through our bodies – I listen attentively during our conversations to the content and the melody of what he says. I recommend to him that he lays out a boundary, a breathing space, around him with stones which I keep ready in a container for this purpose. The stones mark out his space. Where in his body does he perceive that the distance he has marked with the stones is correct? Most of us have an inner and outer tolerance. The issue of proximity and distance is one that can be experienced and discussed with this simple exercise.

What we are currently experiencing resonates back to our earliest experience of closeness and the point at which closeness becomes inundation; of distance and the point where distance starts to feel like abandonment. This can be noticed afresh in the here and now. This is a steady practice of 'giving in to lying down'. As expressions of our vitality, all emotions are everyday occurrences and therefore 'normal'. In our bodies, emotions take the form, intensity, modulation and function that 'they' want. We are always in the particular mood that we need at that moment. This is what happens when we trust in our selves. Here, we listen to our inner voice. Valuing our emotions in the way they deserve allows us to develop self-esteem. 'What does your inner voice have to say? What do you perceive?' We go from one emotion to another, and to the images which present themselves to him as we go along, playing it by ear. Deep breathing has a supportive effect: bending my legs, feet a shoulder-width apart, breathing deeply and fully into the upper chest (the 'sympathicus' of the autonomous nervous system). Everything else is as relaxed as possible. When I breathe out, I relax my lower jaw, push into the ground with my whole foot from the heel to the tips of my toes; my pelvis tilts when I am grounded like this. When I breathe in it swings back; when I breathe out, it comes forward and up. We usually practise this form of deep breathing ten times. Then a pause, and three or four normal breaths – letting the breath come and go – to see what has changed in the body. My eyes are closed. I 'look' into myself and take notice of what's going on.

My body is the boat of my existence in this world. With this exercise we make it easier to access the core of our being. There we sense where the false self covers the true self like a thin membrane. The false self feigns to protect the true self, but through the years as we grow older, makes the true self more and more into its prisoner. I live in a golden cage – the door is open, but I can't fly out into life. It is necessary to sense this. Here we turn our misery over, like a farmer turns his hay, until it's dry. Then it is brought home. Now, we can touch the wound or the anguish and at the same time grasp it in an adult resourceful way. Thus a momentary regression is made possible, with the transitory reality that accompanies and empowers it.

Being 'good enough' as a therapist means conveying a maternal message to the patient: 'I see you, I hear you, I get you, by paying attention to you'. The young child (or the patient) is able to draw on his inner world, creating what Winnicott termed the 'transitional space', a realm – transitional reality – that bridges the gap between inner world and external reality. Being good enough, being with and not doing for the patient, is a difficult art. Once I've mastered it – it can take up to ten years – it is no longer artificial, that is, directly informed by learned techniques, sentences of psychotherapy school dogma and identification with one's master psychotherapist. The patient, in this 'supportive' presence of me as psychotherapist, can have a corrective, healing experience. This offers a new way of living. To experience being able to live differently – this is something which takes a while to become a new habit. An old habit is driven out only by a new habit. Through practising these psychotherapy exercises (experience is practice), one gains the insight that change is possible. Changing your own beliefs is only possible through the somatic experience of a discipline. Psychotherapy is just one among many.[5] Only when we can take a path that will lead us to a new way of living, one that we have actively chosen, can we give up the comfort of the false selves (being a Shaman, in James' case) which have protected us and ensured our survival. This requires courage in our own truth and the desire for mental health. Once a course of psychotherapy is over, a person is responsible for using her or his own practices to keep up this newly found integrity. This requires a discipline to sustain integration.

Autumn comes and James passes his entry exam to the renowned school for clowns. This knowledge of results relieves him greatly. He has thus given himself a new perspective. In total we see each other for 14 sessions in the first year. The themes we follow take in the need for admiration, to be seen and heard, as well as the libido and other vitality in his body which aim outwards towards expression. James practises lots of 'kung fu'. Spring comes and goes. In June 2004 his father joins us for a session. For two weeks his parents observe once again a 'psychotic episode'. I organise, in agreement with James and his parents, a first visit and then entry to the therapeutic community setting 'Soteria Bern'. After a while I hear from his father that he was thrown out of Soteria for hitting a female psychiatrist. James then went to live in the psychiatric clinic Waldau, Bern. I pay him a visit there (a three-hour journey) and we take a stroll in the ancient clinic's compound. 'I have given up the clown school', he tells me. 'Ah well, you do as you please', I reply, 'but why did you hit the woman psychiatrist?' 'I wanted to know how she would react', was his reply. 'Now you know', said I.

After his release from the Waldau, he desired to come back into psychotherapy with me. It is September by now and he describes how his relationship with his brother has developed positively, that he has visited his new girlfriend in the Valais and feels lots of vitality within himself. We continue to do mainly integrative body psychotherapy. Opening himself up he experiences his being newly in love with another woman as motivation to express his emotions in a truthful and trusting way. In the spring of 2005 James has a dream, where he meets his last year's self with dreadlocks on a flat roof. 'My second I' he calls this. He has gained a freedom to look at himself from a higher vantage point. I refrained from interpretation in terms of the 'true-' and 'false-self' systems. Undoubtedly, James' true self emerges there while his false self, generally seen as a soul's self-healing response to wounding in childhood, recedes.

He stops further psychotherapy, as he moves into the Alps until August, to work as a shepherd and enjoy the new sights on the horizon. Upon coming down into the valley he will begin a traineeship in a special needs pedagogy family. In the last session we speak about his psychotic episodes and how sometimes the new feelings dry up in his well of emotions. This can be one of the effects of psychopharmacologic treatment which his female psychiatrist has ordered him to follow. He takes Prozac, an antidepressant and at the same time, so as not to get too high, Zyprexa, a neuroleptic mixed in with Temesta (a benzodiazepine tranquilliser) to bring him down. Not surprisingly, as a result of this chemical sandwich James feels himself always a bit tired, not quite in the here and now.

By March 2006 he is back and I give him a copy of Peter Lehmann's (2002) book *Coming Off Psychiatric Drugs*. His father gives James' psychiatrist a copy of this book as a present. I usually keep a few copies of this book in my practice, in order to lend them out as guides to successfully reducing and coming off drugs. A month later he is free of medication, works and has a daily routine including a siesta. Together with his parents we review the so-far 43 psychotherapy sessions, spanning three years. His sense of self-worth and self-esteem is good enough; he has a new relationship with a woman whom he initially met in Soteria Bern. Off he goes on a planned journey to Italy. Then back to Switzerland, to earn more money to enable him to travel to Scandinavia. Farewell then with his joyful self-realisation as a 25-year-old adult.

A year later (2007) his father writes to me with good news: 'James is now in a good space after a six-month traineeship. He is being creative [his father is a goldsmith, his mother a painter]. For a month he has been living in a steady relationship with a girlfriend. After the summer break James will begin to study Pedagogy at Basle University. We are very relieved, that he has found a new perspective.' In autumn 2008 James visits me in my practice for tea and a chat. He is in the fourth semester at University and is doing well. This was the last time I would see him.

In 2011 he sends me his Master's thesis based on his experience in psychiatric institutions. In spring 2013, his father gives me a call out of the blue, asking me to suggest a few colleagues of mine in Basle. James' lady friend is pregnant and he is taken over by depressive mood. The next communication I get, in August, is an invitation to attend James' funeral service. He has said his final farewell, and I am reminded once again how an emphatic resonance between two people often cannot alleviate all childhood sorrow, rage and despair. In the innermost regions of the soul and psychic life there will always remain a field of the unknown. In *Suicide and the Soul*, James Hillman (1997b) cautions us fellow therapists that despite the insights gained through diligent psychoanalysis or analytical psychology, the wish of a person to go to an early death, as a phantasy of the self to realise the unconscious healing urge to hasten to Samsara (or Heaven or Valhalla, whatever this imagined state after death is likely to be called) and say farewell to the mystery of the lived, remains a possibility. Human life is lived, like the cosmos too, so much in the darkness of sleep and unconsciousness.

> The closed vessel is the receptacle for the transcendent, impersonal force of the psyche which produces the healing. This healing is prepared behind the curtain in the swings. ... This therapeutic drama is one long mythological epic in which the Gods and the patient and the analyst take part. (Hillman, 1997b: 178–9)

Was James afraid to be the father he became? Had his shunning a new life's responsibility driven him slightly crazy? Was he afraid to hold his own child in his arms while the child within did not recognise his adult? The final curtain went down on his *Sturm und Drang* period. My joint negotiations with James, to find his rightful path in this life, accepting thereby the facts of his life, trusting his inner voice and letting it be heard, are now stripped of their honours. The archaic and anarchistic self James embodied has cast rage and despair onto the principle of indecidability,[6] that which points towards the civilised humanity of our domesticated and still-wild instinctual animal nature and further helps me to make use of the distinction between the true and the real world. The 'real' personal and social world we live in is, and remains, impermanent and finite. In truth, in this silence, the fire of my sadness turns to acceptance of this final act of James' living.

III. Approaches and concepts

Body psychotherapy

The basic concepts used in my therapeutic style, which I used with James, were as follows: In integrative body psychotherapy (IBP) as well as psychoanalytical psychotherapy, I follow a holistic approach, taking body, self and soul as inseparable aspects of our being human.

It focuses on the somatic, emotional, social, and spiritual energetic experience, and the way these are expressed in the therapeutic (and other forms of) relationship. IBP is an eclectic approach to reducing and alleviating mental suffering. Jack Lee Rosenberg and his team of therapists in Los Angeles developed this method over a number of years between 1973–96 (Rosenberg, Rand & Asay, 1985; Rosenberg & Kitaen-Morse, 1996). Rosenberg brought together and integrated the most effective elements of independent British forms of psychoanalysis,[7] Gestalt therapy, Reichian psychotherapy, cognitive behavioural therapy (CBT), and various humanistic psychotherapy processes (Itten, 2002; Itten & Fisher, 2002). Combining these various psychological and psychotherapeutic experiential methods and theories, which legitimate them, enriches and simplifies my daily practice as a psychotherapist. In IBP we consider the following seven areas, which are always present in every psychotherapeutic encounter and situation.

1.   *The present, boundaries and inner support.* The aspects of being embodied through being in the present moment, boundaries and inner support (emotional containment) help me to sense my embodiment. How do I perceive my boundaries? As a patient I can make myself conscious of these through laying down a boundary. I thus give myself enough breathing space. I respect my boundaries and those of others. How can I keep emotions, impulses, tensions inside myself? How present am I in the meeting with the therapist? Questions that must be clarified each time we meet afresh.

2.   *What are the current everyday occurrences and troubling situations in my own life?* Which worries, behaviour patterns, and difficulties I have experienced (old family movie) and emotional issues determine my current way of coping with day-to-day life? To what extent can variations on a constantly repeated theme (repetition compulsion) be recognised? The basic fault issue also has to be dealt with.[8] The fault in the base of our being is that our human and our animal natures lie in close proximity, and flow into each other. There is no escaping this existential tightrope. In Balint's words:

> In geology and in crystallography the word fault is used to describe a sudden irregularity in the overall structure, an

irregularity which in normal circumstances might lie hidden but, if strains and stress occur, may lead to a break. (Balint, 1968: 32-3)

The basic fault could be called, more playfully, the 'paradise complex'. Each and every soul is cracked in the process of becoming human, being incarnated.

3. *The issue of transference and countertransference is taken into account.* By this we mean the therapeutic relationship between patient and therapist. What each party brings to, and projects onto, the therapeutic relationship will be looked at, discussed and resolved. It's about having a discourse and a clarity over what happens in psychotherapy. At the same time it is a metalog (a talk about our talking) to the therapeutic relationship as a relationship of practice. In a course of psychotherapy I am encouraged to try out new forms of relationship and release myself from my old relationship patterns (mostly those set in and from my childhood).

4. *The primary scenario.* In the area of the primary scenario, we look at what first shaped us when we were born into our family. This concerns our own mental history, and the history of our emotional embodiment. 'Secret themes' and childhood patterns are analysed. The same is done with the way roles and types of behaviour within the family are delegated down the generations. In a short regression, prenatal factors can also be brought in – informing a history of our personality that is still open, which has passed its expiry date, but which still by force of habit shows up in our patterns of emotion and behaviour. A great deal of our mental resources and vitality can be committed to this, taking them away from creating a fulfilled life in the here and now.[9]

5. *The forming and living of our 'character style' and our treatment of others, as in 'other agency', contrasted to 'self-agency'.* Our particular character style is a development from the style of survival strategy we have had to adopt to get on in the family we have been born into. IBP differentiates between three character styles, which are shaped by the quality of a person's emotional relationship to their principle caregiver in the primary scenario: abandonment, inundation, and abandonment and inundation. According to our style, our behaviour is protective, clingy, or avoidant in our interactions with the world. This is where so-

called 'ego identification' happens, which then matures in the person or character we become in our adult lives. Our treatment of others (other agency) is contrasted with our treatment of ourselves. I must do something to help others (at first this is usually the mother or father), so that they will love and care for me, otherwise I won't be able to grow mentally or physically. Later, when we no longer live with the primary family, this necessary survival strategy becomes a pattern of behaviour, which constitutes a habit. Self-oriented behaviour comes from the innermost core of our being, and is only possible in a family where we are cared and provided for well enough. Patterns must first be recognised for what they are. Only then can we free ourselves from them.

6. *Our sexuality and the eroticism of emotions.* Sexuality and the eroticism of emotions are a wider area that we are always observing, directly reflecting upon and mapping. This is an area of life that directly determines both our physical activeness and our vitality in our relationships to ourselves and others. Rosenberg established himself as an original thinker and adviser in this area with his books *Total Orgasm* (1973) and *The Intimate Couple* (1996).

7. *Finally, our existential themes are addressed.* With existential themes, we are dealing in the realm of myth, religion, and the larger, cosmological connections. Here we look at the facts of life: accepting the fact that I am a mortal being, and engaging with the questions of meaning that unfold from this through meditation and the practice of other spiritual disciplines. Our psychotherapeutic stance and approach is deeply ecumenical. The aim is to create a greater and smoother sense of wholeness both within oneself, with others and existentially with the cosmic powers that be. Whatever the content in a system of faith, it is a holding and containing (therapeutic) environment with a certain model of change and spiritual world of consolation.

My other major psychoanalytic concepts are taken from the tradition of the major players of the British object relations school. These are as follows: interpersonal experience, process and praxis, intelligibility, ontological insecurity (engulfment, implosion, petrification and depersonalisation), the embodied and unembodied self, the false-self system, authenticity and inauthenticity, alienation and mystification, self-consciousness, modes of interpersonal experience (phantasy, communication, pretence and elusion, the counterpoint), forms of interpersonal action (complementary identity, confirmation and disconfirmation, collusion, false and untenable positions, attributions and injunctions), primary data and family scenario (operations, rules and metarules, mapping), dual unity and ego-boundary, the tie and the cut-off, embryologems (patterns through conception to infancy), psychologems (patterns and habits of behaviour learnt through family and social conditioning), and mythologems (patterns of faith in interpreting what is represented as our world and planet in a cosmos), recession and regression, procession *and* progression while in psychotherapy and experienced transgression, mystical experience and liberation, all form parts of the real life. In summarising his work for the *Oxford Companion to the Mind*, Laing wrote:

> There is so much that goes on between us which we can never know. The necessity of this ignorance, and the impossibility of any satisfactory criteria of decidability when it comes to the validation of particular attributions of a personal and interpersonal order, have led those who wish to cultivate the art of the soluble to abandon this area of uncertainty and enigmas. However, this domain does not evaporate because the objective look does not see it. The great divide between fact and feelings is a product of our own schizoid construction. In reality, the reason of the heart and the physiology of the brain coexist and must be interdependent. We cannot construe this reality, however. We cannot explain it; much less can we understand it. (Laing, 1987b: 418)

Ultimately, what Laing was referring to can only be lived, not conceived. Often we learn the hard way, to become more and more tolerant that we cannot modify our behaviour patterns despite all the insight gained by having undergone psychotherapy. What we can do is reflect on how we live these and to dis-identify ourselves from those familiar habitats (mostly family) which set them going in the first place.

IV. Style

Heraclitus' straightforwardness is gentle: You are *how* you are. Thus what I do fundamentally is live my style as psychotherapist and psychologist. As we all know, character style is fated, is set as a habit, continuously reinforced with sentences of faith, wherever they initially came from. What is then open to change? How I live the person I have become and will be, embedded in the self, rooted within a given family-clan finding itself in a society, culture and religious pantheon. Soul determines all and in silence is the basis of our music or song of life. 'Silence is not only present before the beginning and after the end, but during the piece' (Brendel, 2002: 173). As a psychotherapist I practise being in company in an undivided attention, clarification, reframing, co-presence, cultivated intuition, spontaneity and sensibility. Our world, our experience of the world and our selves are one. Silence can be such a delight, especially when the inner voices grow calm and refrain from their interminable chit-chat. True, there is one of them, the so-called inner voice (which takes the lead) who confers on each one of us – like the unconscious beings we are – a set of truthful instructions of what is to be said and done. When I follow this inner voice or calling, this talent will set me free in my individuation. In case I decide to ignore and go against this truth, voiced from the soul, this not hearing will turn against me and make me ill or harm me otherwise, with panic, put down, low self-esteem and, obviously low self-confidence. Here is the weed in the imagined garden of health and healing.

> We could not fear and hate health until there was a will to the health we fear and hate. Until or unless we have a clear vision of the answers to these six questions, embedded in the sentence: 'Who, or what, needs to be healed, of what, by whom, how?' we won't get far along the Way. We shall just be taking a stroll down another garden path which ends in another cul de sac. (Laing, 1987c: 84)

Yes, we in the PA cultivate and nourish a sense of wholeness, some like to call it a gestalt, to understand how we live our life, and how we are lived, by the unconscious, what the trouble is that disturbs our calm smooth sailing. We tend to reframe content and form, view context and matrix, to sense again, that each person is a whole, in relationship to the whole.

One useful principle of clarifying our experiences, both in dreams and in waking life, is to accept the reality of being one-self and someone-else at the same time. The Jungians call this the subjective and the objective part of the dream, since we can see a dream like a drama of the soul, a mythologem, as well as the subjective presentation of different aspects of one's present identity, a psychologem. Huxley (1961), who worked closely with Laing for over 20 years, argued that there is a close bond between what we feel in our natural, biological body and what we dream about. Psychotherapy, as a ritual of initiation or rite of passage towards becoming oneself (what C.G. Jung called 'individuation'), does affect us as it affects our body image. Only through these means can 'it' free our imaginations. Our self-image is the basis of our creativity. The vision freed through our imagination guides us through the field of myths and mysteries, both of which are at the root of our everyday habits and way of life. Remember John Yossarian in Joseph Heller's (1961) *Catch-22*: if he flies (as a bomber pilot) he is crazy and doesn't have to fly; but if he doesn't want to fly bombers he must be sane, and thus has to take off. That's some catch, don't you think? A psychoanalyst returning from Vienna to Haifa port tries to smuggle in two sacks of best Demel coffee. Customs officer: 'What have you got in the sacks?' He replies: 'Bird feed.' So they ask him to open the sack and see the coffee. 'Since when did birds eat coffee?' 'Ah well', so he says, 'they eat it if they want, and if they don't they won't.'

Endnotes

1. Laing, RD (1984a) The Tao of Therapy.
2. Two friends of mine – who have been a couple for forty years – dreamt, the very same night, about naming the shade system. Inge Santner & Ada Holl, personal communication, 2013.
3. 道
4. The Italian-speaking area of Switzerland.
5. A woman (or man) who changed her mind against her will is of the same opinion still (as a British saying goes).
6. 'The fact that we are considering not merely the private unshared autistic inconceivable delusions of single-cut-off crazy minds may mean that more of civilized humanity is still more immersed in deepest darkness than we would like to believe. On the other hand, the laws of what goes on outside our lived world cannot be assumed or be expected to obtain within the world we actually live in. Our human experience is conditional, relative and limited. Within this conditional, relative, limited field, as we always are, we cannot determine unconditionally, absolutely or finally the scope of its conditionality, relativeness and limits. Call this the principle of indecidability' (Laing, 1983: 81).
7. Rayner, E (1991) *The Independent Mind in British Psychoanalysis* concerns the group of formidable analysts such as Milner, Rycroft, Bowlby, Winnicott, Fairbairn and Laing.

8.   The Hungarian doctor Michael Balint (1896–1970) transformed the notion of original sin into a concept of the basic fault in humans in his 1968 book *The Basic Fault: Therapeutic aspects of regression*.

9.   I came to call this 'the old family home movie', following the schema and modus of therapy relayed to me by my wife Evelyne Gottwalz-Itten.

Chapter 4

Playing:
Theory and praxis

There is more in a human life than our theories allow.
(James Hillman, 1996: 3)

Sages are upright without causing injury, honest without hurting,
direct but not tactless, illumined but not flashy.
(Lao Tzu, in Cleary, 1993: 45)

Both of us work as researchers in psychotherapy and psychology as well as psychotherapeutic practitioners and teachers. Theodor participates as a clinical psychologist and psychotherapist in field studies, such as the recent Naturalistic Psychotherapy Study on Outpatient Treatment (2007–12) in Switzerland.[1] As well as teaching, Ron's work has spanned psychotherapy, epidemiology and psychology, a bit of counselling and most recently critical social science. In this chapter we look, with open playful eyes, at the unexpected difficulties of life, even our own. We practise, as clinical and social psychologists, putting into the world what we know. In this practice we are also exercising the art of counselling and psychotherapy. Theory carries the shadow of expectancy in understanding the world and praxis is its counterpart, not only in providing the test of theory but in being the life force of experience and wisdom of the heart. For us it is axiomatic that the basis of any theory making is experience. Theory might be arrived at ad hoc, through intuition, or after discussion, to be tempered by the results of observation and experiment, our conclusions always tentative – with preliminary conclusions eventually leading to recognisable theory. As the Ancient Greek meaning of *theoria* θεωρία – is to witness or behold, our theories are in effect acts of witnessing the world.

In psychology our intentions in theory, are to tune in to the facts as they offer themselves, or rather as we construct them to be in a given context and time, and to use our given framework to articulate the works of the soul, figuratively speaking – to know ourselves through our eyes on the world. This encompasses the human condition in its collective as well as individual settings. We no longer fall into the trap of psychotherapeutic idealism (a pleasant defence strategy) which '... seeks to uncover the true self or the inner child and put the patient on the creative track by freeing genius from hindering ... abuses' (Hillman, 1996: 254). Our reflections come from forty-odd years of professional life, freely embracing the inevitable and vast changes that come in any lifetime. We have endeavoured to remain in touch with what is going on in our professions – but given their contemporary size and scope this desire to remain 'up to date' is an inevitable struggle. As the water through which revenge is drowned comes always from one's own tears, so the search for knowledge from both societal and individual vantage points involves struggle and pain. Thus in any worthwhile attempt to get to grips with the key issues in contemporary psychological and scientific endeavour, we must peer into the dark waters of knowledge – a murky place frequently imbued with the myths of Big Science.[2] But it is important not to drown in these waters or be seduced by the gentle lapping of crashing waves or the lure of fame or the dollar for that matter. Just as theory and practice are always context bound, the basis of sensible psychotherapy and psychological research is having a good-enough setting which can be a 'facilitating environment'.[3] How one defines this of course will depend on one's values. One of the approaches to the soul, which is less materialistic than contemporary psychology and accordingly is less in thrall to the industrial, magnetic power of natural science, is to accept that there are 'bigger things' than what meets the eye or can be measured.

> A passion to cage the invisible by visible methods continues to motivate the science of psychology, even though that science has given up the century-long search for the soul in various body parts and systems. When the searchers failed to find the soul in the place where they were looking, scientistic psychology gave up on the idea of the soul. (Hillman, 1996: 92)

Almost 20 years on from Hillman's remarks, colleagues, as they have done for hundreds of years, continue to look to the central nervous system to deliver answers to our questions concerning emotions and consciousness. As they do so, we feel it necessary to state for the record that we find it somewhat disingenuous that many of our colleagues continue to use our professional titles – psychologist/psychiatrist/ psychotherapist – as their professional and scientific nom de plume yet fervently deny what this implies. These titles now embody a systemic lie and etymological fraud. The majority of practitioners no longer think and consider that the 'soul/psyche' refers to anything 'real' of substance yet continue to use this Greek word as the logos of their activities. The word psychology literally means 'study of the soul' (ψυχή, *psukhē*, meaning 'breath', 'spirit', or 'soul'; and λογος, *logos*, translated as 'study of' or 'research'. The Latin word *psychologia* was first used by the Croatian humanist and Latinist Marko Marulić in his book *Psichiologia de Ratione Animae Humanae* in the late fifteenth or early sixteenth century (see Brysbaert & Rastle, 2013). The earliest known reference to the word 'psychology' in English was by Steven Blankaart in 1694 in *The Physical Dictionary* which refers to 'Anatomy, which treats of the Body, and Psychology, which treats of the Soul'.[4] Given this, it is probably true to say that there are few authentic psychologists and psychotherapists today. There is a way out of this systemic lying however. This book is our own humble contribution to ending the catalogue of deception, pretence and misuse in our 130-year-old profession.[5]

I. Playing praxis

Normality, floating on a surface of apparent reason, is no guarantor of sanity. To the question 'what sort of psychotherapy do I (TI) practise?' I might point to a specific dream as an answer. The Taoist philosopher Chuang Tzu's speculations about his identity aside,[6] the ability to distinguish the dreaming life from the waking is part and parcel of sanity. Does our mind then balance itself perfectly on the sleep line – a line that is impenetrability itself? Across the line lies a pool of subconscious sketches of tabooed topics. Francis Huxley writing in *The Invisibles* (1966a) encourages us to connect to the rich knowledge of this underworld where daily events and ritual ceremonies have their roots – 'the unknown lying on the other side of reason' (Huxley, 1976: 88). These forces of life (*bios*) help us to live not only on the surface of awareness, but to be aware and beware of the mystery of what one cannot, but perhaps two can, do. Here is a refuge of transcendental probabilities where many powerful social and economic forces are present. A dream vignette from TI:

Flückiger is a garden architect. He visits me in my consulting room. As soon as he sits down on the couch he begins to talk and mutter in a strange way about his moods and the problems of living, the way he 'does' his life. After listening with undivided attention to the story he tells, I get up and give him my accordion. I help him to hold it properly, and then we find ourselves in the garden behind my consulting and practice room. There he tenderly begins to play. After initial inhibitions he no longer holds back, now jumping up and down, pulling and pushing the accordion in great anger. He runs to and fro over the vegetable and flower beds, dancing wildly to his own music. The scope of his actions is limited only by the garden fence. When he runs violently towards it, threatening to break through the boundary, I stand in his way and offer a containing resistance with which he humorously plays. He is playing with the limitations of this garden (process) of growth. He jumps on me, bounces back, and then repeats this again and again. The music and our voices mingle with sweat and tears. Windows fly open in the neighbouring houses and people look out to see what's going on. I wonder that they might think: 'What sort of therapy is this?' I feel an answer suggesting itself: It is drama and dance. Here is his music; we are becoming attuned to one another. We are together in his element, the garden. It is like a ritual fertility dance. He plays the accordion in accord with how he feels, and we communicate in the open air as ably as we possibly can. I am protecting him and helping him to cultivate his ability to respond. Call it 'drama therapy' or 'art-of-living therapy'. Once back in the consulting room, panting with exhaustion, breathing deeply, we reflect on the experience of what we have just been through together. We speak about our deepest desires, feeling 'the breath of the psyche', flowing freely through us. We give voice to it;[7] feeling free to experience its boundaries and limitations in our embodiment. We have been and are still on common ground; we heard the music of his heart's desire which provided the rhythm and pulse for our mutual experience. We were experiencing the innermost desire, spirit and fire of the child within.

Implied in my dream question, 'Is this therapy?', is a continuous musing over the various proclamations regarding therapeutic methods, which in itself does no harm, a part of the often grotesque longing to be secure in a delicious wisdom of life, to wake up into being one's self and not a second-hand copy of someone else. In contrast, the compulsion of comparing – more often than not in a competitive mood – the variety of talented methods and schools of psychotherapy is frequently paralysing and contradictory. These old divisions have often brought new confusion in their wake – to the lives of patients, families and friends, as well as the therapists engaged in this competitive 'one-upmanship'. It certainly obscures our professional and personal longings for certainty, for a secure base, a home; a vital need of us therapists as much as our fellow human beings who are in our company as our patients. At the beginning of the dream we were two strangers, meeting to explore what it was, in terms of disturbance and privation suffered, what it was that motivated him to come and see me. As we became 'attuned' to each other we found ourselves in the place of his professional competence. There he felt safe to let go and experience guided emotional release as a creative act. When he headed for the fence, I provided a protective boundary and containment, so that the playing could continue. Then came the central question about what I thought was going on. I projected myself outside, looking as if I were someone else (the neighbours) peering into the garden of therapy, seeing and naming the risk – to hurt and be hurt, to lose and be lost, to disturb and be disturbing – that was involved in being together in this way. Finally when we became exhausted, we returned indoors to my familiar sphere of competence to reflect on what we had been through: a choreographic movement from interior to exterior – integrating opposites – or from introversion to extraversion, soul as personal to soul in the world! At the end of the dream, we are back to where we started from, yet somehow changed.

As skilled healing artists, we solve riddles, masters of the impromptu mode of performance, as shown in this dream. We sometimes have not the slightest idea to begin with, what a specific life's puzzle is all about. One way to cope with this immediately is to let out a sigh, since the limit between what is sayable in words and what can only be expressed through emotions (and movement) is thin. What cannot be thought or reflected directly ought then to rest on this thin boundary. It is '... the limit itself, which is therefore not peripheral but central' (Huxley, 1976: 10). Speechlessness as we often experience it within ourselves – whether as patient or psychotherapist – is hooked into our linguistic attitude. As a good amateur psychoanalyst, social anthropologist Huxley expressed his admiration for the art form, the 'performance' of free association: 'it being at once logical, romantic and extempore ... In Nonsense,[8] then, one never knows what one is going to say until one has said it' (Huxley, 1976: 12). Life then, unbeknown to mainstream psychology, is continuous invention. We psychoanalysts and psychotherapists of various persuasions and modalities can profit by clarifying some

hasn't read anything (this is about eight weeks into the course – the work is due in two more). In that case I tell her I don't think there's much to discuss. I don't want her to reproduce my ideas in her essay, I want to hear about what she thinks. She is annoyed with me. I suggest a range of reading she can begin from and say she should come back when she has done some. It is a brief meeting. She reappears the next day. I am surprised. I've read one article she says. I tell her one article is an insufficient basis for an essay at this level. 'Come back when you've done some serious reading' I say. She is visibly annoyed and frustrated. She wants to be told what to do – to follow a prescription, the rule-based approach to life and to learning promoted in too much of the UK education system. She wanted to be told what to do. Her autonomy is to her a weight, a burden, something to be avoided. She doesn't reappear.

Amongst many things, psychotherapy has in the past been considered as an educational undertaking (Szasz, 1965/1988), the reverse of this, teaching – though it is true its pastoral dimension has been acknowledged – has rarely been considered in the same breath as psychotherapy. This is surprising given the generally understood aims of education to shape minds and mould future possibilities. In fact it is precisely because of these intentions and the sheer scale of state education that the education of young people has been so politicised. While I was growing up, the goals of education were more likely to be disseminated to the general public as promoting independence of mind and personal development. The reality of course was something more complex and getting a decent job at the end was certainly included in the mix – however it was not the be-all and end-all of education. If one believes what one reads in the press and sees on TV, it is all about one's future 'earning power' – a fairy story to deflect attention from the immense debt currently incurred.

Back at base camp academics are charged with 'enhancing', and students are encouraged to reflect on, 'the quality' of 'the student experience', something which has now been fetishised beyond belief. The paradoxical nature of this is apparent to anyone given a moment's consideration. The barometer for assessing this 'experience' – and note that nowadays all experience has to be assessed, quantified and graded – is the National Student Survey (NSS). Every year, up and down the country academic managers salivate at the very prospect of the latest NSS scores. 'Good' scores, read as extolling an institution's virtues, are greeted with an almost orgasmic ecstasy, displayed to the public as evidence of a local earthly paradise. 'Bad' scores on the other hand are likely to be succeeded by a plethora of new management initiatives, rules and procedures, born out of desperation to 'guarantee' future NSS success.

None of this is motivated by a concern for the welfare of students. Much like the proverbial time traveller who, knowing his/her eventual fate, travels back in time in an effort to change the course of their history, only to find that everything they do to prevent the undesired future in actuality hastens it; such initiatives to improve the student experience render it more unpalatable. And why is this? Precisely because the desire to live well, and treat others with respect and care, a part of treating oneself well, must come from within; actions which flow from a desire to have a fully human encounter with another, to treat others as one would wish to be treated oneself, are of an altogether different nature than those driven by a fear of failure to comply with an external threat – usually contained in management orders or a fear of the consequences if the end result is not delivered – a perspective which leads inevitably to an instrumental view of students, one which has it that students' responses must be 'engineered' to ensure that the authorities are happy. I say all this because the relationship between staff and students in higher education and how each of the parties will experience it has thus been politicised.

Coinciding with the increased politicisation of higher education and the massive reorganisation of state funding, since the late 1990s I have undertaken a series of studies investigating the impact of student debt on physical and mental health (Roberts et al., 2000), the wellbeing of student parents in this climate (Gerrard & Roberts, 2006) and the nature of students' increasing participation in sex-work (Roberts, Bergström & La Rooy, 2007a, 2007b; Roberts et al., 2010, 2013). None of this paints a reassuring picture – psychology students themselves appear to come to their studies with a considerable number of issues – and sadly relevant stakeholders in higher education (the UK Government, the National Union of Students, and the universities themselves) have shown little appetite to either debate what is going on or respond to the needs of students. This is the broader context within which teaching occurs. With that said a few more words about 'teaching'.

I learned, and this was first of all from my own experience as a learner, and secondly having this reinforced from my time in co-

counselling, that learning thrives when one feels respected – that one feels liked helps too – and having (relaxed) high expectations set for oneself. Also, as I have said elsewhere in this book – it is OK to fail, to get things wrong – to make mistakes, without this how can one learn anything? Finally, one must be able to deal with the emotional fallout that comes with 'failure', from dealing with the threats, challenges and excitement of new information and new vistas, and recognising that students often have to contend with others' unreasonable demands and expectations – not to mention on occasion their own internalisation of these. All this of course makes the relationship between staff and student sound somewhat like a psychotherapeutic encounter. If emotions are not dealt with – in the classroom, lecture theatre or office, they will impede learning and create frustration on all sides. Academic psychologists' problems in this arena are potentially huge. Many have little idea that their job is fundamentally about human interaction – having had years of training as academics they have been trained to place all faith in reason, to distrust emotions as a wild untamed creature. These difficulties are compounded, in my experience, by the training people have in specific areas of academic psychology. A good many of the theoretical approaches to hand encourage human beings to be seen as things – whether as dysfunctional organisms, complex biological assembly lines or information-processing apparatus. Theories of mental health predicated on these perspectives too, are of no use whatsoever in dealing with another human being face to face. A story:

> Many years ago one of my students, I'll call her Eileen, a mature woman in her early fifties, came to see me. She had come to university late, convinced she was not up to the job, that she couldn't do statistics because she was no good at maths, was afraid she would fail the research methods component and her dream of getting a degree would thereby go up in smoke with it. She couldn't see a way past this and was clearly stuck. I gave her the space to be upset while holding out the firm belief that she could not only pass but do very well. I held this out as a firm possibility for her, all the while discouraging 'rational' reflection and 'analysis' on her part which repeated the mantra that she was bound to fail. I reminded her that the present reality was not only different from whatever was contained in her childhood memories of maths, but that one didn't need to 'do' maths to be a good researcher. I remembered my old maths teacher who had always made himself available. I told her anytime she doubted what I was telling her, to come and see

me and I would remind her that she could do it. I stuck to imparting this simple message with complete confidence. She came to see me several times, I forget how many – each time floods of tears would prevail as she implored me to believe the contents of her distress. Of course this was just testing me out. She was asking me – was I serious? I stuck to the simple truth – she could do it and I had complete confidence in her. She put the work in, eventually passed her degree with flying colours, overcame her mental block about research and went on to successfully do a Masters degree.

Is the above teaching or psychotherapy? Does it matter? In a way I don't believe it does, but I think it important to remember that one does not need to be trained in a variety of esoteric skills in order to assist another human being. This is especially so when she, like Eileen, aims to become a psychologist. We will go on to treat other people who become our clients or patients as we were treated in our own formative years as psychologists/psychotherapists. As so many have said before and no doubt more eloquently than myself, there are no rules for this. 'When we act based upon what arises in *this* moment – rather than upon what we hope, or expect, or pretend – we no longer need a script or set of guidelines to follow' (Hagen, 2012: 262). This is to be oneself, which paradoxically may involve forgetting all about one's self and just doing what is appropriate, what fits with reality there and then. Educational institutions are only one place where people have difficulties. It is fortunately still conceivable while there – though this is becoming increasingly difficult with the micromanagement of virtually everything that takes place in a university – to propel oneself to the outer limits of self-prescribed possibility. Teaching is about far more than imparting subject-specific knowledge. It is, as *educare*, to bring out what is within a pupil and student, to get her or his 'genius' at work. If what is within a given person is brought out – aided out by the educator – that which will come out – the outcome, will make that person whole. Teaching has always been about the twin possibilities of changing oneself and the world. Are we not inseparable from it?

III. Research

Some years back RR conducted work with Lesley Fallowfield exploring the then nascent field of oncology counselling, examining available sources of support (Roberts & Fallowfield, 1990a), working conditions and responsibilities (Fallowfield & Roberts, 1992), as well as the aims and goals of the counsellors (Roberts & Fallowfield, 1990b). At the time the field was undeveloped (75 per cent for example had had no professional training), underfunded (posts were largely paid for by charities although where they were funded by the NHS, salaries were greater), poorly understood and evaluated. The work, principally a national (UK) survey of all those working in cancer counselling, was supported by the Cancer Research Campaign, and set out the case for better training and supervision of counsellors, in order that ultimately, counsellors not only understand what is required of them in delivering psychological care, but in the act of so doing avoid contracting the very problems they are entrusted to alleviate in others. When TI was a member of the council (2003–11) of the Swiss Association of Psychotherapy (ASP) and from 2008–11 its president, he was engaged not only in writing about research findings as editor of various professional journals,[10] but also actively participating in research. *The Professional Competencies of a European Psychotherapist* is a work in progress by the working group of the European Association of Psychotherapy (all seasoned psychotherapists from four different modalities). This vanguard project was given a ten-year lifespan to first of all describe the need for, and secondly to establish, a set of professional competencies necessary for an independent profession of psychotherapy in Europe – this as a prerequisite for the free movement of professionals across European countries and to differentiate between the work of psychotherapists and the overlapping professional work of clinical psychologists, psychiatrists and counsellors (Young et al., 2013).

Other research practitioners, like Mick Cooper, of the University of Roehampton (London) and John McLeod of the University of Abertay (Dundee), have argued vehemently in favour of instituting a pluralistic model of training and practice (2011). Both come from the field of counselling, and argue, as we have here, that there is simply no one right way of practising psychotherapy or doing counselling. Different clients or patients need different interventions, at different times and in different spaces. Their take-home message is that we practitioners trust our own modality as well as a variety of other therapeutic methods which most of us have acquired through continuous professional education and supervision, in order to be as flexible as can be. In that way we can 'fit' into the needs of patients and clients, giving our experience and knowledge fully to the service of recovery and healing.

This argument is elegantly confirmed by the PAP-S study in Switzerland (Tschuschke et al., 2010) showing how the modality and technique applied is not critical, as we thought or were told it was while in psychotherapeutic apprenticeship. The main factor is the holding relationship, meeting the other as the other, knowing that the difference is between people, once we have been able to form a collaborative 'being with' the person in psychological dire straits, looking for guidance and companionship. Often there are no short cuts, even so after several sessions (up to eight) the presenting issues are alleviated and the first alternative coping strategies put into place as a new possible habit, driving out the old unfit one. Modern psychotherapy research refers to this as a process of cognitive restructuring. Nevertheless it often requires long-term psychotherapy – 90–120 consultations – to restructure a person's life, modes, characteristics, complexes and schemas in a lasting way. The success of a course of psychotherapy is dependent on many factors. Health, level of social functioning, the length of time symptoms have been in place before the start of psychotherapy, age, sex, class, education, religion, work situation, family history etc., are all of enormous importance. In Switzerland, practitioners of Jungian psychotherapy spent eight years conducting empirical tests. Their empirically validated results are available (Mattanza, Meier & Schlegel, 2006) and are relevant to a wider psychotherapy audience than 'merely' those with interests in depth psychology.

A particularly challenging piece of research was done by Rosmarie Mendel et al. (2010) from the Department of Psychiatry, Technische Universität München. They asked psychiatrists to take the point of view of patients: 'What would you do if you were me, doctor?' This question is often asked by patients unsure whether a specific treatment is really good for them, and their inner voice gives them a different directive following the experience gained in psychiatric therapy. Patients, so the researchers assume, want their psychiatrists to put themselves in their shoes and not to give a set of 'standard recommendations'. This is, after all is said and done, the 'golden rule'. I imagine what I would feel like to be one of my patients and I treat them in the way I would like her or him to treat me if I were in their position. This is the practice and cultivation of reciprocity of perspective we all have inside us, like the inborn ability to sing. The aim of Mendel's study was to find out if this open question really leads psychiatrists (they asked

515) to reveal their personal preferences. What the researchers found was that the psychiatrists, when choosing treatment for themselves, predominantly selected different therapies than they normally recommended to patients when asked in the 'regular recommendation role'. They were less pharmacologically oriented towards themselves (preferring the 'talking cure' more than taking mere pills), and when choosing medication, were apt to consider lower doses than for their patients.

The authors of the study concluded that psychiatrists are not motivated to leave their professional recommendation role and to take a more personal perspective when seeing patients – in other words, 50 years after *The Divided Self*,[11] orthodox psychiatry still views the patient as 'other'. Another conclusion might be that what is scientifically right might actually be ethically wrong (Laing, 1983). This possibility is scarcely addressed in modern medicine or psychology. The fundamental clash between value-free science in search of value-free facts and the ethical treatment of human beings in research is effectively taboo. The scientific fraternity enamoured by their success and power simply don't get it. Michaela Amering and Margit Schmolke (2009) with overwhelming evidence to hand, argue convincingly that it is to the advantage of both patient and therapist in reaching recovery, that they follow the guiding principle of the 'golden rule of treatment' (do to others as you would like them to do to you, or rather be with others as you like them to be with you). Truly person-centred care and user involvement requires it.

The lived experiences of users regaining their mental health and equilibrium are used as the basis for a grounded theory to define the state of the art today. Overwhelming evidence in treating mental suffering by harmless yet successful means is collected and amassed in the second edition of *Models of Madness* (Read & Dillon, 2013). It is time to leave behind the prevailing damaging and scientifically false (or faked) biological models of madness and accept the social scientific evidence, that hallucinations, delusions, illusions, strange behaviour, etc. are favourably (for the healing) understood as understandable and at times appropriate reactions to adverse life events (whether trauma, sexual assault, parental or authoritarian brutality, etc.). The many authors in Read and Dillon's collection conclude that social psychological and psychotherapeutic approaches (like community therapy) are safe and statistically, as well as from the subjective perspective of the users, effective. A mark of respect for the other human being as a fellow creature of our species is a foremost ethical iconic imperative. It is high time for politicians with an interest in mental health to also heed these results and instigate wide-ranging policy changes so that what we have is an honest mental health practice rather than one the ideologically supported pharmaceutical industry props up by sales pitches and advertising. This may be a long way off – but it may also be closer than one dare imagine.

Just imagine, had Samuel Beckett been treated by a neurobiological psychiatrist, and not by the young Wilfred Bion (Beckett was in therapy from 1934–5), he might have been lost to the psychiatric maze, deemed 'invalid' as a person, and not the brilliant writer and artist of words he is fondly remembered as. Let us not forget 'psychotherapeutic action happens within and between individuals, and inheres within individual experiences' (Miller, 2013: 38). Aderhold, Gottwalz-Itten and Haßlöwer (2010) have shown in their research at the University Hospital of Hamburg, how, by involving patients in a weekly treatment conference, as the experts of their experience and subjective positions, the outcome is much more effective than conventional inpatient (chemical) treatment. Those who insist on seeing everything from a reductionist perspective would do well to remember that what most affects our chemical balance is other people. Of course, we – as specialists in attentiveness and awareness – know from experience how we can affect and be affected each by the other.

As psychotherapist and psychologist respectively we endeavour to practise authentic meetings between human beings. Aderhold and Gottwalz-Itten (2013) provide an example, using the expertise of the patient's experience, of how this can be done successfully in family therapy with individuals who have been diagnosed as suffering from a so-called psychotic episode. Bob Mullan (1996) has interviewed psychotherapists from all major modalities and shows the actual work of healers of the soul. His anecdotal research provides a good insight into the contemporary psychotherapeutic enterprise. Intuition is of the utmost importance in this. How it works in psychotherapy (it is associated with positive outcomes) can be researched in vivo with empirical phenomenological data (Itten, 2011a). This is why it is so important for us psychotherapists that we make a priority of our own wellbeing, and ensure that our souls are well healed.[12] What happens though when we feel that playing it by ear no longer attunes us to the voice of experience of our patients? Over 85 per cent of us go back into personal treatment – the psychotherapy of therapists is thus a meaningful way to get tuned in again. Geller, Norcross and Orlinsky show that 'therapists enter personal treatment an average of two to three times during their careers – and probably for and during developmentally propitious crises' (Geller, Norcross & Orlinsky, 2005: 8). Our health (body, self and soul) is in its wholeness our indispensable foundation to work successfully, just like a musician has to be able to practise and perform her or his instrument. These real-life domains – how we live our own life in the socio-economic field of living – have to be addressed continuously in order to sustain our own wellbeing.

My cousin Thomas (Aramaic: the twin, the doubter) suggested to me in a dream: 'Why don't you cultivate sobriety as a magic to clarify what is going on in our relationships, in and outside of our family'. *Sobrius* in Latin means not being addicted to intoxication of any sort, be that words, silence, ideology, hallucinogenic drugs or methods, models, theories and so on. It also means to be unhurried and thoughtfully calm. In fact the concept of *sobrius* can gather together all the qualities needed – even for psychotherapists – to deal with the confusion and disturbance of the social, intellectual, emotional, spiritual, somatic and religious aspects of life (see Bellah, 2011). In my native German the word for sobriety is *Nüchternheit*, holding, within itself, the sense of night (Latin: *nocturnus*) and daybreak, dawn. 'It dawns on me', I say, and remember how as a tender of the soul, I am in an old monk-like tradition, which includes an early meditation before we sit for breakfast, reviewing our excesses, our fantasies and emotions, filled with a prejudice which we have acquired in and during the course of daily life. In therapy we can calm emotional, intellectual, somatic and social turmoils, we can play, we can circle round our human faculties, examining them and making sense of who we are with, why, and in what way. In this way we practise the art of 'Satisampajanna', which is an essential psychotherapeutic skill, unconditional attentiveness, the cultivation of being aware of what is going on, without projecting our own phantasy system upon it.

We endeavour to live the balance between practice and theory and Theodor has addressed, in an essay in *Alternatives beyond Psychiatry* (Itten, 2007), how psychotherapy is still a real and sensible alternative to psychiatric pharmacotherapy. Young (2012) has added to this endeavour by considering body psychotherapy as both an effective art of healing and an empirically informed human science. I (TI) have also discussed in a special edition of the *International Journal of Psychotherapy* (Itten, 2009) how various approaches to depression can be fitting for different patients. The largest social psychological study I conducted, with a small group of independent researchers, was done in the summer of 2006 in Switzerland, asking almost 600 people about their personal experience with sudden rage (Itten, 2007, 2011b). The surprising result: 20 per cent were the victims of their parent's rage as children, and 24 per cent of those surveyed experienced rage themselves. This unregulated and affective way to live this strong and intensive emotion is a widespread source of unease and can be successfully dealt with in psychotherapy. With a team from the Swiss Association of Psychotherapy (ASP),[13] I researched the literature and curricula from various European universities already offering BA, MA/MSc and PhD degrees in psychotherapy. We wanted to see how the paradigm shift is being achieved at this moment in time, viewing psychotherapy as a house on its own within the social and human sciences, with rooms for psychology, philosophy, ethics, religion, anthropology, neurology and history of psychotherapy and depth psychology. Together with Peter Schulthess, we assessed the radical changes in psychotherapy in Switzerland, which showed a profession in flux and future oriented, while new legal measurements (passes into law on April 2013) were fixed on bygone professional standards and vested interests (Schulthess & Itten, 2008). The work is ongoing.

Filz and Young conclude their argument for psychotherapy as an independent activity, on the road to being a fully independent profession in the near future (an equal next to psychiatry and psychology) as follows:

> As psychotherapy develops its independent status, and works to establish this politically across Europe and internationally, we are working to create a strong theoretical foundation of its own, which would be common for all modalities. (Filz & Young, 2009: 10)[14]

Psychotherapy thus is on the road, freeing itself from what Laing in the mid-1970s had called the control of psychotherapy by pseudo-medical procedures and pseudo-scientific terminology designed to make commodities of our experience.[15] Richard

Bentall (2009) has opened the eyes of many who desire a human, healing approach to madness. In unmasking the illusion of progress peddled by pharmaceutical companies he exposes the vacuity of the unsubstantiated biological myths which they sponsor. Bentall argues for placing trust not in medical 'reps' but in the judgements of those who seek their recovery through enhanced autonomy. This is the way forward. Our broader aims must be to work with others to make our human cultures enablers of the art of living. However as the psychotherapeutic project grows we must beware the sting in the tail. As psychotherapy risks becoming another European game without frontiers,[16] it must take care to ensure that in freeing itself from the cold hand of medicine it is not seized by the even icier grip of managerial bureaucracy. If we are not to be imprisoned by the mores of the professional social systems in which we reside – then we must have some guiding lights to chart our course through stormy seas. These can be personal values, moral-ethical systems or even humanistic theories or some combination thereof. Whichever they are – at root they must contain some idea of what is a desirable way to treat human beings. Scientific practice though it may inform such thinking cannot be its source. Instead we must draw on the notions we have garnered through life about we would like to be treated in our own struggles with the contingencies of existence. Armed with these, the task is then to put our desires into practice – to produce what we might call therapeutic compassion but which is really a compassion for life.

Endnotes

1. PAP-S: A naturalistic psychotherapy outcome study on outpatient treatment in Switzerland. (PAP-S stands for *Praxisstudie Ambulante Psychotherapie Schweiz*.) This was a research project of the Swiss Charta of Psychotherapy in cooperation with the Clinical Centre of the University of Cologne and School for Applied Psychology at the Zürich University of Applied Science.

2. 'Big Science' refers to the developments in industrial nations both during and after the Second World War whereby science increasingly revolved around large-scale projects funded by government, groups of governments or corporations. This scientific progress becomes increasingly identified with corporate and capitalist aspirations (see http://en.wikipedia.org/wiki/Big_Science Accessed September 2013). We argue throughout this book that the values and practices of a psychology predicated on the mores of

Big Science stand in opposition to one predicated on a respect and love for human experience and existence in the world.

3. D.W. Winnicott's concept for psychotherapeutic phantasy work and good-enough parenting.

4. See http://en.wikipedia.org/wiki/Psychology. Last accessed 26 March 2014.

5. Psychology was at home in the house of philosophy, theology and mythology for thousands of years. The first steps to rebrand psychology as an experimental social science began in earnest with Wilhelm Wundt (1832–1920) at Leipzig University in 1879.

6. Chuang Tzu: 'Once upon a time I, Chuang Chou, dreamt I was a butterfly, fluttering hither and thither, to all intents and purposes a butterfly. I was conscious only of my happiness as a butterfly, unaware that I was Chou. Soon I awaked, and there I was, veritably myself again. Now I do not know whether I was then a man dreaming I was a butterfly, or whether I am now a butterfly, dreaming I am a man'. http://en.wikiquote.org/wiki/Zhuangzi. Last accessed September 2013.

7. In *The Voice of Experience*, Laing (1983) encourages us to admit that sometimes we can neither explain nor understand certain experiences, 'as it is impossible to contain what contains us' (Laing, 1983: 69).

8. 'Nonsense' is a game in Anglo-Saxon attitudes (Huxley, 1976: 189).

9. Rules from *A Game in Anglo-Saxon Attitudes, Called Nonsense* (Huxley, 1976: 189). The rules mentioned are numbers 1, 6, 7, 9 and 11.

10. *à jour! Aktuelles für ASP Mitglieder* (Zürich); *Psychotherapie Forum Supplement Schweiz* (Springer Verlag, Wien); *International Journal of Psychotherapy* (European Association of Psychotherapy (EAP), Wien).

11. We both have written on this issue in *RD Laing: 50 years since* The Divided Self (Itten & Young, 2012).

12. Readers will we hope forgive the pun here.

13. (2010) At that time as president of ASP and chair of this working group: Psychotherapie-Wissenschaft (PTW) – Bericht über die Entwicklungs-möglichkeiten eines eigenständigen PTW-Studiums und eines integralen Konzeptes für die wissenschaftliche Berufsausbildung. Psychotherapy science – a report about the possibilities for development of an independent degree in psychotherapy science and an integral concept of a scientific professional training.

14. Alexander Filz, University of Lviv, Ukraine (associate editor) and Courtenay Young, Edinburgh, Scotland, (editor) are in the editors collective of the *International Journal of Psychotherapy* (IJP), of which TI is executive editor. In its seventeeth year, IJP publishes vanguard research and practice papers. http://www.ijp.org.uk/ Last accessed 26 March 2013.

15. Elaborated in depth by Daniel Burston in his second book (2000) on Laing, concerning the crisis of psychotherapy.

However, is this merely 'curing' what we do not want to see? The miserable situation might anyway change, from the outside in. Yet we also live our lives from inside out. As social anthropologists and psychotherapists we tread the paths of the unknown when we accompany those who have searched out our company for a while. Usually they want to change something about how they go about their lives. In front of us lies an unmapped landscape, with scarcely a familiar landmark in sight. A few however are known to us – bequeathed to us as myths, a pantheon of legends large and small. They serve as a handy cosmology, a vast invisible umbrella over our individual existence, conferring an illusory sense of protection by making some sense of what is happening. By such visions and imaginings we alleviate the fears of the soul. Some seek a rapport with this unknown realm, calling it the collective unconscious; they project a grand vision of the dark and unwelcome side of our personality that lies in the shadows.

By practising the healing art of psychotherapy I am opening up a place (space) and time for another human being, coming into a meeting with me. She or he can then begin to talk freely and securely in confidence. First of all, there is trust, that as a patient I will not be harmed by those I am consulting. In a therapeutic conversation there is always already compassion from the side of the therapist, holding the floor, maintaining the ebb and flow of:

> ... rhythm, tempo – the timbre and pitch of the words that are in the *paralinguistics*. There is ... a music of words. There are, as well, *kinesics* – concerted movements involving arm, hand, finger, leg, the positions of our bodies in the chairs, set at 90 degrees to each other. (Laing, cited in Amantea, 1989: 141)[1]

Laing's words here come from his videoed presentation at the first Evolution of Psychotherapy Conference, in December 1985, where he conducted an in vivo therapeutic intervention with a card-carrying 'schizophrenic' women, called Christy.

Laing continues:

> The paralinguistic and kinesics – the *music* and the *dance* were much emphasized ... but most 'professionals' are amazingly impervious to all that. It is a question of the complete opera, with singers, costumes, sets, backdrops and orchestra, versus the mere libretto. You are publishing the libretto (the verbal content) without the music (the pitch, timbre, rhythm, tempo, the paralinguistics)

and without the choreography (two symmetrical chairs placed
precisely as intended) and the ballet (*kinesics*). ... There is a lot
of technique there. Many people like Christy do not connect with
'content' alone, if the sound and movements of the therapist
are, in effect, *autistic*. That is, if the therapist in his/her presence
manifested through sight and sound is effectively selectively
inattentive to 99 percent of the sight and sound of the patient/
client. (Laing, cited in Amantea, 1989: 142)

Laing in effect demystified a transpersonal reality by communicating
with Christy in an interpersonal way – projecting into awareness a
transpersonal field, so to speak, that envelops our encounter, that is
the encounter and which in the normal course of things we seldom
dare to know. There are more things in heaven and earth than are
dreamt of in *our* philosophy.

In the ensuing question time, Christy mentions the reason why
she is doing better than before the interview with Laing. 'I think that's
because you know how to share minds, it's because he knows how to
tap into other people's minds. (Looks at Laing) You know on a subtle
level – not by asking questions' (ibid: 160). Laing found, she said, the
place where her mind had wandered. He affirmed her perception of
reality before giving her a chance to consider changing it. Thus she
quit putting mental energy, as she remarked, into a conspiracy model.
Psychotherapeutic passion is, when good enough, an experience of
communion.

There is an abiding temptation within the community of social
scientists to try to define the undefinable – a task we might better
leave to philosophers. With 15 books under his belt, H. Peter Rickman
(1918–2010), my old friend and seasoned philosophy and humanities
teacher at City University (from 1978–82) considered the usefulness
of philosophy:

Though the progress of the different human disciplines
answers many questions about human life, it can never replace
philosophical speculation on it. Not only is a general conception of
man always presupposed in research, but it is also needed to guide
and to impose a unitary picture of man from the jigsaw puzzle of
pieces provided by the specialized disciplines. It is also needed to
remove confusions and inconsistencies that impede the progress
of knowledge. (Rickman, 2004: 18)

This is an endless quest, the Arthurian challenge to know our self.
Philosophers of the social sciences, like Rickman, remain cheerful as

there are always more 'golden apples to be gathered, more stables to be cleared'. To search amongst the hidden depths, be alive to visions from the unconscious. Though we cannot be certain of their truth value, 'it matters' Rickman remarked, 'that we continue' (ibid: 19) and on this path '… see and hear more at each end (of the ordinary range) … to explore, to find words for the inarticulate, to capture those feelings which people can hardly ever feel because they have no words for them' (T.S. Eliot, cited in Rycroft, 1991: 4). In psychotherapeutic time and space we entertain deep subjectivity, both in service of and in trepidation of 'objectivity'. Embarking on this journey into the underworld we discover, with the help of trust and therapeutic commitment, how subjective reflections on our experience are not to be violated by reasoning objectivity.

A daring familiarity with such deep subjectivity characterises all of Laing's travels through this terrain; utilising the tools which the late Roger Poole (1939–2003) catalogued as 'description, comparison, deployment, perspectives, sympathy and re-organisation of sheaves and profiles' which have enriched us with a measure of 'truth about the *totality* of the psychic background' (Poole, 1972: 128) of the families Laing and Esterson (1964) studied.

Laing was strongly influenced by Kierkegaard, especially the *Concluding Unscientific Postscript* (1969), which assisted him in his desire to establish a rapport with the subjective reality of the person before him, someone who was, in the language of his chosen profession, first and foremost a patient. This became a necessity when faced with someone who was living in a state of 'ontological insecurity', swimming in dire straits, closed down, despairing and desperate for respect. With Kierkegaard to hand, Poole (2005: 105) writes: 'Laing has now what he needs for the analysis of despair, the battle between "the self" and "the false self"'.

Trusting his fellow witness in despair, sickness unto death, confusion and existential dread, Laing practised variants of what Poole termed both direct and indirect communication in order to comprehend even the most seemingly odd behaviour and see in it the person's unique answer to the problem of insufferable situations. Laing perennially reached for authenticity, the gold standard in psychotherapy. In *The Divided Self*, he wrote:

> This provides striking confirmation of Jung's statement that the schizophrenic ceases to be schizophrenic when he meets someone by whom he feels understood. When this happens most

of the bizarrerie which is taken as 'signs' of the 'disease 'simply evaporates ... The main agent in uniting the patient, in allowing the pieces to come together, to cohere, is the physician's love, a love that recognises the patient's total being, and accepts it, with no strings attached. (Laing, 1960: 180)

Laing ventured into this territory, but unlike Freud, with no defensive sword in hand, a leap into a boundless empty space between, where the healing relationship of patient and therapist could come to be – a place where love is indispensable to making sense of the world.

Practical wisdom of the heart

Anthropology in the Modern World, Claude Lévi-Strauss' (2011) work was first written and presented in Tokyo in 1986. It remains hugely relevant today, not least – in an age of increasing racism – his view that human characteristics are the same everywhere – without exception we all possess language, arts, technology, religious imagination, a structured system of knowledge and exist within a social and a political order which organises our everyday living situation.

As the 'psy' industries proliferate, the production of psychological knowledge intensifies, reaching ever-increasing numbers of people – who in turn demand more. This demand feeds back into an escalating system of desire for 'better' mental health. Thus, as psychotherapists we serve an ever-growing health market, one of many markets created to pacify, and nurture insatiable demands and unlimited desires. What happens in the end is that more and more people are drawn towards the big cities and metropolises to be trapped within an artificial urban life habitat, prisoners of an urban space which day by day estranges one from 'natural human nature'. As we are now virtually all cosmopolitan city dwellers, how then do we denote, signal, imagine or create any sense of our longed for uniqueness and originality?

Anthropology gives us the opportunity to study the human spirit amidst an incredible diversity of settings and collective endeavours – to learn how we manage our difficulties under the various geographic and historical givens within which we face the challenge to survive. For us psychologists the details are vital, and we would do well to pay close attention to those details which make a difference. What are the collective moral and ethical motivations, about which an individual member might not have an inkling, which make a tribe (native or city dweller) successful? Collective life in a social setting is always about what happens between individual people, their language ability, family strings, social and institutional ties, unfolding within a traditional pattern of verbal communication which often is not written up. Social anthropology is aiming for a total view of what is taking place at any one time in a society under conditions of 'objective' participant observation. This requires balancing the degree of autonomy within a given tradition (both inner and outer) with the way of life authentically followed, that is the philosophy of life by which the members live their desires.

Psychotherapy can also be a technique to become, as a patient, a 'stranger to one's self', so that I can then witness and understand 'me', with all my habits, modes of behaviour and schemas of experience. Outside in is as valid a take on this as is inside out. The main advantage of social anthropology for members of the helping profession in Western advanced societies, and for Laing, Francis Huxley was indispensable in this, is to give us humility, and a scepticism about the 'rightness' of our ways of being. When it comes to reaching an enduring balance between natural environment and human demands, our own receptivity to practical wisdom (what the Greek philosophers called *phronesis*) does not compare favourably to the tribes of old.

> Careful studies in Australia, Melanesia, South America and Africa have shown that two to four hours of activity have been ample to secure survival for all the families in a tribe. The rest of the day could be spent in story telling and giving imagination and myth a field day. (Lévi-Strauss, 2011: 52)

How can we fulfil both our biological and our spiritual desires in modern social settings? A variety of ideological explosions, as Lévi-Strauss calls them, have certainly not contributed to the wellbeing of humanity, in the long run. For a brief period of time, these ideological dictates have enriched leaders of social reform or revolutionary movements. Capitalism, Marxism, totalitarianism, have all ended up as vast and deadly betrayals. Their brutal murderous destructions – two world wars, decades of global conflict, the 'great leap forward' in China – have largely removed people from any stable healthy mode of living.

Each society has habits, rituals and institutional sentences of faith, with lots of people following their leaders with a devotion which they may see as god given or 'natural'. Authority as biologically or divinely ordained. It has always been like this, and cannot be witnessed or completely understood from the outside. So whatever belief and habit is followed, this makes sense only in the context of a given social setting. To outsiders who come with a natural scientific stance, the behaviour might seem mad or crazy. Yet despite our devotion to logic, classification systems like *DSM-5* and *ICD-10* are artificial methods, hoping to make sense of experiences which need to be understood in the context and content of a given society. Only in our society do we see certain behaviour and experience as natural, for others this is not so, as a matter of course. We can aim, like Lévi-Strauss and Francis Huxley, for example, to look out for 'universals' of human nature, adapting to a habitat and its social, political and religious management. It is not only 'to be or not to be' that is in question – to endure and/or to change, is of equal importance – in living together as well as in psychotherapy. Permanency is what we often long for, be those in the realm of habits, myths, faith or strategy. The unexpected therefore must always be managed and the 'potential difference' amalgamated into our socially hierarchically organised society. As our 'culture contains the totality of relationships which human beings within a given civilisation cultivate' and that 'this society rests on the relationships, which these human beings have with one another' (Lévi-Strauss, 2011: 91), there is a perpetual dynamic equilibrium, a total field of reverberating human activity, constant in its change.

Thanks to such anthropological knowledge and vision I can appreciate the variety of difference and the difference of variety, a variety which is always a threat to those who like to minimise, monopolise (mono-police) and be in the lead. Psychotherapy offers a vast repertoire of imaginations, which too can express themselves in the form of rituals and myths, and their multifaceted combinations. Myths can be seen as ordering stories of the otherwise inexplicable experience and cosmic happenings that permeate our existence. The myths, it matters little if they are social or natural scientific in their character, give us an enduring comfort and security, in time. Even scientific myth making, as Rupert Sheldrake (2012) demonstrates is full of 'givens' for how our experience and knowledge of the world must be regulated. This domain is the political philosophy of experience. All past issues and patterns of thinking and behaving, even in psychotherapy, inhabit our present thinking. This is no more than a grand constructed phenomena, sculpted to deliver sentences of belief which determine our present cultural inheritance. This side of the divide in the new politics of experience appears to be developing much quicker than human genetics. Living conditions, which have helped us to survive in the past – peasantry, handiwork etc. – might in hindsight seem primitive, yet they were well enough suited for human beings in their own specific temporal and cultural environment. Despite our immense scientific knowledge we are much more alienated in terms of social evolution. In the present day and age, economic growth, genetic experimentation, chaotic modification of the biosphere and political folly on a grand scale all threaten to derail the human project and destroy the experiential rhythms of life.

Before Dawkins, Lévi-Strauss asked whether evolution (of both humanity and the broader biosphere) is a game genes play on us. However, as soon as culture came into existence, it was this, and not nature, which consolidated and directed the habits of human thinking and behaving, and thereby shaped the politics of experiencing. Biologists, social anthropologists and psychologists agree that in all times and places, human beings have created a rich and diverse survival repertoire. But it is culture which has continued the unfinished business of creation and elaborated our astonishing capacity for resilience. Like natural selection, culture works upon difference, the products of human creativity situated within shifting trans-generational familial and social fields comprised of traditions, value judgements, motivations, beliefs, interests and imaginings which have taught us about our history and the future of our civilisation. Implicit in this system of determinants, are subtle influences which make it difficult if not impossible for most of us to actually have a clue that the cultural reference system which we follow is only one among many possible human ways of being. The psychological dangers consequent to this are obvious.

To reckon with the hidden variables which shape a given culture's position in relation to the checks and balances provided by its natural environment is to engage in a calculus of truth and morality. Looming large and visible in this reckoning are the dilemmas posed by globalisation, and world civilisation, yet there are plenty of other factors to throw into the mix – not least the variety of cultures and multitude of experiences possible within them. The game, such as it is, may be open or closed, free flowing or in stasis; it may proceed in phases, or be phased out entirely; it may be fragmented or fermenting. When we are facing our way of living in psychotherapy, we face our lived reality, the drama we play amidst our politics of experience. As long as we psychotherapists do not mask our practice with shields of theory or plaster our experience with concepts, we can, like many a novelist, face up to life in the heat of a given civilisation.

Therapeutic passion

> For Socrates, the unexamined life was not worth living, the examined life can be pretty rotten too. It all depends who is doing the examining. The unfortunate individuals whose minds attract the scrutiny of the modern state usually find the experience profoundly traumatic, and sometimes disturbing to the point of permanent psychological debilitation. (Hawkes, 2013: 7)

To attend a joint examination of life with passion is to be patient. To hear the etymological sound in compassion, we find the Latin root in *passio* meaning the endurance of ill or illness, suffering. Hence compassion is to suffer with another, to feel pity (Partridge, 1966: 475). More often than not, experiencing an imbroglio in living can be harrowingly painful. Since a lot of people have complained to me after they have been to mental hospitals/psychiatric clinics of how, in the grip of their hopelessness, they were treated in a condescending manner, we want to make you, the reader, aware of how madness can hinder and stifle *all* action and engender profound upheaval. How then to hear authentic communication, when it is most needed? The late James Hillman[2] (1926–2011) was a daring expert in present age journeys to the underworld of the soul. Madness, if not shunned away by anxiety, is a profoundly ancient experience of a gargantuan emotion. Let's hear what he has to say:

> From its point of view, it's walking in the door with a message, but you sit in the room and it knocks the door down and you think, 'Shit, this is only bringing me disruption', but what does it carry in its hand? I think what it's walking in the door with are the Gods. I think the madness is the messenger of the Gods. And that's Plato, not Freud. Different forms of what Plato called mania, each of them associated with a different God. So the madness is calling us to the Gods, in one way or another either as frenzy or as a love or as a ritual initiation into a new kind of life. Something more important than usual life is going on. It is drawing us out of one thing and toward something else. (Hillman & Ventura, 1993: 169)

Viennese author and critical theologian Adolf Holl brought this platonic notion of madness into play in a mental hospital in Vienna, in his book on *Compassion in Wintertime*, where Fips, a free-spirited patient and Socrates meet to share and discuss their respective slants on madness. Socrates invokes the fate of Pentheus, in his madness torn apart, an experience at the hands of the wild women in the mountains. For Fips, 'schizophrenia' is to be torn away from one's heart and soul in the world. The holy madness of Eros has to be served, otherwise, the profane silliness of everydayness catches up with confusion. Holl's prose brings in the four players of the Gods of madness: Apollo, Dionysus, Aphrodite, and the poet's muse, the so-called White Goddess (Holl, 1985). Socrates mentions to Phaedrus, that in days of old, madness was held to be a valuable gift. True, some saw it as an evil:

> but in reality, the greatest blessings come by way of madness, indeed of madness that is heaven-sent. It was when they were mad that the prophetess at Delphi and the priestesses at Dodona achieved so much for which both states and individuals in Greece were thankful; when sane they did little or nothing. (Plato, 1978; Phaedrus, No. 244b: 491)

With Jung we have learned again, against the protest of modern psychiatrists, that the Gods are in the disease. Called or not called, they are always there whether you believe it or not. For Hillman and Ventura insanity is the description of:

> what the human being does in relation to that mania. That is, it follows the wrong God, or it serves its God in the wrong way. It doesn't understand the ritual, or it literalizes the ritual. It gets inflated, it takes the mania to itself, takes credit for it, 'the thoughts that come through me are mine, not the Gods'. (Hillman & Ventura, 1993: 169–70)

Or it says, 'I am an instrument of the Gods, I'm their favourite son or chosen person'. Of all the definitions of madness, Theodore Roethke's (2005: 116) is a firm favourite; 'What's madness but the nobility of soul at odds with circumstance?'

Roethke's example was found in a poem, but there are other perhaps less charming ways of thinking about insanity and madness which use various language games to prop them up. We know them as the biochemical, neurological, genetic, sociological, psychoanalytical, childhood dysfunction and abuse models. From description to reality – one suffused with contradiction – where people snap at the point of no return. I turn now to the story of Angel, one of immediacy in the search for the hidden dimension to life.

Experience with Angel

Jeff called. It was a lush evening in the summer of 1979. He described his problem with Angel, his former lover, who visited him over Christmas. Now she keeps throwing tantrums, shouting in the house, being a burden on his housemates. She can't stay any longer. He would like, together with Angel, to drop in on us in the Villa Therapeutica, a place in Islington, North London. He asks me to put some time aside for both of them. Maybe Angel can even stay at the Villa Therapeutica, temporarily of course. They arrive in the late evening. They tell their stories. After two hours it's time for them to depart. Then Angel stands up, shouts louder and louder, throws her hands in front of her flickering eyes. 'Where am I? What am I doing here?' she asks. What answer does she hear within herself? I ask her in return. 'I need a room, a quiet place to think. I don't want to carry on playing other people's games. I want to be protected. To stretch out my hand, and touch another hand'. Whilst she is answering, Angel plays with her hands in front of her eyes. The silence that follows takes hold of our hearts. This is enough for a first time.

A few days later Angel comes to visit again, eyes filled with fear. 'I don't have anything left', she says. 'I just see a hole'. Whilst she tells stories about her life, she weeps, and gesticulates as if conducting her mental melody. After an hour and a half I have to leave her. She sinks to the floor, says 'now you have just killed me'. Silence! I kneel down next to her and massage her back, gently and slowly. Angel calms down. After a while she gets up and leaves. I see the many dimensions of her story of suffering vanish into one another like breaking waves. The symbolic roads! I am Angel's audience and listener. In this way I become part of her story, and her secret stories, told here for the second time, a part of me. Which great story plays host to our own individual ones? Angel wants to empty herself, talk herself free, and talk right to the end, in the here and now. She is afraid of this.

I wake up. It is half past three in the morning, and Angel is standing in my rest room in the Villa. 'What's wrong?' I ask her from the in-between world of dreams. 'I'm frightened', she says, 'of the voices downstairs in my room and of my thoughts as well. I can't sleep. I'm exhausted'. 'Angel', I reply, 'light a candle'. She does so. I go back to sleep. After several hours, she wakes me. 'I'm going', she says, 'the dawn (Eos) is coming. I'm not frightened in your room, so now I can sleep downstairs in my room too. Can I take a candle with me?' 'Of course.' Angel and I found ourselves in a therapeutic situation which allowed her experiences, and the stories which until that point she had repressed, to flame freely. There are no more self-defence games. She is exhausted.

'Those people who make others feel guilty using the dictatorial words "you should, you must, you could", are bastards.' The woman who says this in a public lecture is Vera von der Heydt (1899–1997), my first Jungian analyst. I attended this lecture in the week that Angel spent living with us in the Villa. Vera says: 'There is only "there is".' Where love is, there is also pain and care, shame and death. We are loving creatures, who can also wound.' There are places we linger as we wander through the country of the mind. It's Angel's last day. She wanders about the Villa, alert and bold. She calls me from the airport. 'I need another few francs to get me home. Can you help me out?' Although this takes the biscuit, 'sure', I say, 'I'm on my way'. I go there on the Honda 340 and hand over the money. 'Have a good journey.' Back to the cover of *Time Out* magazine, this week's title: 'Blind Faith'. Is there any other sort of faith? Over the course of this single week, Angel moved along the path of experience, from going crazy over newfound emptiness and quiet, to a new departure on the road homeward to herself.

Anthropological interventions

We met in the living room of Arnold's shared house. In June 1979, this is where the meetings of our association – the Philadelphia Association (headed by Ronald D. Laing) – took place. On this particular evening, where the following story began, Loren Mosher (1933–2004) was our guest. He had arrived back from Italy. He was there to give us his impressions of the Democratic Psychiatry movement in and around Verona and his experiments in the Soteria project – where spontaneous, slightly mad people were successfully treated without medication (Mosher & Burti, 1989; Mosher, Hendrix & Fort, 2004). Francis Huxley, a member of the executive committee, introduced Loren. As the latter began to get into his story, Arnold, a rather stocky, 26-year-old postgraduate in humanities, interrupted him. Arnold commentated on this in the style of a newsreader. Loren Mosher and several of the listeners seemed irritated by this. What Arnold said: 'For my mind, finishing psychoanalysis is the same as emerging from adolescence. To do this successfully you have to internalise your family sufficiently well. We have to come to terms with our strengths and weaknesses.' Following on from which, a few statements about group dynamics: the group here feels 'out of context'. Cautiously, Arnold leaned back in his armchair. Loren Mosher carried on speaking. He was in full flow when Arnold jumped in again and gave a short commentary on what was going on in the here and now, from his point of view. Francis Huxley politely asked him to stop doing this. I could see that this confusion was more than just a student's fit of over-enthusiasm. Mosher managed to finish telling his stories, but most of the listeners left dissatisfied.

The following evening there was a seminar scheduled on the topic 'The mythological spirit' with Francis Huxley, anthropologist and mythologist. Huxley's basic question in this seminar was 'how can we be direct and spontaneous with people who are filled with madness?' What do we learn from a cultural comparison? Some societies still nourish and cherish a formal religious system – mythos – like the people of Haiti and the African religious voodoo system, documented by Huxley (1966a) in his book *The Invisibles*. What happens if a member of their community is possessed by madness? The ritualisation of madness can be seen as a possible route to healing. When I arrived at Arnold's home, he was still in the same mood as the previous evening. Over the past weeks we had been discussing in the seminar the myths of being disassembled. They always have, as we learnt, something to do with sex, gender confusion, incest taboos and violence – becoming detached from the habits that bind us to our fellows in everyday life. In the absence of a route to somewhere where we can reorient ourselves; our panic carries within it the danger of a mental and social breakdown. Arnold broke his shell. His demonstrative masquerade, in the panic of not being able to say everything he thought, to show everything he felt, to dance out everything that moved him, brought him into an unusual stream of life. If he had been a stutterer up until then, he now stood trembling on the threshold. Here, therapeutic ideas were transformed into actions. Now Arnold spoke fluently. Francis Huxley asked those who were present if they would like to put mythology into practice. We could thus discover together whether mythical stories could give us hints as to what Arnold was now experiencing.

We are familiar with the stories of Chronos, Isis and Osiris. After a brief, clear discussion, the majority of the 15 participants agreed not to shut Arnold, and the things he showed and revealed to us, out of the meeting. Huxley had brought a rattle with him, which emitted a rich, full, gurgling tone. He stood up and began to beat a rhythm with the rattle. He thus tried to raise our own rhythms and slow Arnold's down, an adjustment in our mental kraal. Arnold now had our full attention. His continual wandering about in the flat caused us to move about as well. Now he sat down at Francis' feet, and asked Gale, his girlfriend, and Chris, to hold his hands, to create a half moon. Arnold said 'my sexuality is a mess. I feel homosexual. I feel a bisexual fear. I am in the womb. I feel my father copulating with my mother. I realise that I have not given birth to myself, or conceived myself. I am concerned for us all: I want us to be a loving, caring community. That is all I have to say, and now I'll be quiet.' Arnold leaves the group space. 'Now he's quiet, we can talk' says a woman whose name I have forgotten. We have hardly begun our conversation when he's there again, touching people he is more closely acquainted with. He says, 'my mouth is my vagina, my tongue is my clitoris.' Huxley starts to hum. Arnold tries to stand behind him. Huxley doesn't allow this. Now we dance. We hum together. Arnold rocks himself into a tantrum, is pushed into the centre of the dance, shoved, and rolled about. From this emerges something like a re-birthing ritual. Then the neighbours arrive. They ask us to calm things down a bit: their baby can't sleep. Francis Huxley asks for a bath towel and a fresh flannel dipped in cold water. Whilst he washes Arnold's face and neck, he talks. 'Now you are reborn and washed. Up and out onto your new path.' With this little celebratory act, Arnold becomes calmer. We calm down as well. Francis Huxley has guided us through this 'rite of passage' ceremony. As the master of ceremonies, he looked at the chaos and made it his mission to guide us through this mental storm (Itten, 1979, 1993).

It is not only that we have secrets. The real secrets, as Jung thought, also have us, which is a jolly good example of the voice of experience and self-presence in psychotherapy. Francis Huxley and Ronnie Laing first met at a conference on ritualisation, held at the Royal Society, London, in 1965. Organised by Francis' father, Sir Julian Huxley (1887–1975), son of Leonard Huxley (1860–1933) and Julia Arnold (1862–1908) daughter of Matthew Arnold (1822–88) whose book, *Culture and Anarchy* (Arnold, 1869/1979) was a formative influence on Ronnie Laing. Julian Huxley had coined the term *ritualisation of behaviour* in describing the mating habits of birds. As one of the renowned polymaths in the cultural and scientific life of the last century, he was instrumental in setting up the Department of Biology at the Rice Institute, Houston, Texas, fellow of New College, Oxford, and professor of Zoology at King's College, London. He was director of the Zoological Society, thus the London Zoo, and became the first director general of the United Nations Educational Scientific, and Cultural Organisation (UNESCO).

With a taste for outlandish places, Francis Huxley went as an undergraduate to investigate hippos in Gambia and the birds of Jan Mayen Island. He had served as a lieutenant in the Royal Navy during World War Two, after which he veered from zoology towards anthropology and spent some six months living with the Urubus, a tribe of the Tupinamba peoples, who live between the roughly north-eastern courses of the Pindaré and Gurupi rivers, in the Amazon jungle of Brazil (see Huxley, 1956). In the two years following his return Huxley held the position of assistant curator of the Liverpool Museum; he then worked as a social anthropologist in the Weyburn Hospital, Canada and for five years was research fellow at St Catherine's College. From 1974–82, Francis was principal of studies of the Philadelphia Association, London.

When Francis and Ronnie first met, (at the conference on ritualisation, mentioned earlier) Ronnie Laing was 37 years old, in private practice as a much sought after psychoanalyst, and at the time still at the Tavistock Institute of Human Relations as principal investigator, Schizophrenia and Family Research Unit, and fellow of the Foundations' Fund for Research in Psychiatry. 'Ritualisation and abnormal behaviour' was the title of his talk. He pointed out that as social norms shift, and they certainly did in the mid-1960s, so shift the demarcation lines between what most people regard as normal and abnormal. He gave examples of para- or anti-ritualisation, private rituals that seem to be self-gratifying or self-rewarding, aiming at anxiety reduction and destructuring the usual social structure of communication. Laing said, with Francis Huxley among the audience:

On closer understanding, however, the ritual may be found not only to be self-directed but also to have a socially directed message, conveyed in a privately elaborate code. It becomes the psychotherapist's task to decode it. Sometimes, if the patients trust one enough, he will decode his signals himself, or explain them retrospectively after he has given up the ritual. (Laing, 1966: 332–3) be actualised or cultivated. This was done by a process of incubation. This took place underground, in snake holes, where the patients, after cleansing and singing rituals, spent a day and night of healing sleep. Some say it was for three days and according to other writers, involved the use of psychedelic substances, as well as the company of snakes. On re-emerging the patient would tell their healing dreams and visions to the therapist, who often did nothing but listen attentively with unconditional love. The content of the healing dreams would direct and form the basis of the treatment. In an interview with the Greek journal *CHIOS*, Laing (1984b) had this to say:

> I call my type of therapy Integral Therapy, because integral means the whole and that means that I don't confine myself say to practising so-called psychotherapy or psychoanalysis or any particular method ... I regard myself as a priest of Asclepius ... a method of healing which is incubation ... the skilful method of helping people out of catastrophic states of mind that they want to be helped out of themselves. That is therapy. And the main factor in this skilful means, in this method of therapy, is one's own presence, one's own relationship to the universe. (Laing, 1984b)

A stay in the Villa Therapeutica is usually in three stages: the first one is generally in the swing of rushing about, doing things frantically. The second is a spiralling down, a journey to the bottom of core issues. After one has reached the bottom as the ground of one's core or true self, one moves slowly into the third stage, where new initiatives become apparent and people start to find their own pace and place in life. It is important not to resist any active impulses coming from within, to let one's self go, so that one does not become the prisoner of one's own past conditioning experience. I have experienced, on a personal level, that there was an up and down of spiritual and physical discipline, the lack of which leads to a point of boredom with no initiative whatsoever. Then comes the moment of begging, where as a patient one only wants things done for oneself. If they don't materialise, let's find a scapegoat to be blamed for the state one is in. There is a soul swing between wanting to be open and tolerant to those in severe distress, and yet, if someone should rock the boat too much, and personal self-interests are endangered, like a balanced household, then there is no way that a person like that could stay on too long. The courage to say no in the first place is called for as an important therapeutic key, to realise one's own personal limits and boundaries.

Finally, I would propose to you to imagine someone allowed to go through a psychosis as a natural cycle, as a breakthrough to the true self, as the beginning of a healing journey. Furthermore you as an aide or professional helper can partake in this adventure of natural healing, without the interference of chemical straightjackets; to experience a reality based on the authority of one's own psyche, rather than power- and theory-based authority. As long as we practise human camaraderie, this can be, as Laing mentioned in his biography, 'the *sin qua non* of "treatment"' (Laing, 1985a: 145). He goes on to remind us:

> The misery of a person in extreme mental misery is usually apparently related to their relations with other human beings. Indeed, we sometimes almost take it for granted that most people seem to go on most about their relations with others. (ibid: 146)

Thus, the way we treat each other is the therapy. We can think about reframing our experience and mode of living, we can be co-present in a courteous and harmless means as compassionate psychotherapist in rapport with our patients. They are invited to drop their past suffering, change their habits in a self-determined and free fashion, knowing that due to living and being lived (by the unconscious) we have new moments to get stuck. The art of living is to get out of the place we are caught in first. This is the beginning, middle and end of the process and experience of metanoia (see Laing, 1972).

To date the iterative journey through our own lived experience and the practical and theoretical developments (which have connected themselves to them) has largely considered the art and 'science' of psychotherapy. The human beings who venture into psychotherapeutic encounters seeking assistance however, begin their journey to that space through the accumulated wealth (or poverty) of their own life history. How they got here (often – though not always) lies thus beyond our own direct experience. This is where we call on theory beyond our own structured imaginings of what it means to be human and what human beings require from one another in the world. This is where we require theory to explicate what can happen to human experience in the shadow and complexity of other people's presence. In the following two chapters we return to Laing's work with families. Our purpose in doing so is twofold: first to examine what we see as neglected aspects of earlier analyses – the gender and historical dimensions of family life, and second, to extend the

the Berlin Wall and the reappearance of modes of thought buried under decades of communist rule (Hewer & Kut, 2010). Memory can now be envisaged as a reconstruction that flows through people's interactions with each other, with institutions, places, monuments, and information archives (Hewer & Roberts, 2012). This is an active ongoing process subject to continued negotiation, renegotiation and contest at all levels of social organisation. Thus, how a nation recollects its past and orients itself to the future (e.g. Liu & Hilton, 2005) is in principle no different from how any smaller grouping such as an organisation, institution, community or family organises its own identity and corresponding *raison d'être*. The same processes of affirmation, avowal, disaffirmation, denial and forgetting (Connerton, 2008, 2009) can be found wherever one looks in the social hierarchy.

Laing's emphasis on the intergenerational re-enactment of specific family identities, power roles and psychosocial dynamics across time points to an aspect of social memory which has not always been made explicit, that the recollection, recall, reliving and re-embodiment of the past in the present is often more unconscious than conscious, present more in behaviour than conscious awareness – a memory transmitted through the acquired patterns of relating between members. Our present collective misery, subservience, hopelessness and obedience to authority can all in some measure be viewed as collective memories of personal and social historical submission – similarly our continued resistance to the systems of organised malpractice in which we live (sexism, racism, classism, able-bodiedism, psychiatric oppression, to name but a few) are constructed wholesale from the successful lessons of the past and how they are bequeathed to those who will come after us will depend on the forms of memory transmission we enact. To elaborate, such identities as may reoccur across generations of families, embodied in different individuals who may carry family role traditions, for example, black sheep, clown, naughty child, eccentric, lunatic, brains, etc. may be nothing more than the behavioural tip of a memorial iceberg that has travelled downstream generation after generation, melting slowly and inexorably into our basic assumptions and ways of seeing.

Institutions, politics and memory

As in the family, so it is in the workplace – a neglected site when it comes to studying the manufacture of madness. The following I (RR) hope will clarify the creative possibilities for understanding the relocation of irrationality from the social to the individual which resides there. In an attempted discussion in recent months to resolve a dispute, one of the managerial storm troopers of higher education remarked to me (delivered with insincere bonhomie[5]) 'just because I've written something [in an email] doesn't mean you should assume that I believe it'. How exactly is one, as both employee and human being, supposed to respond to this? To engage in open conflict over this is to risk becoming entangled in a strand of gobbledegook, which could tie one in knots trying to make sense out of something, which from the recipient's point of view, essentially lacks it. It helps to realise that working in a modern institute of higher education such as a university is to be embedded in a phantasy system no less complex and very possibly a good deal more complex than that found in the average family. Of course belief in the existence of the university is founded upon a number of apparently rational factors, thus we are likely to believe that we are working in a university if there is a believable hierarchy of academic prowess on show, that is, that there are students, lecturers and professors, that the lecturers are suitably qualified, teach, do meaningful research in areas of their choosing, that is, pursue academic freedom and challenge existing wisdom, that the students study, engage in debate, take exams etc., that there is in addition a suitable physical geographical infrastructure such as libraries, computers and lecture halls and that these are made appropriate use of. Each institution will also have its acquired history and roll call of illustrious alumni to make everything appear that much more credible. The internalisation of the relationships between these actors, institutional artefacts and institutional history is what forms the basis of the belief that the university is in some sense 'real'.

To the extent that the internalisation of the above relationships accords with what one 'sees' on the campus, the psychological operations which construct the phantasy of the university as object will map transparently onto the reality. What if all is not what it seems however or is considered to be not what it seems? What if the professors and those higher up the academic food chain don't actually possess academic qualifications? What if they don't do any research or have never done any? What if the actions and functions of the supposed academic hierarchy have more in common with the running of a supermarket chain than an institute of learning? What if the central planners behind the current set-up don't actually want academics to do research, detest 'unfettered scholarly inquiry' and want vocational training rather than higher learning (Tucker, 2012: 99)? What if academic freedom has been abolished? What if the students don't study, what if the library has few books and journals? What if students don't write their own essays, and think they buy their degrees rather than earn them through their own efforts? In short, what if the whole enterprise is a gigantic lie?[6] Furthermore what if one doesn't want to exhibit the unswerving loyalty to the institution that one is expected to internalise and display? It is undeniable that since the 'end of history' proclaimed by Francis Fukuyama, history has changed and with it the higher education landscape has actually changed beyond recognition, warped by the transforming power of corporate desire – a lust for learning has given way to a lust for money, power, market share and social control. Given this, ideas of what is a university are changing[7] – and with it gaps are opening up between the present reality and the decades-old (if not centuries) old social phantasy of universities as society's dispassionate truth seekers. How far this fracture between phantasy and reality can proceed before the casualties become undeniable is open to question.

Drawing on his experiences in the UK, Tucker (2012: 101) outlines his view of the modern European university, now envisaged as a way station on a managerially driven corporate conveyor belt to societal intellectual stagnation.

> The corporations ... tell the public universities what kinds of specialists they need, the universities produce them, and the graduates will have an excellent chance to work for the companies. The state will collect and spend taxes, and the corporations will save on the costs of training new employees. However, the interests of the big corporations are not identical to those of students and workers. Corporations prefer to receive welfare from the public purse to save on their training expenses; they prefer highly specialized workers who can start work immediately and cannot change jobs easily. Workers who are overspecialized cannot find alternative jobs easily and therefore occupy a weak negotiation position. If they lose their job when the company collapses or contracts, they have a limited set of skills to offer other employers. (Tucker, 2012: 101)

In this uncompromising vision, academic self-governance along with academic freedom has been abolished. Our factories of learning are the new dark satanic mills run by managers[8] who follow a model 'that resembles the late Soviet model of industry during the Brezhnev era' (ibid: 102). The demise of the ivory towers as places of free thinking and intellectual liberty could easily lead one to surmise that the university is in the same state of obsolescence as the family in David Cooper's (1971) eyes, God in Nietzsche's and the Parrot in John Cleese's – that is, in effect dead. The university, God, and the parrot also share a commonality in that there are people with vested interests in believing in their existence. Unable to acknowledge the death publically we are condemned to live in a state of lucrative[9] denial as unwitting students and their parents subsidise the lavish lifestyles of the teams of bureaucrats who maintain the government/ corporate simulacrum that animates the corpse of the actual deceased university.

> The centrally managed university is a parody of a university, a Potemkin village that has the facade of a university. Instead of teaching, it has cheating; instead of Socratic dialogues, it has bullet points; instead of a community of scholars united by a search for truth, it has atomized individuals suspicious of each other and informers for the manager; instead of intellectual and spiritual life in truth, academic life is devoted to the implementation of absurd, senseless, immoral, and harmful policies that percolate down through an anonymous, unaccountable bureaucratic hierarchy. (Tucker, 2012: 118)

Thus have the bearers of the enlightenment been given a makeover. To keep up appearances universities as they now self-construct themselves in their own brand image are in the 'business' of selling themselves to business for their own survival – in a not too dissimilar fashion to some of the students who populate the landscapes of higher education. Such market activity one can argue constitutes a greater peril to esteemed Western pedagogical values and our remembered way of life than anything *Buffy the Vampire Slayer* dispatched in her weekly battles with the campus supernatural who were, it must be noted, conspicuous in their abundance whilst going unnoticed to all but the Scoobies (Roberts, 2011a). Not for nothing are the undead a recurring motif in popular culture – a theme we will return to in Chapter 10.

As my own (RR) awareness of this has blossomed, so to speak, in recent years I have both witnessed and encountered first hand a set of strategic responses on the part of higher education luminaries which are uncannily similar to those meted out to the unfortunate victims of 'family dynamics' captured in the pages of Laing and Esterson's justified, denied, fantasised, fabricated, objectified and lied about by numerous Serbs on an individual, personal as well as social, political and collective level are recognised in other quarters as the worst war crimes to have occurred in Europe since the Second World War, involving genocide, mass murder, rape, and forced deportations.

All this is of course refracted and experienced through the continuing human interactions between people on different sides of the ethnic divide. The survivors of Europe's latest 'war against memory' (Levi, 1989: 18) feel 'alone, abandoned and forgotten' (Halilovich, 2011: 49). Many of Vulliamy's interviewees describe continuing feelings of unreality, that they are living another life, are not themselves; are 'Nowhere. Lost', think of themselves as 'limbo people' (ibid: xlii) feel 'ruined', and speak of having to 'close' themselves 'down as a human being' (ibid: 107), that what they must deal with is 'strange', 'frightening' (ibid: 179), a disjunctive 'terrible black hole' (ibid: 307) in their lives. There is talk of those who have cracked up and retreated into a world where others cannot reach them, their 'minds defiled, memories overrun and dreams eroded' (ibid: 323). Their agony and destroyed world is described on the Serbian side as 'liberation', (Vulliamy, 2012: 180), their narratives as 'unfounded', or else 'irrelevant' (ibid: 140) and 'disrupt[ive]' (ibid: 144). One of Vulliamy's points – and one increasingly supported by scholarship – is that the people of Bosnia are a forgotten people, whose existence is disavowed by the West, which has disavowed its own role in the unsavoury events which unfolded there[14] (Glaurdić, 2011; Roberts, Bećirević & Paul, 2011).

Those who somehow survived this desecration of memory and remained sane do so because they have maintained their own 'axis of orientation', in disobedience to the nationalist authority of those who would steal their memories and bury them along with the many dead. In part it is also because they have retained an ability to laugh and cry and have developed a sense of when and when not to share their experiences. Crucially they have each other to confirm their sense of reality, and provide that vital 'connective structure of memory' (Brockmeier, 2002: 26) that enables them to make sense of their past and present lives and thereby evade the full force of the strategic lies and attempted mystification sought by their Serbian aggressors. 'We are told by the Serbs who persecuted us that the place to which we have returned is a multicultural place, after they tried to destroy us; and that we can be expected to live together with them but on their terms' (Vulliamy, 2012: 308). The wider international community too has sought to impose its own variety of mystification by seeking to impose the mantra of moral equivalence on both victim and aggressor and with it an imperative that they must 'forgive and forget. Move on'. Through this they remain confused as to why their Serbian neighbours cannot simply apologise and begin the process of reconciliation. Of particular interest in these accounts is that recovery as well as the trauma is seen as extending across generations – 'it's too late for our generation to recover. It's got to the point where we don't want it out of our heads anymore, so that the recovery time is fifty years, three generations' (ibid: 303).

If it will take several generations for the Bosnians to recover, what will it take for their aggressors? Welzer's (2005) research into the transmission of historical awareness in a group of forty German families provides some clues. The study design has many parallels with Laing and Esterson's family research – a social phenomenological investigation in which interviews took place 'in the context of a whole family discussion and in separate interviews with at least one member of the eye witness, child, and grandchild generations in the family' (Welzer, 2005: 2). Eyewitnesses were questioned about their wartime experiences in the period after 1933, whilst their children were asked to relate what they had heard from their grandparents and parents about the same period. The study is therefore avowedly intergenerational in character and provides evidence that even where perpetrators have provided honest accounts of their participation in Nazi crimes 'family loyalties' prevent this information from being absorbed and assimilated. Instead, 'wartime memories are preserved in the family's lore as stories that can be reshaped to an idealized vision' whereby grandparents are transformed into 'people of constant moral integrity' (ibid: 7–8). Their relatives are constructed as 'good Germans' in opposition to 'bad Nazis'.

That succeeding generations have so managed to overwhelm the truth in a society which has unquestioningly done so much to reckon with its unsavoury past does not bode well for those societies which have not. In the Serbian community there has been no reckoning with the state's aggression against its neighbours. We find simultaneous public recognition of Bosnia's territorial integrity with support for the eventual political assimilation into Serbia of half of the country, genocide is still denied (Ramet, 2002) most recently by the new Serbian President (BBC News, 2012), the international courts and

Thus it might make sense to consider the total world system (Laing, 1968) within which all social organisation is captured and all power flows, not only as the level of abstraction where all contradiction is reconciled but also as the repository of all human memory.

Lovelock (2008) proposed the Gaia hypothesis to bring us to see the earth as a living organism – a Laingian psychodynamics of intergenerational memory may give us a look inside the mind of the greater human presence on the planet. Interestingly, Stanislaw Lem's (2003) *Solaris,* while similarly positing a planetary living entity, can also be read as a philosophical meditation on our incapacity to escape from the recurrent dead weight of the past, how its emotionally salient content clings to us, driving us to relive it even while it haunts and imperils us. Caught as we all undoubtedly are in an enormous collective intergenerational memory game, our first steps in constructing for ourselves a measure of freedom from it must be to acknowledge that we are in fact in it. Then we might discover buried in the 'depth of the dark earth' an altogether different vision of the 'the bright gold' of humanity, one which from our present perspective is still 'fathoms down' (Laing, 1965a: 205).

Table 1   The behavioural and 'psycho' dynamics of memory and identity preservation

Domain	Defensive operations employed	Object and desire of defence
Psychoanalysis		
Self (object relations)	Memory control (repression, denial)	Preservation of psyche
	Acting out (self-injury, violence)	Ego integrity, self-esteem
Family (family relations)	Memory control (mystification, repression, denial)	Preservation of family reputation
	Use of psychiatric force, hospitalisation, treatment	Family integrity
Group dynamics		
Workplace (workplace relations)	Memory control (mystification, public relations)	Institutional reputation (community relations)
	Use of force (bullying, dismissal of staff)	Stability of business/financial interests
Geo-analysis		
Nation (international relations)	Memory control (modification, falsification of history, propaganda, diplomacy, public relations)	Preservation of national esteem
	Use of military and economic force: Power	Stability of political/business/financial interests

and reconstituted with every new edition – discussion of past errors perpetually consigned to what Chomsky refers to as the 'memory hole'. The balance in psychiatric assessment accordingly shifted from considerations of phenomenology towards those resembling the compilation of a shopping list. With psychiatric diagnoses now becoming indistinguishable from consumer products[17] one can but note the appearance of new products with alarming regularity. The **planned obsolescence** (the fourth mode of forgetting) thus built into each edition of the *DSM* has meant that considerations of family praxis and process can be safely relegated to the historical dustbin.[18]

Finally we have what Connerton referred to as **humiliated silence**. Successful marketing of belief in the putative biological nature of mental disorders has meant that open discussion of how families operate to produce what is considered to be madness leaves interested researchers at the mercy of their biologically oriented bosses, accused of being out of touch and at risk of career suicide, a clear danger to themselves and perhaps others (mainstream psychiatry). Without consideration of the extensive social memory processes at work, one of the enigmas of post-modern critical psychology would be the continued, and deliberate, neglect of Laing's work in some quarters. His name has been virtually expunged from contemporary accounts of the crisis in psychiatry – a crisis which is not difficult to discern from outside the profession. To invoke his name or his work is to risk serious embarrassment despite the fact that his presence lurks in the shadows of contemporary critiques of psychiatric theory and practice. A striking example of this is present in contemporary invocations to examine the social context, to recover and discover meaning in the behaviour and experience of the mentally disturbed. These are today the rallying cry of those who posit, not the 'anti-psychiatry' attributed to Laing and his followers, but 'post-psychiatry'.

> Contexts, that is to say social, political, and cultural realities, should be central to our understanding of madness. A context centred approach acknowledges the importance of empirical knowledge in understanding the effects of social factors on individual experience ... Post-psychiatry opens up the possibility of working with people in ways that render the experiences of psychosis meaningful rather than simply psychopathological. (Bracken & Thomas, 2001: 726–7)

Compare this with Laing, speaking at the 'Dialectics of Liberation' conference in 1967:

A fundamental lesson that almost all social scientists have learned is that the intelligibility of social events requires they be seen in a context that extends both spatially and in time. The fabric of sociality is an interlaced set of contexts interlaced with meta contexts ... One moves for example from the apparent irrationality of the single 'psychotic' individual to the intelligibility of that irrationality within the context of the family. The irrationality of the family in its turn must in be placed within the context of its encompassing networks. These further networks must be seen within the context of yet larger organisations and institutions. (Laing, 1968: 15)

Bracken and Thomas are the champions of this 'post-psychiatry', a post-modern linguistic subterfuge which transports us to a paradoxical brave new world, where we struggle for meaning, enmeshed in a system of social relationships stripped bare of the struggle for power between oppressed and oppressor. This exercise in 'post-philosophising' constitutes nothing less than the dematerialisation of the extant world in favour of an interiorised world of ideas. This new consumer friendly version of individualism Laing would no doubt have considered an act of mystification, by which he meant:

> ... the substitution of false for true constructions of what is being experienced, being done (praxis), or going on (process), and the substitution of false issues for the actual issues ... If we detect mystification, we are alerted to the presence of a conflict of some kind that is being evaded. The mystified person ... is unable to see the authentic conflict ... He may experience false peace, false calm, or inauthentic conflict and confusion over false issues. (Laing, 1965b: 344–5)

For Laing, as for Marx, the function of this trickery was clear – to enable '... a plausible misrepresentation of what is going on (process) or what is being done (praxis) in the service of the interests of one socioeconomic class (the exploiters) over or against another class (the exploited)' (Laing, 1965b: 343).

In reading the post-psychiatry of Bracken and Thomas, it is nigh on impossible to find signs of conflict, or discrepancies in power. Instead, what we *are* offered is yet more psychiatry. For them post-psychiatry:

> ... does not seek to replace the medical techniques of psychiatry with new therapies or new paths towards 'liberation'. It is not a set of fixed ideas and beliefs, more a set of signposts

> that can help us move on from where we are now ... and an
> increasing number of psychiatrists are becoming interested
> in philosophical and historical aspects of mental health care.
> (Bracken & Thomas, 2001: 727)

Bracken and Thomas fail to realise that this interest in 'philosophical and historical aspects' is the sign of a dubious paradigm (Kuhn, 1970) and a sure-fire indicator that their discipline is in crisis – a point made by Charlton (1990) some years before. Post-psychiatry then heralds no quest for liberation and no end to psychiatry – their lip service to 'philosophical aspects of mental health care', is an acknowledgement 'post-Laing' that people's problems do mean something but their mantra is to 'keep taking the tablets' anyway. So, despite having earlier (Bracken & Thomas, 1999) called on medicine to abandon psychopathology, remove schizophrenia from the lexicon, and set in motion a fundamental shift in the power relationship between doctor and patient, one can only be amazed that they continue to countenance any role for medicine and drug-wielding psychiatrists, in any imagined 'alternative' to current arrangements. They perpetuate the humiliated silence surrounding Laing and as a result post-psychiatry offers more confusion than enlightenment and, as a brand of psychiatry, nothing new – as some commentators from the right of the discipline have acknowledged (e.g. Smith, 2001). Humiliated silence however describes not just the professional, institutional response to what Laing offered – it also succinctly describes the plight of mental health service users who, when asked, consider family relationships as foremost amongst the causes of mental distress (Molvaer, Hantzi & Papadatos, 1992; Read & Dillon, 2013).

Endnotes

1. Bowlby considered it to be the most important book published on families in the twentieth century (Burston, 1996).

2. In Chapter 10 of Mullan (1995) Laing discusses his research into so-called normal families which was originally intended as a companion piece to *Sanity, Madness and the Family*. This never saw the light of day for a number of reasons, one of which was that Laing found the material excruciatingly boring, 'an endless drone, about nothing', in which 'fuck all' ever happens (Mullan, 1995: 281).

3. The *Times Educational Supplement* (cited on the back cover of *The Politics of the Family*). See Addendum on page 118 for a discussion of the different social memory processes at work in producing this particular form of cultural amnesia.

4. An excellent discussion of the re-enactment of our hidden behavioural past and how to deal with it is contained in the book by Anne Anceline Schützenberger (2004) *The Ancestor Syndrome: Transgenerational psychotherapy and the hidden links in the family tree.* London: Routledge. Further avenues for exploration exist in the biographical works of famous families, e.g. the Huxleys, the House Wittgenstein or the Kennedys. Sadly the poor do not have the means to leave us comparable details of their legacies.

5. I stress from my perspective. The individual may believe in the utmost sincerity of what comes across as utterly insincere. A psychoanalytic examination of the possible alienation and auto mystification of one's own experience that may be going on here is beyond the scope of the present discussion.

6. Even stalwarts of the profession such as Jerome Kagan (2012) have begun to question just exactly what has come out of it.

7. Higher education was first subject to 'market discipline' by the Thatcher government during the 1980s. It has proceeded unabated since – the RAE (Research Assessment Exercise), TQA (Teaching and Quality Assessment) and escalating tuition fees form a grim procession.

8. 'failed academics, and clerical and secretarial staff' according to Tucker (2012: 108).

9. Lucrative, that is, for the state and corporate sector as students in the UK pay eye-watering fees and in doing so effectively pay for their own training.

10. I could provide personal communication here or else cite legal affidavits submitted on behalf of colleagues, but let us just say, there is documentation to back this up and leave it at that.

11. Dare we call these the 'white shirts'?

12. In my current institution at least, courses in NLP have been a consistent feature of induction into the managerial hall of fame. In this context NLP may even be seen as a perverse form of psychotherapy 'light' – an intervention designed to hold the present at bay which in time can be forgotten about now.

13. During his trial at the ICTY, Milošević told the court that it was the French and the Bosnian Muslims who had masterminded the massacre at Srebrenica. A seasoned ICTY commentator remarked dryly that for Milošević 'truth holds no value' (Ramet, 2007b: 117).

14. 'Srebrenica was not simply a case of the international community standing by as a far-off atrocity was committed. The actions of the international community encouraged, aided and emboldened the executioners' (Rohde, 1998: 250).

15. This view charges that the ICTY has unfairly singled out Serbs for prosecution. Ramet (2012) cites a poll conducted in July 2003, which found that 59 per

cent of the 1,545 Serbs polled felt that Serbia should not cooperate with the tribunal.

16. Tennis player Novak Djoković, 'arguably no greater patriot in sport … believes … passionately that his country has had an undeserved bad press'. 'I believe', he said, 'my country deserves more than it gets at this moment press-wise and hopefully it is going to turn around.' The article in *The Independent* (Newman, 2012) entitled 'Novak Djokovic: Patriot's game' found time to mention the NATO attacks on Belgrade, whilst studiously avoiding any word of Serbia's role in the wars in Slovenia, Croatia, Bosnian and Kosovo. The hapless reader could be forgiven for wondering why Serbia has a bad 'reputation' at all.

17. Of course one wonders who is doing the buying and selling here – as the 'customers' have the products forced upon them by the bureaucratic state-sponsored vendors.

18. See Chapter 9 for further discussion of these issues.

Chapter 7

Feminism, madness and the family

> It is impossible to write as a feminist about R.D. Laing without acknowledging the importance of his analysis of madness as a female strategy within the family. For a whole generation of women, Laing's work was a significant validation of perceptions that found little social support elsewhere.
>
> (Showalter, 1987: 246)

> Ronnie stood in for all the times in my life when I felt unseen, unheard, with my experience unacknowledged.
>
> (Semyon, 1995: 195)

Introduction

'Feminism', wrote Juliet Mitchell (2000: xix), 'is about confronting emancipation in the heart of darkness.' In the 1960s many saw this heart of darkness beating in the killing fields of Vietnam and the riot-torn streets of the US. Those who read Laing at this time could also see it beating firmly within the bricks and mortar of the family home, a tell-tale heart dedicated to the destruction of youthful and not so youthful liberty. Eleven case histories, all of them involving young women, form the substantive core of *Sanity, Madness and the Family* (Laing & Esterson, 1964) and comprise the foundational work for virtually all that has been said about Laing and the family. Given this selection of material however it is more than a little surprising that little comprehensive assessment of it has been undertaken from a feminist perspective, save perhaps Mitchell's examination of the Laingian project in two chapters of *Psychoanalysis and Feminism*.[1] Added to this is the curious fact that save Hunter-Brown's (2008) survey of psychodynamic psychiatry in 1950s Glasgow, none of the numerous biographies and critiques of Laing's work (e.g. Burston, 1996; Collier, 1977; Friedenberg, 1973; Howarth-Williams, 1977;

Kotowicz, 1997; Raschid, 2005) has been written by a female author.

Before we embark on an exploration of the emancipatory possibilities which this work of Laing's offers women however, it is perhaps necessary to distinguish such analysis from any examination of Laing's or his colleagues' personal behaviour. Certainly legitimate questions can be raised with respect to the personal and political concerns, and indeed notable shortcomings, of the so-called anti-psychiatric coterie who briefly threatened the ruling psychiatric fashions – fashions which have since resurfaced with an institutional and pharmaceutical vengeance. Laing and David Cooper in particular have had their inadequacies laid bare – notably by Szasz (2009) in perhaps his final withering condemnation of the errors of the anti-psychiatry movement.[2] Such an enterprise, he argues, stood in the way of a sustainable and viable critique of the bogus medical nature of psychiatry. Though it is unfair to hold Laing completely personally responsible for his media elevation to psychiatric guru, it is nonetheless true that he had long sought intellectual fame (Beveridge, 2011) and when it eventually arrived was readily seduced by it. It is also true that the practitioners of what Cooper (1967) declared to be anti-psychiatry, as Szasz (2009) and Showalter (1987) maintain, were doing no more than offering another version of psychiatry – one in which coercion had yet to be completely banished and talking and listening to others – the care of the soul – masqueraded as cutting-edge medicine. Laing disavowed the title of anti-psychiatrist, though embraced what he described as 'the anti-psychiatric thesis' that 'psychiatry functions to exclude and repress' (Laing, 1985a: 8) elements of society. This ambiguity meant that the 'practice' of anti-psychiatry remained cloaked in the shadow of its ostensible parent discipline and as such, at least in the minds of the public, it served only to reproduce both psychiatric power structures and psychiatric identity.

Analysis of Laing's personal failings, whilst they may be relevant to an historical analysis of the fate of the Laingian projects of the 1960s and 1970s – and readers with such interests now have numerous biographical works at their disposal to aid their study – does not exhaust an examination of their continuing worth. To think otherwise would be akin to rejecting the insights of Marx, currently reinvigorated by the unfolding political, economic and social tsunami provoked by the banking crisis, on account of his inability to escape the gendered behavioural standards of his day or, on a grander scale, the emancipatory failures of the communist revolution in Russia. Accordingly these critiques should not be the last word. Laing's openness to what women had to say, also evident in his critique of medicine's mechanistic approach to childbirth[3] meant that there was considerable scope for women to draw support from his writing. Griffin (2012), for example, writes how she drew great inspiration from Laings' work as she lent her own voice to the burgeoning women's movement. Similarly Mitchell (2000) sees Laing as having furnished the women's liberation movement with some of its language. Showalter's remarks above and Appignanesi's (2009: 406) below testify to the fact that Laing was an 'astute and radical ... listener to the voices' of women, even if he was unable to connect these voices to their plight of gendered social and economic subjugation. For Chesler (2005: 152–3) too, although Laing 'described the phenomena correctly' he did not 'fully understand ... their significance', remaining 'throughout the book ... unaware of the universal and objective oppression of women and of its particular relation to madness in women'.

Chesler's own recently published dialogue with Laing (Chesler & Laing, 2012), while illustrating Laing's sympathy with Chesler's approach, does lend support for her view that he did not fully appreciate the universality of women's institutional and structural subjugation. Ussher (1991: 130) concurs – viewing Laing's work as flawed but as 'an essential part of any deconstruction of women's madness'. In Laing's defence Collier (1977: 136), writing in the immediate aftermath of the Laingian heyday, rejected the charges of sexism levelled at Laing, and argued that 'one should not expect to find the theoretical basis for feminism in his work', seeing Laing's criticism of the family as 'distinct' but 'not opposed to that of the feminists'. All told it is undeniable that the feminist movement of the late 1970s, with its repository of sensitivity groups, consciousness raising and self-help therapy groups drew inspiration from Laing and the psycho-politics of the day.[4]

Before turning to the content of *Sanity, Madness and the Family*, and the continuing lessons as well as limitations the work embodies for understanding the lives of women, it will be useful to distinguish between avowedly female perspectives on Laing's work and those which are explicitly feminist. Appignanesi's (2009) oddly celebrated history of women and the mental health professions over the last two centuries makes such a distinction necessary. Undeniably richly researched and replete with interesting anecdotes about the lion-hearts who have fought the psychiatric crusade as well as those who have been slain by it, both intentionally and unintentionally, Appignanesi's narrative sadly wants for an injection of passion. Lost somewhere between brisk storytelling and the anodyne misguided myth of dispassionate science her tale is ultimately devoid of any critical spirit. As a self-confessed outsider to the 'psy' game she has been seduced into unquestioning acceptance of the language and customs of medicine applied to the existential, social and political struggles of 'the second sex'. From Virginia Woolf to Marilyn Monroe, she sees these women's often desperate attempts to live and make sense of their lives as 'signs' and 'symptoms' of various 'diseases' or 'conditions' they supposedly have. Upheavals in their lives and disturbances to their psychological equilibrium are framed as bouts of 'illness', or 'relapses', interventions from the 'knights of reason and order' (Faggen, 2002: ix); to rescue them are 'treatments' and in a telling phrase, Zelda Fitzgerald's efforts, through dance, to bring a measure of peace and order to her unruly life, merely actions which keep 'the chemical system in balance' (Appignanesi, 2009: 261). All this might be expected from diehard advocates of the medical model, wedded incorrigibly to the concept of mental illness but from someone purportedly championing the female cause one would hope for more.

As Laing (1965a: 31) wrote in *The Divided Self*, 'to see "signs" of disease is not to see neutrally'. The alternative which Laing put forward – to suspend the formal petrifying gaze and see behaviour as 'expressive of [one's] existence' seems lost on Appignanesi. Just as Judith Herman's work on trauma, duly cited by Appignanesi (2009: 482) referred to Freud's work as being 'founded on a denial of women's reality' so too in a curious manner is her own. Like Binswanger's treatment of Ellen West, discussed by Laing (1983) in *The Voice of Experience*, Appignanesi seems hell bent on burying her subjects alive 'screaming in their tomb of words' (Laing, 1985a: 62). As an historicised but not de-medicalised account it is lacking not only in empathy, but also in understanding of the significant scientific, philosophical, political, and moral critiques of the mental health industry. Under the combined dominance of Big Pharma and the medical men,[5] this industry, driven by an insatiable urge for power and control and accompanied by what Ussher (2011: 95) sees as a 'deep seated misogyny', has granted few favours to females.

In stark contrast to Appignanesi's work, Ussher's (1991, 2011) is premised on an explicit understanding of the socially constructed nature of all psycho-diagnostic categories and labels. Accordingly she adopts a similar stance to Laing and Esterson's in refusing to countenance notions of illness, pathology or madness as either legitimate or unproblematic when applied to women's distress, seeing the function of such terms as setting 'the boundaries of behaviour for the good woman' (Ussher, 2011: 7). Indeed psychiatry's fundamental role in society, is to not only police and sanction what behaviour is deemed tolerable and acceptable in a given society but to provide the lexicon for people to police themselves. In his conversations with Laing, Mullan (1995: 258–9) asked what is an all too infrequently asked question – 'Why is psychiatry so reluctant to let go of its ineffective techniques?'

Laing replied:

> They are not at all ineffective. They are only ineffective from our point of view, but are effective from their point of view. Jenner [6] put it to me very clearly one evening round at Francis Huxley's house: he thought that I was going on and getting a bit worked up about this, so he said, 'It's perfectly simple Ronnie, what we psychiatrists do is that we stop undesirable perceptions and experiences and undesirable conduct. And what is undesirable is what society says is undesirable. We are the people that society appoints to stop people seeing things and hearing things and feeling things that society thinks it is undesirable for them to see, and hear and feel' ... We use a medical model because that's the tactic that is currently most acceptable to justify this activity in our society. (Mullan, 1995: 258–9)

Sanity, madness and the feminine

For the eleven families which feature in *Sanity, Madness and the Family*, Laing and Esterson undertook 275 interviews in all,[7] amounting to 274 hours of total interview time. The women whose prior careers as psychiatric patients[8] had brought them to the interviewers' attention featured in 208 of these interviews, their mothers in 128 of them, the fathers in 60, siblings in 17, and extended family members (aunts, uncles and grandparents) in 14. Little is said in the course of the book to account for the observed distribution of interview time amongst family members, though it is noted that relatives on occasion vetoed interviews with particular family members and that sometimes specific individuals refused. Laing notes that they were 'generally successful in interviewing all the persons' (Laing & Esterson, 1964: 10) they wished. Consequently the above distribution is probably a fair reflection of both interviewees' availability and the wishes of the investigators.

The strong representation of mothers in the interview schedules therefore probably reflects not only the importance accorded to mothers in psychoanalytic theory at the time – particularly since Bowlby's work – but also the contemporaneously assumed primacy of mothers in the business of parenting and raising a family. Also to be considered is the fact that during this period of time (one of economic prosperity), most fathers worked whilst mothers who did so were in a minority. Additionally there is the not inconsiderable small matter that some of these fathers may have been abusers who had no wish to be interviewed. It is these broader cultural assumptions which are at play when, following the publication of the research, Laing was put under the spotlight for supposedly blaming 'schizophrenogenic' mothers for their daughters' psychological state. In such crude and outright false accounts the considerable time spent interviewing fathers, siblings and other family members is simply ignored, yet it is abundantly clear that all the family members, fathers as well as mothers, brothers as well as sisters, play important roles in the unfolding dramas of collusion, entrapment, denial, threats, blackmail, double bind and blame which engulf the young women centre stage.

Given the nature of the criticisms laid at his door it is somewhat ironic that Laing subsequently admitted that he hadn't 'written anything' (Mullan, 1995: 305) about sex-roles – that is either mothers as specifically mothers or daughters as daughters[9] – that his concern was principally the 'psycho-social interior of family life' (ibid: 304). His view was that to make an appropriate scientific statement about gender in the midst of this work would have necessitated a comparative study of males and females (who had been diagnosed with schizophrenia) and their families. That the final product had come to be written up in such a way that no emphasis was placed on gender was a criticism that Laing acknowledged in hindsight as 'justified'. 'I think now', he reflected, 'I would sharpen up the colour contrast' (ibid: 370). Of course the original intention had been simply to examine the interactional and communicational processes within families where there was at least one diagnosed member. This was with a view to seeing whether the behaviour and experience of that diagnosed person (which had hitherto been taken as evidencing the presence of some essentially meaningless psychopathological process – 'schizophrenia') might actually make more sense seen as one of the outcomes of the systemic communication processes identified; in short an understandable reaction to the complexities of a given situation. This was what was meant by rendering the behaviour in question 'intelligible'.

Madness and methods

With the above context in place we are now in a better position to consider those aspects of the research which accord with contemporary feminist analyses of women's madness (Ussher, 2011). In employing what would now be termed a deconstructionist stance and one moreover which eschews notions of biological determinism, Laing and Esterson avoided the pitfalls of the (still) dominant biomedical approach where women are customarily positioned/diagnosed either as victims of their reproductive biology (e.g. raging hormones) or their inherently vulnerable psychology (e.g. unstable mood or cognitive/attributional style).

As the social phenomenological method is primarily concerned with relationships which exist between people it follows that potential problems with individualism; that is, essentialising defects or deficits within a single person, are also bypassed. The research is one that is concerned with the meaningful consequences of relationships. Because of this one can read from the data, which was systematically gathered, a Foucauldian perspective of how power flows through the family system. This is assisted by Laing and Esterson's expressed endeavour to eliminate all interpretations, both existential and psychoanalytic regarding the motives and intentions, whether unconscious or conscious, of members of the family. This means that the legacies of any potentially patriarchal strands of psychoanalytic theorising should not intrude on any understanding subsequently developed about the plight of the various women. The methodology, because of its potential for sampling material across several generations of family members is, as discussed in the previous chapter, also avowedly historical in nature. Let us now turn to the data.

Madness and meaning

The clear demonstration in the analysis of all eleven families that interpersonal relationships play an important role in the genesis of the mental states of the young women 'patients' is particularly important given the long history of women's psychology being interpreted through their biology, both real and imagined. The 'delusions', 'hallucinations', 'thought disorder', 'bizarre' behaviour, social withdrawal and 'inappropriate' affect located by psychiatrists in the minds of the women all seem to make clear sense in the social (and historical) context of what others are saying and doing to them. There are recurrent features in the interview material which occur across many of the families. These concern the efforts of those who wield power within the family to control the memories, thought processes, identities, social status, education, sexual expression and liberty of those who by and large have little power – and it is evident that in these families it is the daughters more than the sons who lack it. This is exemplified by what transpires in the Blair family. Lucie, the designated patient, for example says of her father 'he doesn't believe in the emancipation of women. He doesn't believe women should support themselves' (Laing & Esterson, 1964: 48). Lucie's view on this, though not much else, is corroborated by her mother; 'I don't like his attitude towards people, especially women' (ibid: 42), 'he doesn't like men supporting women, and at the same time he doesn't like women to support themselves' (ibid: 55). This antipathy to women in the eyes of Mrs Blair appears to run in the family on her husband's side; 'they were far and away behind the times with their attitude toward women' (ibid: 40).

Faced with this, the failure of any kind of alliance between mother and daughter to materialise is central to the question of how Lucie has acquired the role of mad woman. Chesler (2005) provides part of the answer for the mother's betrayal of the daughter in her observation that Mrs Blair, though she 'sees herself as the subject of a forty-year-long persecution by her husband' (Laing & Esterson, 1964: 58–9) is 'too insecure', 'poorly educated' and ultimately 'economically dependent' (Chesler, 2005: 154) to carve out for herself a viable alternative life away from the home. Ruled by fear, 'terrified to "cross" her husband' (ibid: 53), advised by her own mother 'not to try and leave her husband because the difficulties would be too great' (ibid: 38) she had chosen to 'surrender' (ibid: 49) and forget the possibility of resistance– any signs of which in her daughter were to be crushed in a process of mystification whereby active rebellion on Lucie's part against the status quo was considered 'impulsive' and her resignation to it, 'affective impoverishment' (ibid).

With all roads to freedom closed for Mrs Blair, she is compelled in her husband's presence to shore up his repressive management of family life. 'For many years', Laing writes, 'it has been agreed between them that when he is present' Mrs Blair 'must side with him' (ibid: 40). It is inevitable then that Lucie's experience within this family will be invalidated and her behaviour measured by the yardstick of Mrs Blair's own internalised oppression. The death of Lucie's sister ten years earlier, said to have 'intensified her despair'[10] (ibid: 46) rules out the possibility of any other intra-familial female alliance and thereby cements her isolation and her vulnerability to the observable parental dynamics. The parental tryst functions to support Mr Blair's desire to make of her a 'pure, virginal, spinster, gentlewoman' (ibid: 52). The pivotal role of Mrs Blair's internalised sexism, ably supported by her fear, is not just representative of the dynamics of female subordination, but also an exemplar of how all oppressive systems of thought, dutifully sanctioned by money and power, survive and flourish from one generation to the next. As Black Consciousness activist Steve Biko famously commented, 'The most potent weapon in the hands of the oppressor is the mind of the oppressed' (Biko, 1987: 19).

The antipathy to female independence which characterises the Blairs is a recurrent feature in all the family interactions which Laing and Esterson document. Although the specific qualities of this antipathy as expressed in each family can in many cases be tied to the period in which the research was conducted (a period when social norms more firmly located the role of women within the household), it is of interest, given the importance of the mother–daughter relationship in these stories, to understand how micro-social practices rooted in family beliefs, traditions, myths and loyalties sustain the dynamics of oppression and give functional support to the patriarchal status quo above an alliance of female interests.

The Church family provide a particularly illuminating example. From the perspective of Claire, her mother and father were 'not her real parents ... but simply a pair of business partners' (ibid: 63). Demonstrating the usual incapacity to appreciate metaphorical as well as literal truth, the psychiatric system accorded delusional status to these statements. However the Churches were not the only family interviewed in this series to be constructed as a self-contained business unit. In a further volume, in which Esterson (1972) extends the analysis of the Danzigs, it is apparent that Mr Danzig also sees his family much as Claire Church considered her parents saw hers:

> There's nothing unreasonable in asking a child to do certain small
> things to give pleasure. It's a matter of capital investment. Look
> upon it as a practical point of view, as a businessman. You put
> money into a business and you expect some interest. Interest-
> right. If parents sacrifice their life for their children's, it's capital,
> it's outlay. The interest you get back – little – give and take, give
> and take. (Esterson, 1972: 48)

Viewed from our twenty-first-century vantage point however, the
Churches' and the Danzigs' restructuring and repositioning of the
family as business enterprise merits barely a raised eyebrow. In the
intervening years myriad forms of social organisation, the family
included, have been subject to a process of capitalist naturalisation.
Fully accommodated to managerial mores and the logic of compete
and conquer, their raison d'être as ours now, is to advance and
perpetuate the forward march of the capitalist ethic. If the takeover is
eventually complete, family life would no doubt resemble simulated
reruns of *The Dragon's Den*.[11] In the language of the cybernetic drones
who threaten the *Star Trek* universe (and our own) 'resistance is futile'.
The fate of Claire, captured between the twin invalidating business
interests of her family and the state-supported psychiatric status quo,
would appear to bear this out. Whereas in the heady days of the 1960s
the imperative for the Churches and the Danzigs would have been
for the family to be 'managed' as a small business, the inroads made
by capitalist realism into the family domain fifty years on now means
only one thing – the imperative on all is to consume, no matter what
the personal and social cost.

Claire's point of view, from within the dragon's lair, that any
'real parents' would surely put filial love beyond the reach of the
impersonal (and amoral) fashions of business, underscores her
resistance to a set of practices which threatens to sweep aside all
before it. Her struggle illustrates what the human costs can be
when relationships are sacrificed on the altar of profit and loss. Her
mother, she believes, 'brought the business-woman's attitude into
the home' and 'failed' her 'mentally' (ibid: 63). Claire's recognition
that this devotion to business negates human affection accords with
contemporary views that business 'loves money much more than it
loves you' (Applebaum, 2005). Showered with material goods but
little affection, Claire sees little option but to reflect this truth back
to her parents. A consequence of this is that she is seen as psychotic,
displaying incongruity of affect and persecutory ideation. Her

'failure' to follow her family's (and society's) prescription for what is considered normal compliant female behaviour sets her apart from others and cements their suspicions. She wasn't 'the *least* bit interested' (ibid: 71–2) in shopping, didn't subscribe to her mother's interest in dressmaking or her love of 'pretty', 'lovely', 'beautiful' clothes. This gender role disobedience becomes a matter to bring to the attention of the fledgling 1960s thought police in the guise of her family doctor. Because 'her daughter does not seem to like what she likes', Claire's mother believes 'there must be something wrong with her' (ibid: 72). Like Lucie Blair, Claire Church has lost a sister early in life and like her also faces life as a lone young woman lost in a family which behaves in cahoots with a larger social project intent on squashing female autonomy and replacing it with a socially constructed phantasy of docile femininity. Her opportunities for affection – for her girl friends, for men and for her mother have all been placed under the firm control of others – and thereby the potential avenues of support, confirmation and validation which might otherwise have sustained her existentially have been closed off. For her sins she is no longer on the map of dutiful, obedient and sane family members.

It would be a mistake however to see the daughters in these families as the lone sites of resistance. Mrs Church herself provides a compelling example of how the mothers in these family case histories came to adopt particular stances which spelt trouble for themselves as well as their daughters. Far from seeing herself as antagonistic, Mrs Church actually saw herself and Claire as 'very alike'. As Laing recounts 'neither saw much of their mothers', both of whom were 'business-women' who 'did everything for them'. Both lacked sisters, whom they had lost in infancy and both had younger brothers the burden of whose care had fallen upon them. In Laing's eyes, Mrs Church viewed her daughter through 'a film of projective identifications' (ibid: 66), thereby invalidating her own forlorn attempts to connect with her daughter and forge a sense of solidarity with her. Her actions mean that Claire's whole existence has to be forced into a preset mould; one which had been forged intergenerationally and into which Mrs Church herself had already been set. Claire's mother sought an alliance with her on the grounds that they both acquiesce to feminine powerlessness – a strategy which Mrs Church had learnt from her own mother. For this to function as smoothly as it had for Mrs Church in relation to her own mother, she had perforce to sabotage Claire's rebellious strivings, through the combined weight of her denial of 'her own perceptions' and inducements proffered for 'Claire to deny her experience' and 'moderate her behaviour'. This is a double bind into which Claire is tightly bound, locked into a no-win scenario in which 'the validity of rebellion, which Mrs Church was reaching for in herself, is invalidated by *her* when Claire begins to endorse her mother's own rebellion and to express any rebellion herself' (ibid: 79). Mrs Church 'struggling desperately within the limitations set ... in turn by [her] parents' (ibid: 77) thus sought to hypnotise Claire as she herself had been hypnotised by her mother, no doubt unaware that what she was doing was inducting her daughter into an intergenerational socially sanctioned aesthetic of pleasing others. Claire, unwilling to be so hypnotised but unaware that she was, was trapped; endgame and a journey to the psychiatrist's chair. Mrs Church's failed attempt to build common ground with her daughter is illustrative of many lessons, not least that emancipation cannot be won by conformity, obedience and sacrifice to others.

In summary, within the Church family, it is the internalisation and attempted transmission of capitalist patriarchal norms that has prevented the development of any true female solidarity. This process is still relevant today. The evolution of global super-capitalism in the intervening years has seen these norms imposed as worldwide desiderata. As significant collective feminist resistance in the West has also emerged and developed over the same period there have been concerted attempts to weaken and dilute its impact. These counter revolutionary campaigns have been waged with the full weight of the media behind them, propelling into public consciousness images of capitalist super-women, successful businesses and well-adjusted children in tow, bestriding the world stage with glamour that would not be out of place in a Bond movie. As we marvel at the sheer impossibility that one can really have it all we are simultaneously fed a diet of hyper-sexualised and objectified junk icons from the celebrity worlds of pop culture and pornography; a corporate licence to both thrill and kill, simultaneously feeding unerring dissatisfaction with one's lot. How this dynamic feeds into the micro-social practices of the contemporary family is barely understood as priorities seemingly lie elsewhere. While the corporate world wages an undeclared war against emancipation, the discipline of psychology offers up 'positive' psychology. This in Hedges' view 'is to the corporate state what eugenics was to the Nazis' (Hedges, 2009: 117), by which he means an ideologically supported 'quack science', that is 'no more helpful in solving real problems than alchemy' but is 'effective in keeping people from questioning the structures around them that are responsible for their misery' (ibid: 119–20). Laing's analysis suggests something more is possible. The orchestrated, obsessive objectification of women through their physicality and the consequences of this however are decidedly absent from the Laingian analysis which would benefit from a suitable upgrade in appreciation of the body's importance in affairs of the psyche.

Sanity, madness and the female body

To recap, Laing and Esterson's work, in both theory and method, strongly suggests that the presence of extreme psychological disturbance in people can be rendered comprehensible by an understanding of family dynamics. To produce disturbance, they propose, such dynamics encompass a number of key facets. These are: (1) Conflict of such a nature that important family roles and traditions are challenged or undermined; these may be previously understood (by the parents) ways of conducting family business or maintaining family order (e.g. parental or patriarchal authority, denial of filial autonomy). (2) The employment/enactment of particular political manoeuvres and tactics in the face of this conflict that aim to maintain or restore the desired status quo. Political operations to address this must involve denial, mystification, and invalidation of the experience of family members deemed to be responsible for disturbing the favoured family axes of orientation and denial that the actions of those family members are mystifying, invalidating etc. (3) The absence of sufficient support/solidarity within the family to oppose these operations such that at least one person is rendered alone, confused and uncertain about what is real and what is not.

The above model is one which is largely gender neutral and as such delineates only one of the means by which women's subjectivity can be denied, recognising neither the gender specific ways in which women's experience may be invalidated, nor the gender specific insults and traumas that females must contend with, nor the pathologising of what are 'reasonable, understandable and sometimes adaptive responses' (Ussher, 2011: 129) to how they have been treated. This is important as the entire basis for diagnosing mental disorder in the *DSM* rests on the notion that people's responses must not be 'expectable' responses to particular events. This, of course, assumes complete knowledge of what kind of responses can be expected in the face of a potentially infinite range of physical and psychological insults. Do we know for example what the expected responses are to being threatened with violence throughout childhood or being sexually and physically abused or subject to routine humiliation and invalidation? The answer of course is that we do not and that is before we address how responses may vary with factors such as gender, age, ethnicity, physical size or impairment, position in family, socio-economic position, early social environment, one's history of career/educational success or failure, existing beliefs, being told one is mentally ill, fearing one is mentally ill, the changing values, attitudes and beliefs predominating in a culture over a period of time, not to mention lack of knowledge of other cultures' preferred 'ways of seeing' (Berger, 1972), and how this lack of outside understanding interacts with existing psychological distress. In short, women in distress must contend with a nonsensical system which prejudges, in the absence of adequate information, how women in a patriarchal society ought to respond to the difficulties they face.

As well as underscoring the inadequacies of the *DSM* checklist diagnostic system for decontextualising women's responses to sexual abuse amongst other things, Ussher (2011) highlights the litany of statistics which point to the extreme objectification of women in society, the 'normality' of physical and sexual violence against women[12] and girls and the strong relationship which exists between violence and abuse and subsequent psychiatric service use. For example, child sexual abuse, in which girls outnumber boys by around two to one,[13] carries an elevated risk for most psychiatric disorders. The list includes post-traumatic stress disorder (PTSD), suicide, depression, anxiety, low self-esteem, somatisation, dissociation, obsessive compulsive disorders, phobias, paranoid ideation, substance abuse, eating disorders, and personality disorder (Roberts, O'Connor, Dunne, Golding et al., 2004). In addition, numerous studies attest to a relationship between hallucinations/ hearing voices and a prior history of physical or sexual abuse (Hammersley et al., 2003). Ellenson (1985) for example reported the presence of hallucinations could reliably be used to detect a history of incest; Ensink (1993) found voice hearing (30%) and visual hallucinations (43%) were common in a sample of women who had been sexually abused in childhood, whilst Honig et al. (1998) found high proportions of voice hearers (more than 70%) in those diagnosed with schizophrenia and dissociative disorder.

Numerous authors (e.g. Ensink, 1992; Heins, Gray & Tennant, 1990) have argued that the contents of hallucinations in survivors of child sexual abuse depict symbolic representations as well as flashback elements of their traumatic experiences. A vast amount of data thus points to predictable deleterious psychological consequences in those subjected to sexual violence who, as indicated, are more likely to be female.

Where the aftermath of sexual violence against women is concerned, processes of mystification, invalidation and denial are not confined to the interactions within families but extend well beyond them in processes which are also institutionally, culturally and socially mediated. In light of some of the evidence presented above, the psychiatric system's continuing insistence on viewing psychological disturbance through the lens of a biological causal framework can be construed as one form of institutional mystification and denial, particularly given the paucity of data to support the biomedical model. Women pursuing justice for sexual crimes committed against them must also contend with legal systems which throughout the world place considerable obstacles in their way, obstacles which may include protecting the perpetrators of sexual violence in the home, counsel that readily resort to blaming the victims, accusing them of having provoked their assailant, and not being averse to bringing the victim's previous sexual history and mode of attire into courtroom proceedings. Added to the medical and legal denial of the reality of women's experience, the entire corporate system advertises itself on the back of sexualised images of women, as opposed to the reality of being female. Such ubiquitous social representations create a world in which girls and women must not only contend with their own objectification and alienation writ large but also deal with the reactions of their male counterparts to this objectification. Out of this melting pot emerge the prescribed codes of femininity and masculinity that must be dutifully followed if the gendered requirements for sanity and madness are to be met.

Against this backdrop, there emerges in both men and women an internalised Orwellian system of self-policing. This may mean that anything from one's overall mental state and moods (sadness, anger and fear are high on the list for monitoring; boredom, surprise, interest are low), temperament, personality, physical state, health and wellbeing, to the quality of one's relationships, sexual 'performance', level of physical activity,[14] career advancement, and recognition in society are put under regular scrutiny by both self and others. One of psychology's roles in service to our current economic and political masters is to sell expert narratives to the masses which encourage such surveillance under the guise of being totally responsible for one's fate. In women this surveillance system is focused specifically on the body – what it does, when and with whom, what is put into it or taken out of it. This obsessive observation of women and what they do with their bodies is evident throughout *Sanity, Madness and the Family*, though Laing makes no explicit reference to it, nor considers the specific effect of such physical scrutiny on the subjectivity of the women interviewed. Let's consider this a little more.

In a footnote Laing notes that 'every family … is full of evidence of the struggle of each of the family members against their own sexuality' (Laing & Esterson, 1964). More often than not though, the struggle in question is against the sexual autonomy of female family members. So we learn in the course of examining the Blair family that Lucie had supposedly suffered from 'diminished sexual control' (ibid: 36). She had previously given birth to a baby girl who had been adopted, had another pregnancy which had been terminated and under what one might describe as the 'excessive' sexual control of others had then been sterilised. One must presume she had little say in this. Lucie's life was in addition lived under the constant surveillance of her father, who fearing that she would be 'kidnapped, raped or murdered', 'watched over all her movements' (ibid: 40). An abortion and sterilisation imposed on her by others are clearly relevant to her expressed 'psychotic' feelings of being 'torn to pieces' as is the general family context just described, to her view that other people 'put unpleasant sexual ideas in her head' (ibid: 35).

Ruby Eden's pregnancy and miscarriage also aroused the controlling instincts of her parents. This led to Ruby complaining that 'voices outside' called her '"slut", "dirty", "prostitute"', and that 'she had given birth to a rat' (ibid: 118–19). Though denied to Ruby, her parents confirmed to the interviewers 'with vehemence and intensity' that they thought 'she was a slut and no better than a prostitute' (ibid: 121). Ruby felt 'at night "people" were lying on top of her having sexual intercourse with her' (ibid: 118), this in the context of an ongoing public exchange of physical and sexual affection between the seventeen-year-old Ruby and her uncle which her mother finds repellent and which her uncle does not, despite his unconvincing protestations to the contrary. Sarah Danzig was also described as 'sluttish' and 'obscene' (ibid: 98). Her claims that she had been 'raped' (ibid: 95), and her 'squabbles' with her father 'about unannounced intrusions into her bedroom when she was undressed, listening in to her telephone calls, intercepting her letters' (ibid: 106–7), not to mention her parents' prescription that 'it was ... all right to go out with the opposite sex ... but naturally nothing sexual must enter into the relationship' (ibid: 113) also begs the question as to what was going on in this family and what precisely Sarah Danzig had endured. Claire Church was another who had the view that her tormentors were 'calling her a prostitute', her sexual feelings tolerated 'only if they functioned institutionally' (ibid: 85), that is, only expressions of affection from her which were preprogrammed and robbed of all spontaneity were acceptable, otherwise they 'were condemned in the strongest possible terms as much as sexual behaviour' (ibid: 85).

In addition to the control exerted over the sexual behaviour and feelings of the women described above we find, in the case of Mayo Abbot, a system of thought control whereby her sexual ideation was subject to a system of almost direct rule by her parents. She is told by them that she neither has 'sexual thoughts', nor engages in masturbation even when she affirms in the interviewer's presence that she does. Denial of control of one's own body may be considered a crucial step on the road to denial of the contents of one's thoughts, both are widely in evidence in the lives of the women whose lives form the core puzzle at the heart of *Sanity, Madness and the Family*. If one's own thoughts are powerfully denied then what can be the source of what one thinks? Reason in such circumstance might lead one to suppose that they are the thoughts of others, reason which would then be consigned to the list of supposed symptoms of the supposed schizophrenia which was said to be ravaging the lives of these women.

Laing's project of sampling the micro-politics of the family brings meaning to the 'madness' deconstructed within the eleven families; but it is unarguable that what has been deconstructed cannot be fully grasped without recourse to the wider society's systemic undermining and disempowering of women. The social construction of gender begins with attention to the primal physical differences between boys and girls, men and women. Mitchell (2000) sees conservatism inherent in the very construction of sexual difference, but is unable to appreciate that her own allegiance to the debunked universality of Freud's Oedipus complex as the primary source of the 'child's sexed entry into his or her world' (Mitchell, 2000: 262) is itself profoundly conservative. She thereby underplays the cultural rigidity of the available means of representation to hand and the extent to which, beyond the family, a given culture is, as is ours, in thrall to the image, the mass produced; that is, institutional, source of alienated happiness and real sadness. Foucault's (1979: 8) argument that our task is 'to discover who does the speaking, the positions and viewpoints from which they speak, the institutions which prompt people to speak … and which store and distribute the things that are said', is thus implicitly rejected.

Despite her feminist credentials, Mitchell sees the parent–child relationship as occupying a more fundamental role in the generation of gendered cultural meaning than all the social institutions of humanity since antiquity. She also distils the importance of Laing's work for feminism down to what it says about the singular paired issue of the 'girl leaving home and the mother letting her go' (Mitchell, 2000: 285). In attempting to defend classical psychoanalysis as an important analytic tool for feminists, Mitchell's oversimplification ends up by supplying those antagonistic to psychoanalysis with yet more ammunition. The numerous case presentations focused on women's lives which occur in Laing's work – from Julie in the final chapter of *The Divided Self* all the way through to *The Facts of Life* belie a much more complex picture and reveal Laing as a thoughtful interpreter of female psychology.

Such praxes, which socially construct gender, lay down the boundaries and the initial parameters within which much misery unfolds, is perpetuated and is misunderstood. By virtue of the psychological enslavement to all things corporeal and measurable we are now privy to an accelerating body fascism in Western popular culture, a dystopian culture now so 'flooded with images of women' as 'sexual commodities' (Hedges, 2009: 61) to be quantified, bought, sold, traded and exchanged, that we are being pulled under by the 'undercurrent of sexual callousness and perversion' (ibid: 73) that permeates the fabric of everyday life.[15] In such times the body and in particular the female body has to be appreciated not as an object but as a site of protest and resistance. Living in such an extreme world, 'we cannot dictate to our suffering and tribulation what forms to take, and sometimes they can take on very strange forms indeed' (Laing, 1983: 165). The inherent violence in the current systems of classification, interpretation and response to human distress requires urgent redress. The need for radical analysis and deconstruction of women's 'madness' thus has not diminished. With this, must come a deconstruction also of men's madness. Both have a contribution to make in dismantling the current set of social practices, ultimately rooted in the pursuit of corporate power and the production of social control, that constitute the mental health system.

As many have argued, madness is a gendered construction, but critical analysis should not and must not stop there. To that, though outside the scope of this chapter, we could add to the mix social class, ethnicity, culture, physical impairment, age, nationality and any of the other myriad demarcations real and imagined which set apart those people who wield systematic institutionalised power from those who are on its receiving end. Littlewood and Lipsedge (1997) took a step forward in clarifying the cultural intelligibility of much that is mistaken for ethnic minority unreason. However in failing to apply the principle of cultural intelligibility beyond the confines of their ethnic minority patients, they presumed the cultural, historical and hermeneutic unanimity of all their ethnic majority patients. Thus their well-intentioned efforts took them two steps backward, reinforcing psychiatric hegemony – and in positioning insanity in Black people as somehow different thereby added to the racism inherent in psychiatry which they sought to challenge. There is much work to be done; the extension of the emancipatory potential residing in Laing's family work has in truth barely begun. The interlocking systems of power which lock in the status quo do so to the disadvantage of the majority. The feminist struggle is but one part of the challenge to these. The methods we use to inform ourselves and to resist are of great importance. In the behavioural sciences we would do well to reinvigorate the study of human despair by making greater use of the painstaking methodology which Laing and Esterson pioneered. One of the tasks before us is to use this methodology to search for, uncover and perhaps rediscover the authentic feminine and masculine possibilities within and between us.

Endnotes

1. Even then, Mitchell's analysis has more to say about Laing's psychoanalytic shortcomings (castigating him for disavowing Freud's notions of the death instinct, the Oedipus complex and the unconscious) than it has about female liberation.

2. The term 'anti-psychiatry' was first employed in the early nineteenth century.

3. Described as a 'psychobiological disaster zone' (Laing, 1976: 64). Laing saw childbirth as an opportunity to prevent the inscription of patterns of physical and emotional distress which later could be played out in the continuous repetitions of adult disturbance (see also Brook, 1976). Around this time the Monty Python team, in *The Meaning of Life* (Jones & Gilliam, 1983) were also satirising the ruthless technical inhumanity of medicalised childbirth. The scene in the film is not for the faint hearted.

4. See for example Ernst and Maguire, 1987; Bertoluzza, Gitzl, & Rasler, 1994; and Segal, 1999.

5. Despite citing Foucault, Appignanesi appears unreflective not to say oblivious to the transforming nature and power of medical discourse applied to behaviour. There are also curious omissions from this history – all from the critical canon – no mention is a made of Szasz's (2006) acclaimed biography of Virginia Woolf for example, nor Poole's (1982) deconstruction of Woolf's supposed madness. Boyle's (2002) deconstruction of 'schizophrenia' also passes without mention as does Wilhelm Reich's founding work in 'sexual politics'.

6. Alec Jenner was professor of psychiatry at the University of Sheffield for 25 years.

7. Esterson did more of the interviewing (Burston, 1996) and Laing all of the writing (Mullan, 1995).

8. The age of the women when their psychiatric careers began ranged from 15–31 years. The length of their careers as psychiatric patients ranged from less than one year to 12 years. All had been given a diagnosis of 'schizophrenia'.

9. Although there is, as Laing acknowledged in the introduction, a focus which is 'somewhat' 'on the mother–daughter relationship' (Laing & Esterson, 1964: 13).

10. Mrs Blair comments of Lucy, 'She wasn't always dominated. She was happy enough when she had a sister' (Laing & Esterson, 1964: 55).

11. BBC TV series in which 'contestants' pitch their entrepreneurial ideas to a panel of businessmen and women in the hope of securing their financial backing. The panel are known for their forthright and often brutal judgements of the contestant's deficiencies. One of many examples in recent years of public humiliation masquerading as entertainment.

12. The World Health Organization (WHO), on the basis of 48 population-based surveys around the world, estimates that between 10 per cent and 69 per cent of women are physically assaulted by an intimate partner. The WHO also estimates that between 15.9 per cent and 51.9 per cent of women report attempted and forced sex by an intimate partner (cited in Ussher, 2011: 118–19).

13. Current estimates suggest between 12 and 46 per cent of girls have been sexually abused with concern that these figures may underestimate the magnitude of the problem as many are unwilling to disclose abuse to interviewers or may not recollect it due to defensive dissociation (Ussher, 2011: 114–15).

14. A zealous interest in this began to develop in the UK during Olympic year. In a move characteristic of the totalitarian impulses pulsating through the Western world, British Prime Minister David Cameron announced that competitive school sports would in future be compulsory. Parallels with the logic behind the Hitler Youth movement are unmistakeable. See http://www.guardian.co.uk/education/2012/aug/11/david-cameron-compulsory-competitive-team-sports?newsfeed=true Accessed 12 August 2013.

15. Hedges (2009) references the link between gonzo porn and the sexualised torture chambers of Abu Ghraib.

Chapter 8

The politics of memory: Field notes from an urban anthropologist[1]

> The idea of an individual memory, absolutely separate from social memory is an idea almost devoid of meaning.
>
> (Connerton, 1989, cited in Kansteiner, 2002: 185)

> Everything we have sacrificed and struggled to build to make this country a better place – our universities, our schools, our pensions, our health service ... [will be] hacked down and the little left ... subjected to the laws and logic of the market, where nothing is valued but profit ... That is the future they want, it is the future we must resist.
>
> (Malone, 2010: 240)

Introduction

Laing's work we have argued is relevant to an understanding of the social hierachy at all levels of complexity – the workplace as we have said being one of them. In this chapter we bring together the twin themes of memory and experience as situated within the rapidly changing higher education landscape. The experiential perspective contained in the following pages provides a crucial link between our previously stated critical views about the nature of the 'psy' professions – rooted in our earlier experience and theoretical analysis – and our contemporary experience of the academic world as it practically operates. For psychology to function as an alienated science this alienation must be continually created, produced and experienced on a day-to-day basis. This is one account of how it is felt at ground zero.

In the fable of Rapunzel, the maiden imprisoned in the tower lets down her golden hair in anticipation of attracting the handsome prince, her ally who will facilitate her escape from the clutches of the evil witch who has kept her in bondage. The nineteenth century tale of female slavery from the brothers Grimm has striking similarities to Persian tales dating back to the tenth century. In the twenty-first century the numerous worker prisoners in the ivory towers have no wicked witch to blame for the contemporary infringements of their liberty, and the relegation of intellectual autonomy to an obscure object of desire. In past meetings with the Vice Chancellor (VC) of one of the educational sausage factories[2] in which UK academics ply their trade, some of the reasons for the intellectual captivity of the modern academic were all too clear.

The modern Vice Chancellor, who occasionally prefers the nom de plume of CEO, typically presides over what has become the workhouse of modern reason. In these dark satanic mills students prepare for the derealisation of lifelong lies and dreams. Their partners in servitude are the staff who, inhabiting a resurrected world of Victorian social relations, must know their place. Facing a bullish arrogance and inability to listen, emanating from on high, academic workers now author publications to be counted rather than contemplated. Work is endless – and necessary to keep at bay the cavalcade of bloodsucking managers, the VC's accomplices in the vampire circus who hover in the air as unearthly reminders of the uncertainties in the labour market. With massive salaries, local perks and Dickensian power, the values promoted by the corporate VC bear striking similarities to the musings of such philosopher used car salesmen as Arthur Daley, resonating with the spirit of the British Conservative party – a party incidentally enamoured by disaster capitalism, the absence of morality and a predilection for the vicious targeting of society's most vulnerable. Such figures now populate the higher education landscape with a depressing frequency – and practise with a passion the managerialism which has infected the body politic of learning (Deem, Hillyard & Reed, 2007).

How I came to be part of this merry-go-round is in part the subject of this chapter. Hence beginneth this rag-tag academic travelogue of memorial oddities and anecdotes culled from my wanderings through the urban academic jungle, a parable concerning the abandonment of virtue and truth-seeking for the seductive vice of corporate and political approval. Inevitably rooted in exploitation, modern corporations such as the 'university' have no interest in their own history. To shore up our fascination with the individual, they have largely been airbrushed from the history of thought, yet their history is part of our own and so we must reclaim it as our own. Standing in the way of this, as Sennett noted, is the immense 'difficulty people have in making an accurate record of what has happened to them in the course of ... political and economic change' (Sennett, 2011: 284). In the sciences and disciplines which lay claim to scientific status – and of course psychology is one of these – the role of politics and economics in truth making has been considered of secondary interest if not irrelevant when measured against the myth of lone genius. Repeated often enough, false histories of our intellectual heritage ensure the disappearance of knowledge regarding the formative influence of political economy on thought. Through this collective hole in our intellectual memories we risk the fate of Paul Verhoeven's *Starship Troopers* – having one's brains sucked out in tandem with the disappearance of fundamental liberties. Sennett's professed antidote to this essentially fascistic malaise was to 'deal with the wounds of memory ... by remembering well' (ibid: 284).

The events unfolding in our institutions of learning, the unprincipled retreat there from what were once our core values, should not be considered independently of our violent hunger for acquisition on the world stage. Both chart the decline of the West and the trajectory of our spiritual malaise. Western society has come to the end of the moral and intellectual train ride that we took to flee the horrors of World War Two. At journey's end we find ourselves back at the beginning. In the new Europe everything is for sale including our cherished principles. It is time to take stock. If not now as Hillel asked, then when? Beset by fear, xenophobia, economic nirvana for the super-rich and nothing but cake for the masses, the dark forces of the last century are resurgent. In the aftermath of Nuremberg, with outward expression of the malign safely reigned in, there was a considered appreciation of what had been at stake and what had been on trial. In the present moment that intellectual memory has receded and behaviours considered unthinkable a few decades ago now grow menacingly in the shadows spawned by continental austerity. This marks a failure of all the emancipatory forces post 1945 to pass on the necessary lessons to the generations that follow. In whatever form organised resistance to the current global crisis develops, at the centre of it must be a realisation that social and collective memory projects have considerable significance and must be worked and enacted outside of any official reckonings with the past. Biographical and autobiographical work must be part of this and comprise a means of speaking across the divides of age, gender and culture, for the knowledge and lessons to be refashioned anew.

What follows are field notes from my own expedition through the politics of truth over the past thirty to forty years – my own attempt to deal with some of the aforementioned wounds of memory, and thereby to remember well. The institutions of learning, Magolda (2000) argues, have received all too little scrutiny from scholars. Consequently I locate this effort within the emerging anthropology of higher education, where the rituals, rites of passage, ceremonies and performances (including power, struggle and resistance) of the academy are all fair game (Manning, 2000; Shore & Wright, 1999).

As with all storytelling, this one unfolds beyond the prescriptive frameworks erected by sciences of the human condition. I hope I may be forgiven for recounting some of my own experiences in an age obsessed with narcissism and navel gazing. I can only say in my defence that this offering is no *mal de corazon* for some ancient academic homeland unbesmirched by the realities of power, but a travel guide to the treacherous landscape traversed by the typical Western intellectual over the course of a generation. It is also an introduction to the socially structured defence mechanisms (Menzies-Lyth, 1960) which permeate the fabric of the behavioural sciences and permit convenient lies to be passed off as truth. The ubiquity of our current institutional crises and the demands they make on our attention have their origins in previous events, events which were experienced, interpreted and reacted to (or ignored) by the actors of the day – distant voices and different lives. To understand how we got here requires some attention to what went on previously. The point of departure for such recollection is necessarily arbitrary. In the following pages, the casual reader of this chapter will notice that I have been embroiled in a good deal of conflict over the years. I do not welcome this. I do however prefer truth, honesty and openness to lies, deceit, and secrecy. I also believe that the decisions taken by those in power should be open to scrutiny and the people who make them held accountable for them. To what extent such democratic values have existed and do exist in the academic community is something to be considered.

Reflections

> Anthropology's predicament recalls that of Joseph K, the protagonist in Kafka's *The Trial*. Part of the reason he was so powerless was because he was never able to identify and therefore challenge the reason for his arrest. And because he never understood the system of power to which he was subjected, all his resolve dissipated and he eventually went meekly and willingly to his own execution. The lesson ... in the new neo-liberal 'trial' is that we have become the agents through which power operates and unless we wish to follow in the footsteps of Joseph K, we would do well to engage in more political reflexivity. (Shore & Wright, 1999: 572)

By the time I first set foot in a university,[3] the rot had more than likely already set in. Accounts of psychology's ministrations for the state – notably in the provision of services to aid torture – certainly suggest it had (see for example Cobain, 2012; Harper, 2007). Be that as it may, in the course of my working life the downward spiral has been marked. I have seen the occupation of university lecturer, a position which I formerly associated with at least a passing interest in encouraging free thinking and challenging received wisdom, transformed into an unhealthily pastime, obsessed with meeting the requirements of the bureaucratic and obedient lapdog of savage capitalism. Academics have been refashioned as corporate avatars, and freedom of thought, the new public enemy number one, all but vanquished, its occasional transient appearance of no greater duration than the fleeting light of consciousness evoked by a firefly in the heart of the black Amazon night. Protesting little, if at all, psychology in the meantime has completed the crossover from the 'manifestly unproductive' (Hudson, in Cohen, 1977: 169) to the manifestly dangerous, a key strategic player in the state/corporate game of total social control. Given the insidious nature of this transformation and the vapidity of any spirited opposition to it within the academic community we would do well to reflect on the nature of thought control, the spiritual and intellectual deaths which inevitably follow in its wake and the personnel who hold responsibility for promoting it.

As conventional psychiatric wisdom has it, delusions of influence may be considered 'cognitive intrusions ... misattributed to an external source' (Linney & Peters, 2007: 2726). But what do we say when our errors of judgement operate in the reverse direction, with external sources of thought misattributed to 'internal' sources and we end up mistakenly believing that the thoughts of others are really our own? Contrary to Shelley's famed fragment[4] our thoughts, as Halbwachs (1992) realised, rarely arise in solitude and perhaps more often than we would be comfortable entertaining, are of this misattributed nature. In the introduction to *The Politics of Experience*, Laing's (1967: 11–12) collection of essays from the early 1960s, he directed his attention to the unfathomable depth of our alienation. 'Humanity', he wrote, 'is estranged from its authentic possibilities.' 'Realisation of this', he went on, 'is the essential springboard for any serious reflection on any aspect of present inter-human life.' Such reflection has been absent from intellectual life for some considerable time. Given this, 'we are' as Laing protested 'all murderers and prostitutes' (ibid: 11) of the truth – none more so than the contemporary university lecturer whose professional duties now appear to preclude any possibility of realising (a) that the struggle of human beings to free themselves from the tyranny of malign and/ or stupid forms of social organisation has not actually ended and (b) that they could actually be taking part in this struggle as part and parcel of their professional life.

Encounters with psychiatry

My desire to engage in thoughtful understanding of the great mystery of existence began when I was very young, encouraged by my parents, some good teachers and a love of astronomy. I have always wanted to know what was going on and why. By the time I had finished my first post-doc job I was already thoroughly acquainted with what might happen to free enquiry when it runs up against those vested interests to whom unbounded curiosity is a matter of profound inconvenience and professional concern.

In addition to my duties as Research Fellow I was involved in teaching on the joint Community Medicine and Psychiatry firm in the medical school, working alongside a psychiatrist and a public health specialist in a weekly three-hour session taught to fourth year medical students. In the allotted session I would introduce the students to a critical perspective on mental health issues, taking in diagnostic, methodological and interpretive shortcomings in the speciality but particularly in behavioural genetics research.

The first peculiar incident during my tenure occurred one afternoon, when in front of the assembled students a local consultant psychiatrist, a stand-in for the regular contributor who was away, took it upon himself to induct the medical students into the sins of psychiatric logic. When his turn to take centre stage came he proceeded to ask me why *he* had never heard of any of the critical work to which I had just referred. Well, an important question indeed.[5] As was my custom in those days I used to carry around an A4 box full of this material so that interested parties could borrow and peruse it for their own intellectual edification. So I promptly offered to lend the said psychiatrist the papers at my disposal for him to read and let me have them back once he'd finished with them. To my and the students' astonishment he proceeded to walk backwards across the room declaring that as far as he was concerned, he'd never heard of the work I discussed, because in his eyes it simply didn't exist. The gaping hole in his logic – that is, the actual physical presence of the literature in the file in front of him and the absurdity of his actions – aroused bemused looks from the assembled doctors of tomorrow. This was a notable day in my own education and I'm sure the students', but I couldn't help wondering what kind of a deal the good people of this locality, who looked to this supposedly learned man to help them with their life's problems, actually received. Sadly this wasn't the last of my encounters with the dogmas of psychiatric orthodoxy at the medical school.

What was to be my last session again involved a temporary stand-in. To be fair to the regular guy, he had privately said to me that having listened to my talks now for the best part of two years he had come round to thinking that I was making some important and valid points about psychiatric research. Alas his open-mindedness did not seem to be shared by his colleagues. So, it was that during my final class I shared the proceedings with a professor who had not deigned to burden himself with the lowly task of asking any of us beforehand what exactly we had been teaching the students on this firm for the best part of two years. He waltzed in after my own presentation and nonchalantly proceeded to wax lyrical about the virtues of the so-called Danish-American studies[6] of schizophrenia. Having just heard a deconstruction and critical assessment of these from myself, I'm glad to say the students were having none of the intellectual laziness which the professor thought was adequate that afternoon. They proceeded to lash this big brains of psychiatry with their own views about the methodological shortcomings of what the professor considered (and no doubt still does consider) to be a beacon of established truth, shining in perpetuity from this 'landmark study in the history of biological psychiatry' (Snyder, 1976: 24).

After the class the professor approached me and began discussing the possibilities of the authors of the Danish-American studies taking legal action against their critics to silence them. Clearly he was not happy with any challenge to the received articles of truth and the next thing I knew I was in receipt of a letter on the headed notepaper of the medical school, from the Dean no less, thanking me for my contribution to the firm for the previous two years and letting me know in no uncertain terms that my pedagogical services would no longer be required. Letters of protest to the Dean duly followed and the worthy efforts of Ruth Wallis from the Department of Community Medicine, now director of public health for Southwark and Lambeth, all fell on deaf ears, cementing the triumph of the old boys' network, the intellectual demise of the school and my own exit from the system of medical education there.

Two interesting footnotes should be added to this tale. Less than enamoured of the professor's blunderbuss intervention in their education, the students sought to organise a public debate between myself and the professorial colossus to consider the merits of our respective positions. The latter declined to participate, an action that in itself told me as much about the underlying strength (or lack of it) of mainstream psychiatric opinion as anything I had read or would later come to read.

Some years later another member of the psychiatric staff – the TV and radio personality Raj Persaud – would come unstuck for what the General Medical Council described as 'dishonesty'.[7] Pronounced a repeat offender in the fashionable art of plagiarising the work of others, Persaud's glittering media career evaporated. His dishonesty pertained to repeating without due credit the truths unearthed by others. Though considered unproblematic by the same institution in which Persaud worked, the professor's actions, involving suppressing the truths disseminated by others, are of an altogether more serious nature and in my own eyes a good deal more dishonest and damaging. Collins and Pinch have argued that 'it is the repression of disagreement that makes bad science' (Collins & Pinch, 2012: 153). The history of psychiatry as a discipline and my own experience of it, illustrates their point by overkill.

Before the curtain was brought down on my three-year stint at this institution, I had another brush, though this time indirectly, and from outside the institution, with practitioners of the science of lies (Szasz, 2010). During this period I was involved in putting together the radical science magazine *Science for People*. This was issued quarterly to members of the British Society for Social Responsibility in Science (BSSRS). One of the members of the team happened to be related to the then editor of *The Lancet*.[8] Through this connection and with the day job being in Community Medicine I had occasionally been asked to write an editorial for the august medical weekly. This intellectual hobby was brought to a premature end in the second half of 1989 as one of the consequences of Laing's death.

I suggested to the editor that this was a timely opportunity for *The Lancet* to do a piece re-evaluating Laing's work and to consider the proposition that many people given a diagnosis of schizophrenia were in actuality suffering the consequences of trauma, interpersonal or otherwise, rather than some as yet undiscovered biological flaw. This, it seemed, touched a raw nerve. If I held this view, the editor lamented, I must be half-cracked. *The Lancet* was no place, I was brusquely informed, to be questioning the parameters of psychiatric diagnosis. If I was so concerned about this I should go and take it up with the Royal College of Psychiatry. A friendly challenge back to the editor that this wasn't really an appropriate response and that a really good opportunity was being missed received no reply, and with that my invitation to write for the journal described on its website as 'independent' and 'without affiliation to a medical or scientific organisation' were already a thing of the past. I later learned that the editor was far from independent and without affiliation to the purveyors of psychological medicine. The editor was married to a psychiatrist!

After my three-year stint in my first post-doc job, my next port of call was the Academic Unit of Psychiatry at a London medical college, there to join the denizens of the psychiatric underworld for a one-year research post investigating the role of cancer counsellors. A dilapidated outpost of psychiatry on the fourth floor of a hospital, the unit was memorable only for its peculiarity. The 'Prof' was notorious for locking himself in his office and pretending he wasn't there, which in a very real sense he was not – certainly not in the sense of fully functioning psychologically.

A few years later I bumped into his secretary on the tube. Looking frightened and in need of a good meal, working at close quarters with another of the masters of soul care had not been to her advantage. The strangeness extended to one of the researchers there, who for reasons which will soon become obvious had best remain nameless. Now a professor and consultant psychiatrist outside the capital; though man of mystery for present purposes he was no swaggering James Bond figure. He accosted me one afternoon while I was glued to a computer fathoming the dark arts of SPSS[9] syntax. He burst into the room where I was working and proceeded to rant for what seemed an eternity, accusing me of breaking into his office and stealing god knows what. The fact that I didn't know where his office was, had never set foot in it, and certainly wouldn't want to, didn't seem to cut much ice. Then again, with a reputation (I subsequently learned) for publishing drivel (this I can attest to) as well as manufacturing data to support his belief that 'schizophrenia' was inherited, his relationship to truth had already been compromised long before he accused me of being a liar. Had Freud been around to witness the spectacle he would no doubt have had a field day. At this stage in my career I had encountered four consultant psychiatrists not a single one of whom, in my view, had exhibited any fidelity to open and honest enquiry or understood the basics of scientific enquiry. They were also without exception rude. I began to suspect the issues were systemic rather than personal. Being still of an impressionable age[10] these perceptions began to stick.

From the insane frying pan of one medical college I jumped into the fire of the Department of Psychological Medicine at another. If I thought what I had previously encountered was off the wall, this next experience would see the walls removed completely. The post involved evaluating an experimental residential facility in East London for young people who had come to the notice of the authorities with either drug or alcohol problems. My boss, a decent-minded and fair bloke, with interests in psychopharmacology, had inherited the project from his predecessor, illustrious media psychiatrist, Anthony Clare. Little did I realise when I took the job, but Clare would be inextricably bound to the fate of the project. So too would another person whom I was to meet on my first day of work – Princess Diana. My research career at this institution thus began with a publicity stunt for Lady Di, accompanied as she often was by a pack of nobodies, press junkies and massed hangers-on. In all I spent about a minute talking with her, a forgettable conversation[11] in which funnily enough neither of us touched upon the cataclysmic changes in East–West relations (this was May, 1990), the meaning of life or the state of her marriage to Prince Charles. I'm also pretty certain that none of the residents introduced her to the joys of ecstasy or the delights of crack cocaine – though in the course of the job they did their best to enlighten me about both.[12]

That was my first day, the ensuing ones over the next eighteen months were if anything stranger still. The manner in which the ensemble of psychiatrists and those in their service whom I was to encounter would wield their grubby institutional power came to exceed in sheer nastiness anything then contained in my occupational memory. I was not ready for it.

Confucius (2000) held that 'those who know the truth are not equal to those who love it'. In the hallowed corridors and dusty offices from whence the psychiatric overlords issued their commands (and their dutiful social worker minions responded) could be found confirmation of this ancient Chinese wisdom. Following a series of in-depth interviews with both staff and residents, coupled with an analysis of the characteristics of residents and the nature of their problems prior to admission, I had concluded that all was not well. Residents felt, with some justification (in my view) that they had on occasion been subject to the arbitrary and unfair exercise of power by particular staff members. I had certainly witnessed some of this first hand – seeing residents subjected to disciplinary measures and withholding of privileges for lateness whilst lateness on the side of staff members had been excused by the lame rationalisation that 'it's different for us'. As a participant observer in much that went on in the facility, this inevitably led to a serious ethical dilemma. Should I remain silent and thereby forfeit the trust of the young people in residence there or speak up and risk the wrath of the staff? I chose the latter course and the wrath duly followed. Having already been told not to keep any confidences with residents it had been made clear where my loyalties were supposed to lie.

Having committed the act of heresy, the institutional consequences soon followed, which ranged from denying me access to residents' files, to contacting other drug rehabs where I had arranged interviews with former residents to ensure my appointments with them were sabotaged. The drug rehabilitation community, it seemed, operated a kind of brotherhood, a Cosa Nostra of social workers whereby a perceived threat to the interests of one were seen as a threat to all – with favours and sanctions operating, like the force of gravity, at a distance.[13] This was unpleasant and on more than one occasion resulted in me calling 'headquarters' and asking them to exercise their authority and demand the locals cooperate with me. Bad as this was, a lot worse was to follow. The analysis revealed that people with drug problems belonging to ethnic minority groups had more serious issues than their white counterparts before admittance (i.e. entry requirements for whites were more favourable). Furthermore a good few of the young people who entered with alcohol problems subsequently left with problems now connected to opiate use, having been educated by their new housemates as to the practices, procedures and personalities of the local drug market. A dispassionate reading of all the evidence accrued during the first 18 months of the research was not difficult – the facility, ground-breaking as it was no doubt intended to be – was not a great success. Not only that, but questions were also being asked as to the connections between certain personnel who worked in the house and wealthy patrons[14] outside of it.

For a project born in the fires of celebrity publicity – and royal celebrity at that – there could be only one outcome. The project had to be a success – ergo if it could not be a real success then it had to be a fictional one. As word went round the tightly knit community of people who had an interest in the project's outcome, this meant that something had to be done. What had to be done however was not a review of the policies and practices; my boss, myself and a person who was overseeing the project from another establishment where I was a visiting research fellow, were summoned at a day's notice to an 'on-site inspection' by the guardians of the foundation who were part-funding the project.

The unsavoury bunch who descended on us comprised a selected company of bullies whose mission parameters included stopping any qualitative work. Their first step on the road to achieving this was to announce that I was incompetent to do the work properly. They were sure of this although they hadn't bothered to read an extensive literature review I'd sent them some months earlier in which I had set out the background to the current project, the problems with conventional evaluations of 'treatments' for drug dependence and the justification for our (qualitative) approach. My boss was more than happy with the review – though despite the inconvenience of not having read anything about what we were doing, the visiting team weren't. Perhaps they feared the rumour mill going into overdrive, or that any further exposure to the lives of the young people there might see me turning native – though I think it was pretty unlikely I was ever going to turn up to work with a few rocks or readymade spliffs. Rather, I think what the leader and his entourage really wanted to see was some controlled routine evaluation in which the poor young souls whose lives were under scrutiny would be the beneficiaries of conventional psychiatric treatment. So, despite the fact that they didn't know what was going on in the institution and didn't seem to care, and despite the fact that we had a contract to continue the work, it was demanded of us that we resubmit a grant application or we wouldn't get 'a penny more'.[15]

I submitted my resignation that day and three months later to my immense relief was out the door. My boss and the overseer accepted it reluctantly and implored me to stay. They were decent people but I was not prepared to abandon what we were doing in order to cook the academic books so that powerful onlookers could be made happier by whatever new 'data' came their way. I had argued in the review that developing typologies of drug users, a key feature of evaluation work at that time, prevented the development of a different approach. This would instead direct attention to the ability and capacity of those in a caring role to deal with a variety of problems and situations – an approach which would see the caring environment as the target of any intervention. Before the investigating team departed, one of them offered me her hand. I declined. I was later told that she had brought her spiteful attitude to the day's proceedings because she was upset Anthony Clare was no longer around either to flirt with or provide celebrity shelter.

I later received a phone call from the next minion who had been drafted in to evaluate the programme. Predictably, out had gone any interest in the subjective realities of the people whose lives were supposed to be helped. Instead those deemed 'vulnerable and transgressive' (see Dobson, 2011: 548) by virtue of their disapproved substance use were to be objectified, regulated and investigated via the administration of batteries[16] of psychological and psychiatric tests, a sort of psychometric guillotine which would be sure to do the job, most effectively, of isolating them and their heads from their immediate context. In that way they could remain within the dominant disciplinary framework – indexed, numbered and categorised so that should their journey through the loving hands of the project turn out to be less than successful, the reason for the failure could be firmly located within the personalities and nervous systems of the unfortunate incumbents.

In his autobiography the famed Cuban leader Fidel Castro (2007: 548) declared himself to be 'totally convinced, from my own experience, that values can be sown in the souls of men, in their intelligence and in their hearts'. History is born of the interplay between the human urge to dominate and the imperative to create. Castro's words speak to the nobler possibilities of human existence, even if his own actions haven't always followed this. The day I resigned was the day my experience convinced me that the values sown in the hearts of academic psychiatry and thereby in academia have been seriously corrupted. By now I was coming round to the view that academic life was more about surviving the arrogance and pomposity of those whose primary allegiance was to power, than the uncertainties and challenges of truth. With the 'Gestapo' tactics that morning, the real history of the place I was sent in to evaluate disappeared. In engineering that disappearance, the psychiatric team in question extended psychological medicine's long tradition of reinventing the non-existence of the past. The treatment facility closed a few years later, sometime between the catastrophe of the Bosnian war and the 'triumph' of New Labour. When its doors closed for the last time a spokeswoman for the drug charity Turning Point lamented that the demise of 'this unique treatment centre is a tragedy for young people'.[17] I am not so sure it was.

The social science jungle

My next port of call took me to a department of epidemiology and public health for a two-year stint investigating social inequalities in health. It was a post in which I have to admit, minor quibbles aside, I learnt a great deal. From there I landed at an institute of human relations – specifically the Evaluation, Development and Research Unit housed within it. Intending to stay a while, my employment there lasted little longer than a holiday romance and was a lot less fun. Of the numerous establishments in which I have sold my labour this one takes the biscuit for being the strangest.

Once there I had two principle tasks – to aid in the evaluation of a pioneering centre for people with HIV/AIDS and to participate in an EU-led project[18] with several partner organisations on software development. Beyond possessing common sense and skills in a few programming languages I was no Bill Gates, but from the outset it was obvious that the intended goal of this project – to establish an algorithm which could automate the generic process of software development – was ludicrous. There was no basic understanding that creativity is not a process that can be mechanised. However this minor technical obstacle aside I soon learnt that the greater of the problems resided in the culture and expectations which permeated the institution. Living on past glories, the management had developed a penchant for exploiting the good and bureaucratic natures of EU funders. Unfortunately, outside of this ability to attract money, they were locked into a rigid mindset in which psychoanalytic concepts were routinely invoked whenever any member of the workforce failed to agree with them.

My first assignment had been to review a turgid badly written 100-page report on the software project. I had a solitary weekend to read this over and narrowly survived being bored to death. Asked to give my views the following Monday I tried, diplomatically, to explain that there were a number of good ideas but the report lacked bite, needed tightening up and should be given a more careful presentation. When pressed I had to point to the almost complete absence of punctuation throughout, and the routine presence of sentences which were as long as the Ho Chi Minh trail. My manager, who it transpired was the author of this mind-numbing document, leapt onto the fact that none of his sycophantic crew had apparently noticed this before. To him, the reason for this was simple; there was nothing wrong with his meisterwerk. Rather than acknowledge that I had a point and the report was a total mess – to him I therefore had to be the problem – my groundless objections emanating from some dark corner of my unconscious mind where they lay simmering for decades, waiting to be projected onto the eponymous author of the said document. In addition, despite being 38 years of age, I was but a 'new boy' and had yet to learn the ropes, that is, adopt a supine position and embrace the mystery of authority. I reminded him of my biological age and threw into the mix that I was equally familiar with the conceptual psychoanalytic bullshit he was peddling and that it was not going to work with me.

During my transient stay on this particular moon base I witnessed the application of this institutional hypnosis turn a likeable Irish economist who worked there into a gibbering emotional wreck. After a single encounter group one weekend he came back suffused with talk of the interesting 'group processes' which had apparently overwhelmed him. Duly conversant with the NW3 newspeak he was unfortunately now confused as to who the fuck he actually was. In the virtual environment of *The Matrix*, Lawrence Fishburne's character Morpheus laments that the ultimate functional aim of the system of artificially intelligent machine control is to turn a human being into a battery. In the unreal environment of this institution, the aim was to eradicate any sign of autonomous intelligence and replace it with the compliance of a battery chicken. Consequently my manager and I never hit it off. I found him to be about as charismatic as Jar Jar Binks,[19] though a good deal more punitive. Retribution for my transgressions duly arrived. I was to be dropped from the party due to visit Italy. As the one member of the party who spoke any Italian, my sanctioned absence, it was admitted, meant that the issue of language was 'likely to be a problem on the trip'.

Things went from bad to worse. My subsequent infractions included objecting to having smoke blown into my face during a six-hour meeting – I was told that the institution was 'a smoking culture'. My acquaintance with the director and founder of the HIV/AIDS centre (I had known him through co-counselling circles for some years) provoked a paranoid response from the institution's hierarchy who began accusing me of withholding information from them ... for what supposed ends I was never quite sure. I was eventually shown the door; a mutually agreeable severance arrangement put in place when my repeated requests to see the official Health and Safety procedures at the institution went unanswered. This was not before I had been accused (and found guilty) of the Stalinesque crime of threatening unspecified members of staff, in unspecified ways, in unspecified places, at unspecified times. News eventually reached me that after the final report on the HIV/AIDS centre was submitted it was returned as 'rubbish'. My next foray through the dense undergrowth of the social science jungle saw me ensconced as senior lecturer in the psychology department at the University of Westminster. At this point (1994–5) it had been well over eight years since I had been in the company of academic psychologists.

Death and furniture[20]

All the events that took their allotted place on the timeline during my five years at Westminster are overshadowed by one, which I have recounted numerous times to all my good friends, and shared aspects of with some who are not. I am unlikely to ever forget it. On Friday 5 November 1999 life was changed irrevocably, even though working from home I was oblivious of what was to come. By its end the day had gone, and for some it had taken many of life's sweet pleasures forever away.[21] Sunday arrived. Lying in bed I was awoken by a call – an unfamiliar voice greeted me and introduced its owner as a member of the Metropolitan Police. I was asked to confirm who I was, immediately followed by whether I knew Elizabeth Stacey (our technician) and Steven Reid (a PhD student of mine and a research assistant in the psychology department). A handful of seconds into this exchange I knew something awful was in the air – duly confirmed by the announcement that Elizabeth's body had been found the previous day and Steven had disappeared. The rest of the day passed in a frantic blur of numerous long phone calls with my departmental colleagues and friends. We, at least myself, John Golding and Tony Towell who co-supervised Steven's research work believed immediately that Steven had killed her.[22] Of course the police did too – it was only some of my boneheaded colleagues who had difficulty accepting it, one displaying his accumulated psychological acumen by declaring that Steven 'loved' Elizabeth. I will leave that statement to the worthy critics of misogyny to unpack.

Within days the murder had been picked up by the BBC for its *Crimewatch* programme. Kept in the dark about this, all and sundry (save those up the food chain) were bemused by the presence of Steven Reid and Elizabeth Stacey lookalikes, at once conjoining the real, unreal and surreal, roaming the department for tasteless filmed re-creations of their pre-death encounters, duly served up in the subsequent broadcast. The gross insensitivities did not end there. A BPS course inspection for the MSc in health psychology went ahead a week later almost as if nothing had happened – with discussions of learning outcomes for specific modules in between assisting the police to identify the murder weapon. This was believed to be the wooden roller for the EEG machine in the health psychology lab where Elizabeth had been found. I felt contaminated by this knowledge. Life quickly became a spectacle within the confines of which one simultaneously observed the flow of events and participated in them. Interviewed by detectives, I understood in a manner I would have preferred not to, Baudrillard's (1994) invocation of reality as a simulation of itself. Whilst veterans may experience the battlefield like a bit part in *Apocalypse Now*, my questioning by detectives became framed within the conceptual boundaries of the then current (and my personal favourite) American cop show, *Homicide: Life on the streets*. I fantasised about being in the box with Detectives Baylis and Pemberton. No such luck, though the occasional asides by those questioning me to refer certain matters up to the 'Guvnor' did provoke a wry smile and reminiscences of *The Sweeney*.[23]

For two weeks the winds of emotional mayhem swirled unchecked. Internal 'public' relations however required an image at odds with this. Emails thus circulated throughout the university declaring – unconstrained by reality – that members of the psychology department were coping very well. They weren't! After some insistence, outside psychological help in the form of the trauma debrief team – Ian Robbins and Gillian Mezey from St George's Medical School – was brought in. This was an event not to be missed. In the course of the two-hour critical incident debrief, one of those present[24] announced that in his view the 'wrong' person had been murdered. He then said quite brazenly that had the victim been either myself or Tony, that would have been acceptable. That single remark sums up as well as anything can, just how dysfunctional the department had become. The team were not invited back – their exposure of the unpleasant underbelly of the department a faux pas against the myth of English middle class academic civility. Ian did however invite anybody to make contact personally if they so wished, an offer I was happy to take up. By virtue of the connection thus established, Ian would later contribute a chapter[25] to my book on psychology and terrorism (Roberts, 2007).

Everything that happened during this period would sit comfortably in a Latin American novella tinged with tragedy and magic realism. After the BBC's intervention John considered using the wanted posters of Steven as a basis for cut-out masks which we could adorn as we went about our daily business in the department. Whilst we were not all Spartacus, the university could be populated by Steven Reid look-a-likes everywhere. We speculated on what we might do if Steven suddenly turned up out of the blue. Inviting him up to the sixth floor for a smoke and subsequently pushing him over the balcony was one of the suggestions mooted. This streak of black humour subsided as Steven's two-week period as Westminster's most wanted came to an end. He eventually turned up in Brighton selling copies of the *Big Issue* and when approached by police claimed his name was Robbie Fowler, then a prolific goal scorer for Liverpool FC. The claim was somewhat incongruous as physically they had about as much in common as Woody Allen and Clint Eastwood. The real-life Fowler was of a relatively small stature – about 5 feet 7 inches, whilst Steven was a towering 6 feet 3 inches. Steven's appearance brought other surreal aspects to the fore. The main picture issued by the police whilst they sought his whereabouts looked nothing like him at all.

The next strand of humour we used to cope was to discuss whether at some point in the past he must have metamorphosed into the person we knew. This raised the possibility as to whether he had shape-shifting powers too and had escaped from an episode of *Star Trek*.

Some months later the trial arrived, attended with a ghoulish fascination by a majority of the department, save myself and John. After an interminable exchange of psychobabble between defence and prosecution psychiatrists, Steven was pronounced guilty of manslaughter on the grounds of diminished responsibility; deemed to have a personality disorder, he was considered not fully accountable for his actions, although days before the murder he had withdrawn all his money, and trashed all the data from a project he had been assigned to work on. As he was presumably not accountable for this either, one wonders whether the bank shouldn't have let him have his money back. Those of us who worked with him, as well as the police, thought the verdict absurd. The judge evidently agreed too, sending Steven not to a secure mental hospital but to prison for what he described as 'a deliberate and planned killing'.[26]

Though Steven's supervisor I was not called to give evidence. Whether this had anything to do with the fact that six or seven weeks prior to the murder I had approached a senior member of the department to discuss Steven being offered some form of professional help – his behaviour suggested something was seriously amiss – I shall never know. My suggestion had been dismissed with little thought. I wasn't the only one to have prior concerns about Steven. Tony had once joked after a supervisory meeting that he would not like to be around if Steven 'lost it' as he might 'put a hammer in someone's head' ... sadly and disturbingly prophetic. I left the university about a year later for reasons not unconnected with Elizabeth's killing. Even after these awful events, the university considered subsequent death threats toward me posted around the campus as unworthy of investigation. The head of the school then committed to paper the view that I was 'partly responsible' for Steven Reid's state of mind – ironic considering I was the only person in the university who had actually attempted to have anything done about Reid's state of mind. I brought a complaint internally and to my professional body – of which the head of school was a member. The former investigation was turned into a witch-hunt against me in which the entire department were questioned whilst being tape recorded. The 'interviews' largely concerned trying to ascertain if I had ever done anything wrong, which encompassed anything from swearing to criticising the head. The eagerness of some of my colleagues to demean themselves and crawl knew no bounds, though the transcripts of their voluntary debasement did provide me with some amusement if also sadness.

As for the complaint to my professional body – the British Psychological Society – this was an action for which the university attempted to have me dismissed for gross professional misconduct. I took them to an industrial tribunal. The university eventually settled out of court.[27]

Since then tuition fees have been introduced to extend the icy and destabilising influence of market forces, begun with the research assessment exercise and aided and abetted by the teaching quality assessments – described by Shore and Wright (1999: 58) as "'political technologies" for introducing neo-liberal systems of power'. Many fake professors have come and gone through the revolving doors of British universities – a few of them were in Westminster. The real, I believe, are now outnumbered by managerial and administrative impostors. I have moved on to pastures new, though not greener, with adventures a plenty. Westminster however was a watershed, certainly as regards my perception of higher education establishments. Elizabeth's death was exploited whether intentionally or not by all manner of institutions and individuals, for entertainment, academic reputation, public or professional image. The truth came a distant second to all of these. It was in Westminster that I began my investigations into student participation in the sex industry, yet another corollary of the global reach of money. The story of that belongs elsewhere, but this point marks the end of the beginning. At this juncture murder, corruption, politics, thought control and high finance had found their place in the ivory towers.

Elizabeth's presence in the university was commemorated by a tree positioned in the ornate marble-covered front entrance – since removed years later. I last saw her the day before her life ended; a cheerful hello on the staircase from a lovely, vibrant, sparkly, young woman. There are now no obvious traces that she passed through the building in Regent Street for a few short weeks. But for me her presence will never leave there. In my imagined South American rendition of the tale she is Isabella, renowned for her passion for the jasmine infusions to be imbibed in the technicians' tea room, outside of which hangs a reproduction of Vermeer's *Girl with the Pearl Earring*. In the days which followed her untimely exit from life one could imagine that the once alluring innocent expression radiating from the half-turned face of the seventeenth-century Dutch maiden had been replaced through a delicate transfiguration of light and colour by a haunted accusing admonition of the dangers of immorality, jealousy and the research assessment exercise.

Endnotes

1. Urban anthropology is a subset of anthropology concerned with issues of urbanisation, poverty, and neoliberalism. It is a relatively new and developing field, which became consolidated in the 1960s and 1970s.

2. Perhaps, given the 'McDonalization of Higher Education' (Hartley, 1995) a burger factory might be a more apt analogy.

3. As an undergraduate I entered Sheffield University in 1974.

4. 'My thoughts arise and fade in solitude,
    The verse that would invest them melts away
    Like moonlight in the heaven of spreading day:
    How beautiful they were, how firm they stood,
    Flecking the starry sky like woven pearl' (Shelley, 1839: 204).

5. See Boyle (2002) and Roberts (1990) for further discussion of this topic. It is a strange question however as it presupposes that I should know why he hadn't ventured to specific realms of the library.

6. Rose, Lewontin and Kamin's (1984) book *Not in Our Genes* contains a thorough critique of these.

7. 'Media doctor guilty of disrepute'. http://news.bbc.co.uk/1/hi/health/7464210.stm Last accessed June 2008.

8. Visit http://www.thelancet.com/lancet-about Last accessed June 2013.

9. Statistical Package for the Social Sciences

10. I was then in my mid-thirties.

11. I have forgotten it.

12. In interviews that is.

13. One could of course write an entire book on the politics of the Institution, though Bakan's (2005) reflection on *The Corporation* can be said to provide a useful introduction. Bakan's review makes it clear that the bedrock upon which all such entities are constructed is one of lies. For further musings see Dostoevsky's (2003) *The Brothers Karamazov*, in which the High Inquisitor tells the re-visiting Jesus, that the church 'will be forced to lie' about his second coming. Orwell's (1946) essay on 'Politics and the English language' is also instructive. https://www.mtholyoke.edu/acad/intrel/orwell46.htm (Last accessed 7 April 2014)

14. In this instance a member of the House of Lords.

15. As this phrase invokes Dickens (from his novel *Barnaby Rudge*), one can't help but see in these actions the resurrection of some of the unsavoury values of the Victorian era.

16. I couldn't help noting the alternative reading of battery (i.e. as a form of assault) as equally appropriate here.

17. Visit http://www.prnewswire.co.uk/news-releases/young-peoples-residential-drug-treatment-centre-to-close-156626375.html Last accessed June 2013.

18. Project Delta

19. From the *Star Wars* movies.

20. The title of an article by Edwards, Ashmore, and Potter (1995). Its sad and ironic use in this sub-section will become apparent.

21. I'll thank Keats (2009: 22) for the sentiment.

22. An official summary can be found here http://www.telegraph.co.uk/news/uknews/1346704/Loner-who-battered-graduate-to-death-could-kill-again.html Last accessed July 2000.

23. Renowned violent British Cop show of the 1970s. Recently remade in 2012 as a film.

24. The same individual whose insights into Steven's expressions of 'romantic love' I've already mentioned.

25. Ian's chapter was 'The War on Terror: The road from Belmarsh to Guantánamo Bay'.

26. http://www.telegraph.co.uk/news/uknews/1355267/Life-for-lecturer-who-killed-his-partner-in-death.html Last accessed September 2000.

27. The *Times Higher Education Supplement* published a reasonably accurate account of some of this, which I believe contributed to the university's willingness to avoid court proceedings. http://www.timeshighereducation.co.uk/news/colleague-of-killer-i-have-been-victimised/153520.article   Last accessed September 2000.

Chapter 9

The politics of truth
in psychotherapy

The human race is a myriad of refractive surfaces staining the
white radiance of eternity. Each surface refracts the refraction
of refractions of refractions. Each self refracts the refractions of
others' refractions of self's refractions of others' refractions ...
Here is glory and wonder and mystery, yet too often we simply
wish to ignore or destroy those points of view that refract the light
differently from our own.
(Laing, in Laing, Phillipson & Lee, 1966: 3)

Our account of the politics of experience thus far has been woven
from the interlocking strands of method, theory and experience. But
as the late TV broadcaster and interviewer Alan Whicker – famously
lampooned by Monty Python – once said, 'what does it all really
mean?' And so in the final third of this book, to complete our case for
the return of experience to the centre stage of practical and theoretical
endeavour, we must deal with matters of truth in psychotherapy and
psychology – the truth of our predicament and what we must do or
can do with it.

We are intentional beings, we have an inner longing to be
seen and heard as truthfully as possible, however differently we
might perceive and interpret the world. The above remark by Laing
invites one to reflect on the wonders of interpersonal perception –
to lay aside one's preconceptions in favour of a dose of humility. Yet
attempts to communicate about communication are always marked
by questions concerning who and what the communicator is, let
alone the whys and wherefores of communication. For students of
psychotherapy, methodologically informed indirect communications
(about communication) more often than not can befuddle, even if
in a positive way. Despite such moments of confusion, we know

from experience that the external is mirrored in the internal just as the internal mirrors what is outside. In this ping-pong game of experience the world may provide us with answers we do not wish to hear. Roger Poole (1993), streetwise in indirect communication, reminds us that there are also answers which have so far not found their questions. The ignorance or denial of the question is a facet of the current state of play, a reflection of where we are currently at and who we are. The politics of our experience always comes suffused with themes of identity.

Can we demand objectivity in this maelstrom? To state this simply: My behaviour is your experience, you perceive my body and its signs, and interpret them according to your learned patterns and value systems. At the same time I experience your behaviour influenced by your experience of my behaviour. We are engaged in the daily art of making distinctions, of perceiving the difference that makes the difference. Truth may have a certain driving force, a truthful momentum, which can occur in psychotherapeutic encounters as in everyday life, occasions where lived sense making, meaningful engagement and questions of truth and falsity are paramount to what one does next.

Truth is the subjective committed symbolic presence in psychotherapy. Our perception is like a duet; a musical composition for two performers, where we hear what is said as 'objective' while hearing how it is said as 'subjective'. We make sense by ordering reality as we are in the throes of experiencing it. This then is what we operationally call our truth. To be truthful is to be naked, unveiled, as the Greek word for truth, *aletheia,* informs us. Aletheia (Greek ἀλήθεια 'Truth') is in Greek mythology a daughter of Zeus and the Goddess of Truth. She was also a wet nurse to Apollo. To be true also means to be loyal, trustworthy and for some, straight as a tree if it was so lucky as not to be bent by too fierce a storm. Life, as we all know it, can put you on your knees. These are moments for calling on the inner trust or faith in one's vital self. When we are truthful, we experience and behave in an open, unconcealed fashion. We are practising the process of opening up. Our innermost or true self is being evident, sincere and real. We elucidate our facts of life, and are no longer ashamed to be who we are and have become and are becoming. But truth and deception often go hand in hand. While truth moves us along, deception keeps us tied town, moving in circles. Roman mythology sees truth as Veritas; the Greek Goddess of Truth is Aletheia, the Uncovered. In Horace's story of Carmina we meet *nuda veritas* (the naked truth), which again shows how uncovered we can become. Truth always finds an echo in time.

We carry within us the wonders we seek from outside. Thoth, the Egyptian god with a human body and the head of a bird, an ibis, was worshipped 5,000 years ago as the inventor of the arts and sciences, of music, astronomy, speech and the written word. Hermes is the Greek variant, becoming the God of logos, the Word. The symbol of this God is the caduceus; the staff of Mercury – the Roman adoption – with its two serpents curled around them. The two serpents are Knowledge and Wisdom, sometimes called Science and Humanism. Of the two, Knowledge is generally the more extraverted, Wisdom the more introverted. As psychotherapists, practitioners in the healing arts, we invite the patient to speak from within, while the symptoms she or he complains about (e.g. lack of sleep, sadness, irritability) express themselves to the outside world. The science of psychotherapy relies on an amalgam of these two serpents, combining thoughtful practice alongside understanding with our senses. The arts side of our trade is rooted in feelings and intuition. One serpent alone on the healer's staff leads to scientific stasis and thus stupidity on a high intellectual level, relying entirely on statistical findings filtered through a researcher's expectancy. This is emotional poison for any society and civilised culture.

We psychotherapists must be able to live and practise honesty with our patients. We are called upon, through our apprenticeship and our own psychotherapy, self-experience etc. to cultivate a good enough and authentic life. We become able, through much practice (generally it take 10,000 hours of practice to master any musical instrument), to accept the richness of life, from the darkest corners of the soul to the most brilliant lights, from being whole (once in a while at least) all the way to being fragmented and back again. We do this as court fools, to the Queen or King who is patient. We are the only ones to address fully and truthfully their madness, folly, stupidity and street wisdom.

So we, together with our patients, recognise, realise and verbalise the given. 'We need but to see through the world's outside and into its soul with which each daimon is bound and which claims our participation' (Hillman, 1997b: 202). Throughout our practice of the politics of truth in psychotherapy, we can give something back to the *anima mundi*,[1] as we are aware that our individual way of being is always already embedded in a collective consciousness of present reality. Experience can be comprehended in the totality of the political, economic, historical, cultural system and eco-environment in which we happen to live. It is our psycho-geographic habitat which offers us the present experience of itself. Truth then, as a moment of revelation, of being uncovered, is the peeling away, metaphorically speaking, of the false-self-layers in a false way of living, the stripping away of romantic phantasy and false hopes from the here and now.

The 'politics of truth': Examples

We two authors have been immersed in the practices of psychology and psychotherapy for more than thirty years. Freeing ourselves from the icy and stultifying grip of the 'science is all that counts complex' has been a lengthy and incomplete process. The major debate that has been going on throughout our professional lives has concerned the fact that contemporary psychology assesses 'normal' and 'abnormal' behaviour from an outsider perspective. This stance produces, at best, partial information which is completely inadequate for a seriously informed politics of truth in psychotherapy.

> Paul McCartney: When I admitted I took acid I got into trouble for being honest. The option was there to say, 'LS what? Never heard of it, sorry'. Certainly no one had ever caught me at it ... I'm not ashamed of it. This is something I have done, something Aldous Huxley had done. (Green, 1998: 181–2).

If it is generally good to speak the truth, there is also a good enough reason to keep some secrets to oneself. Nevertheless, to lie, in such a situation as McCartney found himself, would be to deny who one was and has been. So when push comes to shove, each one of us has to determine our standard of truth keeping. Knowing there might always be another reality does not deter me from seeing the difference between fiction and truth. In her memoir, Edna O'Brien relates how she was not only a patient of Laing's but also a wee bit of a friend. As a poetess, as well as a novelist – she describes Laing, who came, for a while, most Saturdays to her flat, as '... half Lucifer, half Christ, pale and aloof ...' (O'Brien, 2012: 183) – we cannot be sure, as a poetess affirms nothing. She tells the story as she remembers, and there is no reason for me to not believe her version of truth.

When Andrew Collier published *R.D. Laing: The Philosophy and Politics of Psychotherapy* in 1977, the cover was placed in the shop window of Dillons in London, and electrified me. First I thought, as I did not 'see' Andrew Collier's name on the cover, that this was Laing's new book on *The Politics of Psychotherapy*, to follow his *The Politics of Experience* (1968) and *The Politics of the Family* (1971). This autonomous interpretation of the cover shows a wishful failure, where I got caught in a relative extraverted position. His approach, to assess Laing's politics of truth in psychotherapy, was fascinating. He showed the various models Laing played along with. Like variations on a theme – the independent psychoanalytic, the systemic, the existential and free style versions were laid bare. Style was a key to open the doors that no one could shut. Laing and his colleagues in the Philadelphia Association were to reject and playfully distrust the various models of psychotherapy and their argued notions for one unified field theory, to be explained in a meta-meta-polytheistic mode of reflecting. This was to the (often enormous) frustration of social scientists, like Collier, who prefer simple factual, neatly compartmentalised schematic constructions; all fancy stuff, to follow their underlying assumptions of ideological correctness. What does not fit this singularity is discarded as not fitting the truth. But there is no universal form of reflection, observation of self or other that exists outside of its cultural origin.

Peter Sedgwick (1934–83), for a time lecturer in politics at the University of York and a member of the critical libertarian left, wrote one of the more polemical attacks on Laing's psycho-politics of health. Fully soaked in the ideological left style of journalistic writing for the gallery, his bombastic critique included the following:

> The Marxists who applauded Laing's apparent convergence with their doctrines during the sixties ('R.D. Laing is one of us', the editor of the New Left Review remarked to me when Laing was just coming into public attention) must now wonder just what continuity exists between yesterday's anti-capitalist prophet and today's denouncer of Umbilical Shock. The truth is surely that Laing took from Marx and from the New Left only what he needed for his own purpose of argument. (Sedgwick, 1982: 113)

Such a way to formulate a politics of truth was not uncommon in the 'holier than thou' atmosphere of the late 1970s. I know that Laing offered to have a conversation with Sedgwick, who, like Szasz before him, declined to actually meet and discuss their practical and theoretical differences. To denounce Laing as being part of the 'cult of immediacy' in the 1960s and 1970s, is, I feel, when all the dust from ideological arguments has settled, a legacy of that particular (male) generation's (born from 1925–35) competitiveness, rivalry and envy – who is right and who is wrong. On 27 January 1982, *The Guardian* printed an edited extract from Peter Sedgewick's book, *Psychopolitics*, with the title: 'R.D. Laing, the retreat from socialism'. Francis Huxley had succinctly reviewed the book the day after, without knowing that *The Guardian* had featured Sedgewick the day before. He ends his review:

> Anti-psychiatry and other disorders, Ah yes, those were the days. How to construct another such total alternative to the inhumanity of capitalism now is the problem, which is not the same as Laing's efforts to house the mentally ill without categorising them in psychiatric terms. Or is it? (Huxley, 1982)

Laing was initially welcomed as a thinker of the New Left (in the 1960s–80s) out to destroy the repressive elements of bourgeois life, aiming for the actualisation of existential possibilities. 'The process of liberation culminates in this discovery (or actualisation) of a self – a self that had otherwise been stunned or extinct' (Scruton, 1985: 51). And yet, far from being unjustly reproached by so-called left wing writers and their critics, like Scruton, Laing's radical approach to the politics of truth in psychotherapy enabled him to come face to face with people in a compassionate way, who were simply seeing him for their troubles. One of his former apprentices and colleagues, Chris Oakley, describes '… the somewhat controversial psychiatrist and psychoanalyst R.D. (Ronnie) Laing. A sort of Brian Clough of psychoanalysis, if you will, never less than interesting but perhaps something of a bully. Both men living under the sign of hero and troublemaker' (Oakley, 2007: 79). Clough (1935–2004) played as a forward with Middlesbrough and Sunderland and scored 251 goals in 274 games, later becoming an outspoken and controversial manager. Laing played successfully, for 35 years, against the opposition, the champions of 'normality'. Though the recipient of many a red card, he frequently took the game to the opposition, as when he remarked: 'pathology has, or has almost, taken over, and has become the norm, the standard that sets the tone for the society he or she lives in' (Laing, 1990: xi).

When searching out writings containing *Politics of Truth* in their title, I found a number of interesting papers and books. Schacht (1985) in his essay on the politics of truth in relation to the old *Diagnostic and Statistical Manual of Mental Disorders* (*DSM-III*) tried to show how the often veiled vested interests in the (commercial) relationship between psychiatric/psychological sciences and the political economy of pharmaceutical production became clouded in double talk (if not double binds). Mental health sciences serve the economic interests, whilst politicians complain about the growth of costs in the mental health services. Today, with *DSM-5* newly on the market, we know even more how this so-called scientific instrument of knowledge is a sales book for the distribution of pharmaceutical power. Together with Courtenay Young, I have written my thoughts on *DSM-5* in our book on *R.D. Laing: 50 Years since* The Divided Self (Itten & Young, 2012: 252–9). We pointed out that:

> R.D. Laing wrote an article for *The Times Literary Supplement*, originally titled 'God and Psychiatry' but it was eventually published as 'God and *DSM-III*' on 23 May 1986. ... [As an introduction to this] in a recently published book, *The Psychopath Test: A Journey through the Madness Industry*, the author, Jon Ronson, gives a hilarious, but horrifyingly chilling account of an interview with Robert Spitzer, the psychiatrist from Columbia University, who, in 1973, became the chairperson of the task force of the 3rd edition of the American Psychiatric Association's *Diagnostic and Statistical Manual of Mental Disorders*, (*DSM-III*) and thus editor of the latest edition of:
>
> > '... a little known spiral booklet called *DSM*'. 'The first edition of *DSM* had been sixty-five pages!' Spitzer laughed. 'It was mainly used for state hospitals reporting on statistics. It was of no interest to researchers at all!'
> > He happened to know some of the *DSM* people. He'd been around when gay activists had lobbied them to get the mental disorder of Homosexuality removed. Spitzer had been on the activists' side and had brokered a deal that meant being gay was no longer a manifestation of insanity. His intervention gained him respect from everyone and so when he expressed interest in the job of editing *DSM-III*, it was a foregone conclusion.
> > 'Anyway,' he said, 'there was nobody vying for the job. It wasn't regarded as a very important job.'
> > What nobody knew was that Spitzer had a plan – to remove, as much as he could, human judgement from psychiatry. (Ronson, 2011: 249)

We concluded, that in the 60 years since the original publication of *DSM* in 1952, researchers in this field have been unable to demonstrate convincing chains of causation for any major form of mental disorder. An 'illness' to be 'treated' is thus increasingly being created from what is relatively 'normal' human activity. *DSM-5*, as is by now well known, is a political tract, trading in what can plainly be described as the future of an illusion – the illusion being that psychiatric nosology is sound science. The harsh reality is that once the smoke screen has lifted, *DSM* (versions 1–5) has always been a milk cow's guide for stigmatisation as well as enrichment of pharmaceutical stockholders. Laing for one was angered by this collusion:

> Ronnie then gave us his overview of the psychiatric profession in the USA. By his account, clinicians, health insurance companies, and the author/distributors of the *DSM* are routinely trying to deceive and double-cross each other. Insincerity is built into the system. When doctors can not fit the pattern of patients' complaints or experiences into a pre-existing theoretical framework, they give them 'dual diagnoses', sometimes claiming to cure 'incurable' disorders and/or pathologizing reasonably intact people in order to be reimbursed for their services. As far as he was concerned, these duplicitous dealings are profoundly immoral. And to complicate matters, though they deceive one another, to be sure, on another level, there is a certain complicity between them all, evidenced in the enormous disparity between the story that the mental health industry puts to the public, and what really goes on behind the scenes. 'Remember', Ronnie said, in an apparent reference to his current professional isolation, 'Galileo and his rift with the Church and the Science establishment'. (Itten, 2001: 78)

His anger was compounded by the continued misrepresentation of his work by those for whom the *DSM* was sacrosanct.

> I have never idealized mental suffering, or romanticized despair, dissolution, torture or terror. I have never said that parents or families or society 'cause' mental illness, genetically or environmentally. I have never denied the existence of patterns of mind and conduct that are excruciating. (Laing, 1985a: 8)

The politics of truth, lies or deception can make sense and meaning in lots of ways, depending on one's class, consciousness and conflict skills. Looking up a few similar titles, I found the following of interest. Robben (2012) signed off his account of 'The politics of truth and emotion among victims and perpetrators of violence', with the observation that knowing the truth of what did take place relaxes the victim, while secrecy and lies seduce perpetrators into further hostility. In *The Politics of Truth and Reconciliation in South Africa: Legitimizing the post-apartheid state*, Wilson (2001) summarises the process of finding truth in the era of apartheid crimes. Using his fieldwork in the urban community in and around Johannesburg, he found that this particular brand of political truth making had less effect on local ideas of human-rights-informed justice restoration than he had hoped. Then we have Michèle Barrett's (1992) assessment of ideology in relation to body politics, *The Politics of Truth: From Marx to Foucault*, which demystifies the master jugglers of political ideology. This study is an exemplar of how concepts of ideology, when they lack any possibility of bringing their relevance into lived reality, become prisons for thought and emotions, or rather, as we sometimes experienced in the late 1960s and 1970s become a self-sabotaging activity in trying to be politically correct. This often plays out in a form hostile to any spontaneous expression of creativity from within, which is inherent in resolving inner conflicts of truth and dishonesty by self-expression through writing, painting, music making, dance, sculpture etc.

Laing's mentor in political philosophy, and his spiritual and intellectual guide, was Joseph Schorstein (1909–76). In his essay, 'The Metaphysics of the Atom Bomb' Schorstein's (1963) musings took on a Nietzschean slant: 'One man is always wrong: but truth begins with two', he wrote. For him, meta-physics changed with the atomic bombs dropped on Japan. The 'dreadful' had indeed already happened:

> ... man's alienation from himself and from the world. ... The coldness and remoteness of all there is demands the return of the warmth of understanding. If we could become fully aware of the 'dreadful' we might ask: 'Who has done it to us?' and 'Why was it done to us?' The questions gravely asked escape from the inescapable and open up the possibility of choice. Fully aware of his own share in irresponsibility each one of us might choose to respond and to affirm ... In a political party there is neither choice nor responsibility. The general evil of the bomb demands a decision from the individual. In choice there is again hope, but no certainty. What appeared a public problem turns out to be a private one, 'but truth begins with two'. (Shorstein, 1963: 46)

Laing made his choice, following his mentor's suggestion, to be engaged in this world, seeing any practical recommendations in the healing arts as intrinsically political decisions (Collins, 2008).

Psychotherapy, a practice in truth

Knot 1

> They are playing a game.
> They are playing at not playing a game.
> If I show them I see they are,
> I shall break the rules and they will punish me.
> I must play their game, of not seeing I see the game.
> (Laing, 1970: 1)

How the shade system, the underworld of the psyche – sometimes referred to as the collective unconscious – can show up in the interaction between self and others is presented in the following dream of a 38-year-old woman patient of mine, who is a neurologist and a psychiatrist.

> Dream: Ronald Laing came to our therapy session. I was to have one hour with him. I feel very tense wondering what will happen. There he is, slender, delicate and simply dressed. That's him, the master. He speaks very little, he just studies me, thinks about what he sees in me, just as if he were asking himself 'What's the matter with her?' I am very aware of my history, my prehistory and development. How I would like to do things without making mistakes, do everything completely right, and behave perfectly. I try to treat him politely, in the way I think I ought. I try with all my might, I do my utmost. But he just mirrors me – everything I do, all my compulsive behaviour. He tells me why I am doing what I am doing. He says that it's not important that I have lived falsely, or that my family upbringing was wrong. What matters is that I have never valued the essential things in life, and these are what I miss now. I think he would have valued someone more spontaneous, someone more artistic. I have become superficial, nonessential. All that behavioural psychology stuff is nonsense. All this became clear. Now my parents appear. Laing stays in the background, distancing himself, yet still very much present. The only way out is suicide. Anxiety. What will happen now? Is Laing going to sentence me, destroy me? No, he tolerates my 'being-so'. Life continues with a new experience and a new insight.

In this dream of meeting and being with Laing, he is practising what he 'deems appropriate to the occasion' (Winnicott, 1980: xvi), without verbalising her nascent consciousness of what she transfers from her past relationships in the family into her relationship with him. 'He mirrors me', is one of the basic tenets of Laing's psychotherapeutic method, which aims to allow the other to experience his or her false and true selves and the discrepancies between the two. When we talked about what the dream meant she said she felt very strongly held in suspense by the dream 'Laing's' attention to her follies. She experienced the transference as a hindrance, while at the same time, helping her to realise what she was doing.

In other words, in the dream she experienced 'Laing's' ability to mimic people – a very powerful therapeutic tool. She was able to recognise that 'Laing' could be with her in that way without condemning her true self. It gave her a chance to move with 'Laing', bringing with her the fear, anxiety and embarrassment she felt at being 'caught out'. The open-heartedness with which it was done allowed her to look at where her past experience and all her learned 'good behaviour' had taken her. Suicide as the only way out expresses the struggle between the true self and the false self which is vividly staged in the dream. Suicide would free her from having to take further evasive action to stay alive, and from her consciousness of and despair regarding the faults that remained as she attained greater self-awareness. As the neurologist's dream also shows, sometimes it is difficult simply to wait patiently for an authentic meeting of two or more human beings and to recognise how we all too often run away from authentic being in order to please others – which we, in the final analysis, can't actually do, try as we may. Suicide seems to be the only way out in the neurologist's dream. But there is an alternative: we can also wait for another dream, another episode of life – the random factor, to give us something fresh to talk through. A fresh event can open up new possibilities as to where our own healing potential is drawing us.

In this dream, Laing's therapeutic capacity to be open-heartedly available to the other is evident. In reality she had seen him only once several years before when he was giving a lecture. In the dream she was sharing one hour in a room with him in which, to quote Laing himself, 'one human being actually gets into the same place at the same time to meet another human being' (Evans, 1976: 42), and as a psychotherapist, 'to intervene in the hope that intervention will in one way or another bring some clarity to the situation, so that the confusion of the people will be mitigated in some way' (ibid: 37). Obviously – though sadly this is not always obvious, by using harmless means.

Truth telling, whether in the inner or outer world, is more often than not denied, repressed or suppressed – it is as such a matter of politics. This is why Laing was so occupied with what kinds of experience of the world are permitted. Yet, despite what Sedgwick (1982) wanted and made him out to be, Laing himself confessed:

> I was never political in an activist sense. I suppose when people think of me as political, they're thinking mainly of the Dialectics of Liberation Congress. I guess I identified myself by being there, but even at the time I made it clear that I really had no idea what could really come of such an extraordinary conglomeration of people. Politically, I think I'm neutral really. I engage in no strictly political actions – except in the sense of following the Tao. (Mezan, 1972: 165)

Laing had used the term 'politics' in two book titles. Together we[2] discussed plans for a third.

The politics of truth: Book project

A few months before R.D. Laing died (23 August 1989), on the Pentecost weekend in 1989, we met in Going, Austria, to discuss, among other issues and plans, a joint book, with the working title: *The Politics of Truth*. The purpose of this joint book would have been to present a coherent and comprehensive examination of the work of R.D. Laing. It was first conceived by Laing in cooperation with me (TI) (Letter: Laing to Itten, 1 August 1989[3]). The book was envisioned both for readers who are well-versed in the work of Laing and those who are drawn to it by 'elective affinity' (Goethe). In his letter, Laing said that he 'would like contributors to commit themselves to an actual examination of the work of RDL, not vague programmatic manifestos'. It was agreed that the choice of contributors should first of all reflect Laing's wishes, individuals, who would do a superb job, prioritising those who knew Laing personally and valued his ideas; who also made them a significant part of their own lives and work.

The intention was for the book to stand out for its honesty, its depth and breadth, and its eloquence, to create a work that would be true, above all, to Laing's complex and brilliant mind, to take Laing's words to heart and to make 'an actual examination of the work' with respect to the aspects covered. Several sections were envisaged; 'Laing and tradition', would situate Laing's work in the context of tradition, be it Aesclepian medicine, moral treatment, Western psychiatry in the wake of Bleuler, Jung and existential analysis as well as the Scottish school, such as Sutherland and Fairbairn, intermingling psychoanalysis with modern, person-oriented treatment in social and community psychiatry. 'The shift of perspective' would traverse the intellectual terrain all through from the Kraepelin interview in *The Divided Self* to the carefully worded relevant introduction to *Sanity, Madness and the Family* to the point-by-point contrasting vignettes in *The Facts of Life* to the complete de-anchoring from 'clinical' coordinates in the vignettes in *The Voice of Experience*. This would form the central plank of the project and help clarify misconceptions concerning the evolution of Laing's thought. The distinction between praxis and process, concepts taken from Sartre, would be considered in depth as a key means for comprehending what he saw was 'going on' in families and groups and what was 'being done' by various members to each other. This is the expressly 'political' aspect in Laing's work as expressed in *The Politics of Experience, The Politics of the Family* and, the proposed *The Politics of Truth*.

A third section would address 'the focus on person–person conjunction–disjunction', 'as the unacknowledged "cleavage", Spaltung, in the I–Thou non-actualized ontologically possible human connection; again, present from beginning of my oeuvre, to now …' This section would seek to examine questions of what is 'ordinary' and what is 'disturbing' in behaviour, experience, communication and phantasy, looking at the aims of disturbed and disturbing people and how they relate to questions of identity and the old chestnut of authentic being-in-the-world. The social context of diagnosis and diagnosis itself as a social activity and social datum is fundamental to this section.

The fourth section would comprise 'The actual data in the work' using 'the presentation of actual metanoiac transformations & modulations of experience, which "sometimes, not always", as said in *The Politics of Experience*, seems to have a healing value'. Laing notes that 'this metaphor of a "journey" has been persistently treated with scorn & contempt'. Necessary to this part of the project would be an overview of practical experience garnered from the Kingsley Hall and Soteria projects, taking in developments in Community Mental Health projects; a consideration of not only how the experiences and visions from this work shaped and changed lives, but also the reality of the day-to-day caring and being with others undergoing such experiences.

'The theoretical and practical study of social context' would be the natural corollary to the above. Laing's work was amongst the first to stress that whatever happens always takes place within a social, cultural and historical context. It is here that a well-founded philosophical reflection of the theme of social context in the work of Laing would be presented, taking in 'Reason and Violence via Sartre, Oxford Companion of Mind article, Phoenix Arizona article.'[4]

Following Merleau-Ponty's (1964) *The Primacy of Perception*, Laing co-wrote, with fellow researchers at the Tavistock Institute of Human Relations, a book on this theme, *Interpersonal Perception* (Laing, Phillipson, & Lee, 1966), which describes how disturbed and non-disturbed interpersonal perceptions and their meta-level components influence relationships at their core. As Laing put it; 'The Look, the Way of Seeing, as constitutive of what is seen etc., *who sees whom how*' (Itten, 2001: 85). The way we look at disturbance and disturbing people is itself disturbed by how we look. Here Laing attempts to provide a new framework for research, giving examples of his approach and methodology in the course of several case histories/ stories. This flows into a 'Laingian approach' to the analysis of social situations and therapeutic engagement in them, interpersonal relationships and the coping, experience and behaviour patterns of people who come into psychotherapy. For Laing the way we treat each other is the treatment. The love of truth and the truth of love are integral to this. Thus at the end of the project we return to the beginning – the philosophical context of being authentic and finding an ontologically secure basis in dealing openly and honestly with others, an issue with which Laing himself struggled throughout his life (Thompson, 2012). In all, Laing's notion of truth and his search for truth in love explored with a flair for the veiled aspects of his work is surely of continuing importance for the art of healing and a wider vision of communal health.

The politics of truthful psychotherapy

> Do you love me?
> Yes.
> Do you believe me?
> Yes.
> How can you love me if you believe me?
> (Huxley, 2005: 194)

Francis Huxley recalls the above disturbing exchange Laing had with his mother. 'I am sorry to say' he goes on:

that 'The Lies of Love', his latest book, is still unpublished, for those who have read it tell me they were much engaged by its disturbing reports of similar interchanges. Laing indeed detested lies above all things, and would go out of his way to demolish liars. Nor did he ever forget his bafflement when a couple came to see him with such contradictory and yet persuasive stories that he was unable to determine which of the two was lying about what, such a mare's nest had they made for themselves to lie in together. (Huxley, 2005: 194)

This was a cunning example of self and other's pretence and elusion. Could the truth of the matter be brought out by psychotherapeutic intervention? For a long time, I had the following sentence on my waiting room door: 'The good thing about truth is, everybody has one'. Totton (2012) a politician of psychotherapy if there is one, had this to say:

Therapy is a practice of truth; by which I mean not that it claims to reveal an absolute truth – just the opposite, that through the ways in which it interrogates our perceptions and beliefs it helps us to see that absolute truth does not exist, and that everything depends on where we are standing. (Totton, 2012: ix)

Psychotherapy can be a checkpoint of possibilities, for what is at issue is up for grabs. Just how aware are we that our estrangement from our own actions and experience may be such that we cover it up with a suitably false theory? What lies buried in the spaces between the truth and the lie? Here is T.S. Eliot, from 1925, an apt reflection on the politics of truth in psychotherapy.

The Hollow Men

V
Between the idea
And the reality
Between the motion
And the act
Falls the Shadow
                    For Thine is the Kingdom
Between the conception
And the creation
Between the emotion
And the response
Falls the Shadow
                    Life is very long

These are the thoughts he was working on at the time of his passing away. He concluded his interview with Anthony Clare (1942–2007) for the BBC's Radio Four (broadcast 14 July 1985) with an honest lament that he had neither theological answers nor explanations for life and death.

> Laing: What do I think of people who have? Well at the very least good luck to them, and at the very most, if they have found a reconciliation for suffering, life, death and spiritual terms which is consistent and coherent and true, then I very much regret that such a vision hasn't come my way. I'm not unaware of the words that could be used to formulate such a view of things, but it hasn't come my way that I've been able to have that type of joyous clear shining eyes that some people who devote themselves to suffering have. If it's true I hope that I can see it's true, and if it's not true then I would rather be in a state of confusion than believe something that is consoling which isn't true. I don't want to trade in the truth for illusions. (Clare, 1993: 216)

As psychotherapists we can reach a mode of living with a truth that leaves no final consolatory words. Perhaps this is the final destination for all explorations of human nature. Who remembers the Penguin edition of *A Critical Dictionary of Psychoanalysis?* It was the first book by the renowned psychoanalyst Charles Rycroft (1914–1998) that I bought in Foyles. The title was irresistible to a 20-year-old living in London in 1972. While Rycroft was a consultant in psychotherapy at the Tavistock Clinic in 1956 he became Laing's training analyst, before he was to become one of the most articulate and creative voices of the counter-culture and radical psychiatry movement. As I trained with Laing from the mid-1970s onwards, I have always had an interest in my psychoanalytic 'grandfather'. Rycroft wanted open-minded psychotherapists whom he could encourage through his writings. This book tries to serve this tradition, so that we readers can find our own way through the deeply liberating experience of, and practice in, psychoanalytical psychotherapy. What was Rycroft's aim in psychotherapy? Anthony Storr quotes him in his memorial address as follows:

> The aim of psycho-analytic treatment is not primarily to make the unconscious conscious, nor to widen and strengthen the ego, but to re-establish the connexion between dissociated psychic functions, so that the patient ceases to feel that there is an inherent antagonism between his imaginative and adaptive capacities. (Pearson, 2004: 15)

As a medical doctor and a psychotherapist, Rycroft believed in the possibility of amelioration of suffering at both personal and social levels. He always supported the idea of authentic choice seen in the context of one's past. Further notions like 'freedom', 'agency', 'action language' and 'reflective self' were very important in his writings. He believed that once we are able to be clear about our inner frame of reference, through the psychoanalytic process, we can live from the core of a 'true self'. In an essay on the development of Rycroft's thought, we meet other original thinkers of the time – Fairbairn, Milner, Payne, and Winnicott. It was refreshing to read that he did not need to create or claim a theory of his own, allying himself theoretically instead with Winnicott and Fairbairn. For many years, through his numerous newspaper articles, he was the best-known psychoanalyst in Britain. He often asked what is valuable in healing, and aimed to answer this within the bounds of his own 'liminality' since psychoanalysis is not a science, but an art, always in dialogue with its culture. Many writers attest to Rycroft's gifted intuitive sense of the healing grace with his patients. Yet he could also be mischievous, rebellious, deeply serious, and generally aware of his blind spots, which often led to sabotage of his own creative self.

Rycroft knew he could become an international force in psychoanalysis, yet he did not rise to the occasion. His politics of truth in psychotherapy was to de-doctrinise and de-dogmatise psychoanalysis, to cure it of its ideology, to make it common sensual and startling. Rycroft hoped that psychotherapists never forget, in our daily practice, that our clients, our patients, are embodied minds and that the symptoms and problems for which they consult us are '... reflections, derivatives, and manifestations of the great human problems implicit in whatever stage of the life cycle they are in' (Pearson, 2004: 247).

What is the subject of truth in psychotherapy nowadays? Mahrer (2004) found from his research with psychotherapists that most felt it was not something they deeply cared for when it came to their practice. On the other hand, Kottler (2010: 168) argued that we do need to address the issue of truthfulness and honesty in the life of our patients, otherwise we 'miss out on the opportunities for helping our clients live more congruent lives'. As far as he is concerned, by definition:

> psychotherapy is supposed to be the place where people ... [can] talk about things they have never revealed before. It is a sanctuary for that which has not been said – or sometimes ever been considered.

> Clients share their deepest secrets, darkest fantasies and most
> closely guarded vulnerabilities. They take a huge risk and often
> suffer immeasurably as a result at least until such time that they
> reach some accommodation with the 'truth'. (Kottler, 2010: 187)

Once we make up our mind, to clear up our act, as the saying goes, or get our act together, to own up, to walk our talk and talk our walk, to preach what we practise and practise what we preach, to face who we are without shame or embracement, we can become free from the old script of our primary scenario and character style, insofar as we have a new chance and potential to live 'us' differently. One can set a new habit only by driving out the old one, the one we want to replace. Left all alone in the weedy garden of the soul one can easily become unhinged. In psychotherapy we are in someone else's company and no longer have to deal with our often frightening and overwhelming emotions on our own. If this is all too serious then pick up *Therapy* from David Lodge (1996). If not, there is always a train or aeroplane to Vienna. If neither, well brace yourself and read on.

Truth in psychotherapy: Practical matters

Practise what you preach, Laing once said to me, and preach what you practise. Teachings, one's own or from another authority, are easier to preach than practise. Francis Huxley wrote of the myths, the grand stories of being on this planet, that they give us '... human beings, very importantly, the illusion, that s/he can understand the universe, and that s/he does understand the universe. It is of course, only an illusion' (Huxley, 1962b: 17). We can find answers within our selves; sharing them within the collective we happen to find ourselves in. Resentment about other folk's arrangements can stop the flow, and fuel addiction, not to truth but to falsity. This was something Francis' uncle, Aldous Huxley (1894–1963), had discovered earlier on. Much can be gleaned from the intergenerational dramas of the Huxley family. For Aldous:

> neurosis is a fixation upon a single aspect of life, a looking at the
> world through one particular set of distorting lenses, and hence as
> the inability to see a wider angle of life and to perceive realistically
> what is going on around us. (A. Huxley, 1977: 234)

What then is going on? No single interest group can be correct about the most unbearable truths that we in fact do not know. How do we cope with the obstacles and troubles served up to us in life? How do we live the truth of the matter we find ourselves in? Melancholia, one of the four traits of Galen[5] had a field day in several generations of the Huxley family. Francis Huxley's father, Julian, felt this intensely while Aldous Huxley's son, Matthew (1920–2005), was:

> caught between two Aldouses; one who expected him to maintain family standards and another still vexed at the high-pressure education of Eton and Oxford, which Huxley blamed for Trev's (1889–1914) suicide. (Dunaway, 1990: 28)

With regard to which:

> Trevenen[6] ... hanged himself when undergoing treatment for a severe nervous breakdown brought on both by having fallen in love with the chambermaid and having got only a second class honours in his exams for the Civil Service. (F. Huxley, 1999: vii)

This is to say that Aldous had woven a charm round his son, which Bateson called a double bind. Father did not send the son to an established school of excellence, where Matthew could have achieved good results and father-pleasing grades thus securing a Huxley intellectual legacy in his son; and when the son was not achieving, then father was disappointed. No easy ride this, surely. Francis Huxley related to Dunaway the following exchange:

> 'How is Matthew?' Francis was asked by uncle Aldous. 'Well', I said, 'he is complaining that you've never been a father to him'. 'Oh, is he still going on about that?' he replied. He was obviously the last man to be a father to anybody. (Dunaway, 1990: 284)

One of the goals of the politics of truth, as practised in psychotherapy, regardless of the modality, method or technique, concerns our intuitive union with a larger scheme, be this a myth, a religion, a scientific schema, or a larger purpose which fixes daily life into a groundedness. As a psychotherapist my aim is to enable folks to live no longer just in the old family home, but in the 'here and now' of everyday presence. Mystic longing is more often than not an escape from daily living. Monks were after all served by peasants. For Francis Huxley, mysticism and the way of the sacred is a path, like the Tao, and not a method to brew a toxin of escape. It is to be more fully here. What does it take to be at peace with oneself? So that others might sigh and say: 'Wow, Theodor, you are so peaceful'. Might it be the organic unity of body, soul and spirit? Is it a question of unconditionally accepting the self we are and have become? The threshold between consciousness and unconsciousness is in a sense a horrible metaphoric bridge. Unexpressed emotions and truthful perceptions (and lies) can just slip away in the flow of unconscious images. Practical matters, for example, were anathema to Aldous Huxley. He just ignored them and would not have anything to do with them.

Easy then to muse over perennial philosophy, grace and peace, while others hold the broom and pecker up, facing broken promises. A quick self-hypnotic mantra (being put to sleep for seconds) might provoke or invoke, as you please, an unconscious affection for renewal or revision of a pleasant fact of human psychology. For Huxley, the fundamental difficulty in life is that we know (I know) what we ought to do and be, but continue as habit-trapped beings, with doing what we would better let go. If we fall on hard times, we are likely to ask for a psychotherapeutic consultation. Aldous married finally a so-called therapist, Laura Archera. In psychotherapy, our aim is to empty ourselves of fears and ambitions, which are conditioned from the home base. Let's not forget that Margaret Huxley (1899–1981) was the true rebel in the family: the only member of her generation to enter teaching, the only one to convert to Christianity; the only one who was gay. Margaret's professional, religious, and sexual choices alienated the family, and she was cordially (or not so cordially) banished (Dunaway, 1990: 386) along with the ideas of Sigmund Freud. Juliette Huxley to Francis, who wanted to know about his aunt:

> My dear, we Huxley's do not talk about these things ... Aldous did not at all like Freud, principally because he ignored the neurological and biochemical level that so profoundly affects our lives. How can mental disorder steaming from these levels be treated by psychological means alone? he asked. He therefore did not depend on Freud when writing about Swift, whose odious and excrementitious obsession left him fascinated and dismayed. (Huxley, 1999: viii)

Francis Huxley reflects on being with his uncle, as a 33-year-old just-published author:

> In 1956, he [Aldous] and Laura invited me to supper. I had just had my first book on the Brazilian Indians, *Affable Savages*, published and Laura provoked me to say, "So what are they like?" So I started telling stories about these Indians. I dredged up the more

grotesque and remarkable anecdotes that I could think of. Laura
was delighted. Aldous kept on eating his lunch, and he never said
anything. I went away feeling that I had fallen into the adolescent
forms of mania and had vastly disappointed my dear uncle Aldous,
whom I really had wished to impress. I went away very cross with
myself. Two or three days later I went to see Eileen Garrett, who told
me that Aldous had been around telling all my stories and roaring
with laughter as he told them. Then I began to understand Aldous.
(Dunaway, 1999: 114)

Once we have been able to face and realise the truth of the ultimate
drama of human existence – which is that we human beings are
encouraged and supported to live an animal existence on human
terms – psychotherapy in its emancipatory aspects supports us to be
truly fulfilled.

Arno Gruen (1987: 193) describes the aim of truthfulness in
psychotherapy as an attempt to balance inside and outside drives, a
recognition that to keep sane we need to pay attention to both sides
of our skin. Those, like Barbara O'Brien (2011) who experienced
both the inner self and the outer self (some call it true and false)
as autonomous un-integrated modes of living, can experience a
psychotic breaking as a full stop on life: a sudden call to attention on
the inauthentic way of being together in our civilisation. The larger
the rift the greater the anxiety that comes to the fore.

The first night after having begun to read *False Self* by Linda
Hopkins (2006), an account of Winnicott's favourite apprentice and
later writing collaborator, Masud Khan (1924–89), I dreamt that
Simone de Beauvoir's unbeknown daughter was in analysis with him.
What could be the humour of these hints from my unconscious? To
fool around in the transitional reality or transitional relationship
between fictitious patient and literal therapist perhaps? Rycroft
commented that Masud Khan's first wife, the beautiful Royal Ballet
dancer Jane Shore, had a sense of humour that Khan totally lacked.
Together with Michael Balint, Charles Rycroft, Marion Milner, Nina
Coltart, Donald Winnicott and R.D. Laing, Khan was a member
of the Independent Group of the British Psychoanalytic Society,
sandwiched as most of us know by now, between the Kleinians and
Freudians.

Rycroft, ten years Khan's senior, became one of his early friends
and for a while they shared a flat. Kahn's thinking and practice came
straight from Winnicott. Whereas Freud saw conflict as the central

issue of human experience, Winnicott considered paradox (as in coexisting contradictory selves) as the essential human reality. For Freud, resolution of conflict constituted the aim of therapeutic effort, but for Winnicott it was the realisation of paradox without its resolution that constitutes psychic health and creativity. Winnicott's hypothesis of the true and false self influenced Khan and a whole generation of analysts. Laing of course wrote extensively on this in *The Divided Self*. Simply put, the idea is that we all have multiple separate selves. A goal for our personal development is to know and accept irreconcilable differences within oneself.

> Happiness is the capacity to be able to share oneself with oneself and with others ... The analytic task is not so much to eliminate an illness or to render it innocuous, as to put a person in the total possession of his affectivity and sensibility, both in its positive sense and negative aspects, so that he can live to the maximum of his potential and in terms of full awareness of the handicap and illness it entails for him. (Kahn, 1974: 134)

Joe Berke's contribution to this conundrum and his own meditation on questions of truth came in the person of Mary Barnes (1923–2001) who was 'cured' in the course of her 'journey through madness':

> People are more complicated. Mary did not need or want curing. She passed through trials that few individuals survive and had experiences that even fewer people manage. By one criterion, in particular, she was eminently sane. Mary had a remarkable capacity to network: to make friends, establish relationships and influence others all over the world. ... She was a culture hero. She descended into the underworld of the unconscious and emerged unscathed, renewed and bearing a gift of wisdom. By her archetypal journey she confirmed R.D. Laing's ideas, as well as her own, that 'madness' could be a cyclical process that should be understood in its own terms. (Barnes & Berke, 2002: 370)

Break down can still be a break through, if you go for it, supported by a troupe of experienced users and experienced healers of the soul. Hillman cautions us to be as honest as we can regarding our 'healing fiction'. Psyche is at the end of the day imagination, is phantasy, serving with words the pictures and dreams and inner landscapes of the soul. Peter Lomas reminds us that what is going on in psychotherapy is nothing new. To him it is a practice that:

takes place in a setting in which two people meet in order that conversation can occur by means of which one of them attempts to help the other, who is defined as the one requiring help. Until the last century, such meetings usually occurred between priest and supplicant; they were called the Confession. In this case the priest acted as mediator; the source of healing ultimately came from God's capacity to forgive. (Lomas, 2003: 179)

In Lomas' view Freud basically moved 'God' out of the picture, replacing the divine with 'Natural Science' so-called. When we report – and why should we anyway – what took place in a psychotherapeutic hour, the base line is our honesty, accuracy and reporting of reality. This goes for anecdotal case story writings, which still count as a contribution to the art and science of our work, as it does for form filling in naturalistic research designs. Can we count on each other to tell it as it is?

Endnotes

1. The soul of the world.
2. TI and RDL.
3. The following discussion and quotes therein are based on this correspondence. See Itten, 1997: 172–7.
4. Quote from original draft.
5. Choleric, sanguine, and phlegmatic are the others.
6. Aldous Huxley's brother.

Chapter 10

Psychology: Individuals, morality and ideology

It's not who I am underneath, but what I do that defines me.
(Batman: *Batman Begins*)

'Any *theory* not founded on the nature of being human', Laing wrote, 'is a lie and a betrayal' (Laing, 1967: 45). As an undergraduate psychology student in the 1970s I was one of many who were perplexed by the nature of the 'social' psychology we were being taught, faced as we were by a concerted attempt to reduce the entire discipline to study of the perception and cognition of the social world. Discontent also surfaced from within the dusty corridors of the academy itself with murmurings about what had happened to the social in social psychology. Laing's subsequent invocation of Heidegger's famous phrase 'the Dreadful has already happened' (Figal, 2009: 254) refers to the divorce between experience and behaviour which then and now typifies the study of human beings.

The late 1960s to early 1970s marked the high point of the so-called crisis in social psychology (Gergen, 1973) as unhappiness with the direction in which experimental social psychology was going, mounted. Of particular concern was its axiomatic fiction of an individual meandering through a social field stripped of all historical and cultural influence. Though the crisis is now regarded as passé the mainstream has continued its pursuit of the apolitical social cognitive and information processing dream unhindered by principled objection. The result is that there is no longer a unitary discipline worthy of the name. The crisis is unresolved (Parker, 1989) as competing modes of enquiry, rooted in different assumptions, different methodologies, different modes of analysis and different subject matter compete for the name.

What has yet to be fully appreciated however is the extent to which the intellectual and emotional malaise in social psychology has eaten away at the foundations of the one discipline which purports to provide an understanding of human beings as experiencing, feeling, social agents in the world. Greenwood's (2004: 1) acknowledgement that '… a discipline [which] calls itself social psychology does not guarantee the social nature of whatever is considered to be its subject matter' illustrates how rotten to the core the subject now is and amply confirms the disappearance of the social dimensions of psychological states and behaviour from mainstream study. One consequence of the disappearance of the social in social psychology has been the parallel disappearance of the person. The 'golden era' of the person in psychology, duly obliterated from the official collective memory of organised psychology, came to an abrupt end as Laing's project to construct a science of persons ran out of steam and Kelly's once vibrant personal construct psychology, championed in Bannister and Fransella's (1971) *Inquiring Man*, gave up the ghost as a radical force as the charlatans of business and psychiatry stepped in for a feeding frenzy on its intellectual carcass. Bannister and Fransella's once hopeful paean to construct theory now reads in retrospect as a requiem. With the person now effectively vanquished from the psychology curriculum, what we have in its place as the central object of study is the human organism as an evolved biologically programmed, and developing, information processing machine. 'One's relationship to an organism' as Laing (1965a: 21) passionately argued in *The Divided Self*, 'is different from one's relation to a person'. This has profound consequences. Outside of the current dominant narrative fiction, the discursive, qualitative, historical and post-modern approaches (Kvale, 1992) to the human condition remain at the margins of psychology in a different intellectual universe than that which drives the mainstream.[1] Psychology has in effect grown and reproduced itself by virtue of the fraud that it is other than what it is, thriving parasitically on people's desire to know and understand personhood and existence in the world when in fact it has little to say that is coherent on these matters. How can it, when it routinely excludes the context of human behaviour from its formulations (Kagan, 2012)?

The corporately framed object of study which resides at the centre, what we might refer to as the 'neuro-entity', is to be researched and understood within the remit of the modern totalitarian capitalist society by means of a science in thrall to technology and economics rather than life. The tools of the trade which stand in the way of 'the honest study of human behaviour and the means people use to help themselves and others cope with the demands of living' (Szasz, 2007: 149) are face recognition, neuroimaging, computational modelling, diagnostic invention, the 5 per cent significance level, abnormal psychology and the eugenic dreams of behaviour genetics, all of which are deemed more worthy of our attention than the preservation of academic freedom, or an existential confrontation with the anxieties and perplexities of life, love and other people. Sartre's aphorism that 'hell is other people' at least presupposed the 'other' as human. With the 'neuro-centric' machine aesthetic in the intellectual ascendancy, the absence of what was once axiomatic is now paradigmatic.

The reasons for the current state of affairs can be traced to the subordination of academic psychology to the demands of authority. Arguably the compromise of psychological reason can be traced both to the inception of the experimental tradition with its lugubrious fixation with measurement and control, and its long-standing cooperation with military interests. 'War, both real and prospective', wrote Richards, has provided a 'hot house environment' in which 'virtually the entire range of psychology's interests have been co-opted' (Richards, 2002: 319). With this subservient domain of thought acceptance duly came. Outside of the mainstream it is equally true that early psychoanalytic insight into the damage caused by sexual trauma was also subordinated to power – the 'seduction' theory giving way to the Oedipus complex by reason of the economic necessity of having the abusers foot the bill for the therapy and thereby not stand in the way of the nascent discipline (Masson, 2003). Thus what was initially and correctly understood as reality was under the transforming conditions of the market reborn as phantasy. This alone arguably distorted and undermined the potential of psychoanalysis and should have served as a wake-up call. Freud had no words for this process. We might call it tertiary revision. Another phrase is intellectual slavery, as Freud remained publicly silent, as he had to, on the influence of those who were bankrolling him. Whilst the development of medicine can in part be understood through its roots in the public health movement, psychology has no such democratic ancestry, lacking 'any historical roots in projects that have sought to improve the public good or bring radical social change' (Harper, Roberts & Sloboda, 2007: 213). Consequently it has been at the mercy of hegemonic power ever since it took its first breath.

By the time World War Two was underway, social psychology had become a willing accomplice to the refurbishment of the US industrial landscape (Collier, Minton & Reynolds, 1991; Moscovici & Markova, 2006). On this side of the Atlantic two events are perhaps of seminal importance for understanding the current subservience of the discipline to elite interests. Firstly, following the ranking of UK schools, the introduction of the Research Assessment Exercise (RAE) in 1986 provided the means for the wholesale ranking of university departments (and within them academic staff) in terms of research 'quality'. Central to the exercise (now rebranded as the Research Excellence Framework or REF) is the process of assigning 'impact factors' to journals, a dubious practice described as 'deeply flawed' by Schekman (2013)[2] and 'psychometric nonsense' by Hartley (2012: 330–1). What this in effect has entailed is a greater weight accorded to publications specific to the North American continent, where a pragmatic individualistic psychology reigns supreme with the hapless subject trapped within a social structure free zone (Parker, 2007). This latter day form of academic (market) imperialism has profound implications for the type and scope of psychology that one is able to do or the range of 'behaviour' that one is permitted to try and explain.

The necessity for researchers to conform to this 'market discipline' for the sake of their careers has explicitly shaped the content of academic discourse, this in a manner considered to have had '… a disastrous impact on the UK higher education system' (UCU, 2008). Under this umbrella, viable research is that which attracts the attentions of academic entrepreneurs and corporate sponsors. Thus in a kind of 'four legs good two legs bad' scenario – we have 'brain research and personality good', 'psychology of political protest and misbehaviour of political elites bad'. The attendant 'narrowing of research opportunities' (ibid.) is a predictable consequence, another, somewhat reminiscent of the reduced attention span of twenty-first century audiences, is the preference for journal articles over books.

Confirmation of the wholesale adoption of market values in the UK higher education wonderland came in the form of the Dearing Report (National Committee of Inquiry into Higher Education, 1997). For example the UK Government's 'vision of a learning society' envisaged students making 'a greater investment in their own futures'. Investment of course can take many forms – and as the language of the market grows more pervasive – a 'deeply shared and transcendent faith' according to Seabrook (1990: 11), 'capital investment' has come to embrace the social, biological, not to say 'human' as well as the purely financial.

The 'self-interested' student situated in the expanding higher education market, contending with spiralling debt in a shrinking job market made worse by the financial crisis, may turn their hand to making money in whatever way they can. The economic psychology of the contemporary student, now thoroughly disciplined to market realities has not surprisingly incorporated the selling of sexual services[3] (Roberts, Sanders, Smith & Myers, 2010; Roberts, Jones & Sanders, 2013), including lap dancing (BBC, 2008), striptease, escorting and prostitution (Brinkworth, 2007; Chapman, 2001; Dolman, 2008; Whitaker, 2001). A list to which no doubt could be added performance in the vast multimedia global pornography industry. The phenomenon is not confined to the UK, having been documented in the UK, the US (Weitzer, 2000), Australia (Lantz, 2004; Sedgman, 2004), and France (Duvall Smith, 2006). It is difficult to avoid seeing a correlation between this geography of student sexual commerce and the (re)modelling of student as customer and consumer of educational services. The academic 'providers' are the other side of this transaction and university departments of psychology, as with all other university departments, have become, willing or not, *de facto* pimps and of course, as compliant social scientists – at one with the corrosion of academic integrity – are to be deterred from any investigation of the phenomenon (Roberts, 2010; Roberts, Jones & Sanders, 2013).

For psychology to have somehow escaped the violence of the market would have been nothing short of miraculous, however the almost complete absence of resistance from the inner sanctums of psychological power speaks volumes for the mindset which animates the mainstream.[4] All this doesn't simply mean a different educational and economic experience for the staff and students who amble through the average university psychology curriculum. Capitalist logic, as Marx warned, dissolves everything in its wake, thus, the imposition of 'market Stalinism and bureaucratic anti-production' (Fisher, 2009: 39) does not stop at the commoditisation of learning and the internal policing of thought; all 'fixed, fast-frozen relations' including those with ourselves are in the course of being 'swept away' (Marx & Engels, 1888/1975: 37). After just a few years of this, we are not what we used to be. Under the influence of the market, knowledge of ourselves has been added to the list of things made transient and disposable – with even the most profound statements about who we are rendered into junk.

Modern psychology in service to super-capitalist transnational ideology has overseen a revolution in how we understand ourselves. Eliminated from the subject matter of the behavioural sciences, the person as centre of experience has been supplanted by the 'zombie', celebrated by philosopher Dan Dennett (1992: 405) as 'behaviourally indistinguishable' from a 'normal human being' and the perfect solution to the thorny problem of consciousness, 'materialism's biggest problem' (Sheldrake, 2012: 109), inconveniently and still inexplicably lurking within the human corporeal frame. This vision, a theoretical version of the Capgras delusion,[5] takes as its inspiration the cinematic zombie collective, reducing human existence to a serial collectivity ruthlessly competing in an eternal Darwinian struggle for survival; an essentially disorganised anti-social ensemble driven to consume, devouring all comers in its wake – much like the agents behind the international financial system exposed by Bakan (2005) as corporate psychopaths. We are now literally, as well as figuratively, what we eat, and as we consume one another to the relentless and sacred rhythm of the FTSE 100, the trinity of the word made flesh is as Abba sang 'money, money, money'.

While some might find the above rendition of the eternal human mystery into the scientific equivalent of a George A. Romero 'B-movie' distasteful, this has not stopped legions of psychologists from proclaiming the virtues of modern scientific psychology. This is not the first time in the history of the behavioural sciences that the political technological transformation of our ideas of human life – both in its nature and purpose – has posed a dire threat to the established moral order – witness the fruits of intellectual realism to be found under Nazi and Soviet domination. As such it ought not to be forgotten that the roads to the death camp and the gulag, just as in the Bosnian genocide a half century later, were paved by the intelligentsia as much as by the crude totalitarian apparatchiks and out and out criminals.

Scorcese's *Shutter Island* contends that in the twentieth century's great battle between good and evil, the scientific community of the victors may have been more than a little compromised, with behavioural science in general and psychology in particular being the sites of greatest contamination (Roberts, 2011b). Perhaps it was always more than a little fanciful to suppose that the cataclysmic moral catastrophe of the century, erected as it was on the intellectual foundations of racial pseudo-science and genetics, would leave no scars on the discipline. Richards (1994: 457) also reminds us, and we do need reminding, that the psychologists who supported the Nazi regime 'were at the forefront of the recognition of professional psychology'. The resultant organisational apparatus of the discipline has so far turned a blind eye to the political and moral issues of the day; for example, the Bosnian genocide, the illegal Iraq war and the use of behavioural scientists in interrogation teams schooled in techniques considered by some to be out and out torture, to name but a few of the largely discussion-free zones in contemporary academic life (Patel, 2007).[6] Psychology has been a regular accomplice to mass crime, indeed it is a key part of the greatest mass crime in history – the Holocaust – and no doubt will be a part of the next one, courtesy amongst other things of its regular assists to populist criminal regimes[7] such as the UK and US, the surveillance society and able contributions to the reification of all forms of disobedience, whether political, social or interpersonal, as individual dysfunction. Its relentless espousal of the myth[8] of objective science in step to the march of reductionist individualism continues to postpone any reckoning with this truth. A truth that is so 'terrible' one 'must not speak or think about [it] ... even if alone in the forest, where no one is listening' (Vulliamy, 2012: 181). Until the silence is prized open psychology will continue to be a 'dangerous' discipline – though sadly not in the sense that Moscovici envisaged in his use of this term (i.e. dangerous to ruling elites) but in the sense that history, justice, purpose, hope and liberty will remain excised from both its lexicon and political repertoire. So it is that in the shadows of the West's ambiguous triumph, as the reverberations of the human failings that brought us the Holocaust echo down the years, as the end of history is proclaimed and authoritarian capitalist fundamentalism declares itself the only game in town, there is almost no professional interest in our responsibilities as moral agents.

In a typical psychology degree programme, concern with the moral order has been replaced by a concern with 'ethics'[9] which now goes no further than acquiring the wherewithal to push one's research plans through the bureaucratic machinery of a university ethics committee or a denunciation of the Milgram experiments – about which more later. It is no coincidence that the 'conceptual primacy of the person as moral agent' (Szasz, 2002: 140) has been supplanted by a crass obsession with neuroscience whereby it is an article of faith that agency, choice and responsibility can and will be explained away by reference to the material substrate of the brain. The challenges of life – to have good friends, engage in meaningful work and leisure activities, receive and express love, bring up children, have harmonious relationships with others, to respect and nurture the environment, to deal with physical and emotional pain – are not problems which can either be reduced to a purely physical or chemical layer of abstraction, or solved by the application of a set of prosaic rules. These are moral, practical and political issues which, no matter how far one peers down a microscope or how much one gazes admiringly at the latest fMRI artistry depicting one's brain, this approach will never solve. Many students do come to psychology seeking practical answers to their own particular dilemmas.[10] They have scant opportunity to discuss them within the remit of their discipline, and the academic staff charged with the responsibility for their education have, for the most part, no desire or inkling as to how to do it. Indeed they too have been so thoroughly professionally brainwashed into the idea that talking and listening to people about their lives is some esoteric skill, requiring years of specialist training, that they have given up hope of doing so before they start. So, rather than any useful practical knowledge, what the luckless psychology student is on the receiving end of is a lengthy indoctrination into the art of psychological sophistry and the championing of a form of scientific method misapplied to the human condition. From this they emerge with an enhanced vocabulary for how to discuss human behaviour but no real understanding of the vagaries or vicissitudes of experience that lie behind it and which continue to resist the stultifying embrace of quantification.

Sooner or later every psychology student faces the painful experience of their rite of passage into the world of psychological research methods and statistics. These fundamentalist tools of the trade recall Maslow's observation that if the only tool you have is a hammer, pretty much everything begins to look like a nail. So it is with the misuse of statistical reasoning. It doesn't take long before the hapless newcomer to psychological enquiry has absorbed the message that the only questions worth asking are those which are answerable by means of a statistical test, and the 'correct answer' must be a statistically significant result; that is, a result so extreme/unusual that in a truly random sample the magnitude of the given result would only have occurred by chance on one in twenty (or fewer) occasions. There are numerous problems with this, not the least of which is that researchers hardly ever use random samples, so that the entire reasoning exercise with the actual samples is premised on a fiction.[11]

Further problems arise when it comes to interpreting statistical output. On this front academic staff are often as confused as the students. In fact it may be the staff's confused ideas that are the source of the students' apprehension. A colleague of mine (White, 2010) recently carried out an intriguing study into the representations and understanding of statistics amongst psychology lecturers and students. What she found ought to give food for thought to anyone content with the status quo. Not only was there evident misunderstanding of common research principles and procedures but also misapprehension as to what the output from these mean (the Null Hypothesis Significance Test (NHST) coined by Ronald Fisher being just one example).[12] Furthermore an acknowledged cynicism toward the use of statistical rhetoric was observed, coupled with a perceived necessity to employ it in order to follow the rules of the game, noted as essential not just for one's own career progression but useful to cement psychology's place on the lower rungs of the science ladder – which needless to say sees physics gazing down from on high. Something to ask is whether this slavish adherence to a set of questionable disciplinary norms (Morrison & Henkel, 1970) constitutes an example of intellectual corruption, institutional inertia or just laziness?

Widespread publication bias, contributing to what is known as the file drawer effect (Rosenthal, 1979), certainly suggests institutional inertia, but laziness is also certainly part of the picture, given that at least forty alternatives to the NHST have been suggested (Kirk, 1996). Last, but not least, psychology's place in the status quo, its undoubted physics envy and penchant for reductionism as well as the historical role of statistical science itself in the development of surveillance societies (see Rabinow, 1991) means that a form of intellectual corruption cannot be ruled out. There are after all no priori reasons why an in-depth understanding of human beings for human beings should emerge from a tradition which has sought prediction and control over its subject matter, itself a highly dubious aim, or that wisdom in such affairs will inevitably emerge from the language of numbers. The difficulties are compounded when one peers into the muddy waters that surround the replication of empirical results, accepted in the natural sciences as the sine qua non of scientific activity, but a deeply problematic issue within psychology. As the replicability of research findings goes to the heart of what we mean by science, any problems with it must raise concerns about the legitimacy of psychology as a social science and the knowledge claims it makes.

In recent years, the spectacular growth in computing power has led researchers to model both the natural world and human behaviour in more and more complex ways. With the ever present desire to employ statistical rhetoric to boost the market share of one's ideas, a technique known as structural equation modelling (SEM, sometimes referred to quite erroneously as 'causal modelling') has grown in popularity and has come to be seen as an important tool in the multivariate armoury. What the criteria are, however, which should inform acceptance of SEM model replication has seldom been considered in the literature. Miles and Shevlin's (2003) introduction to the technique makes no mention of replicability at all beyond it being 'a problem'. At the time of writing, if we consider one speciality where SEM has been extensively employed (e.g. health psychology), we are not aware of a single instance where such a model has been fully replicated, that is, (1) has been able to explain the same degree of variance in an outcome of interest, (2) employed the same predictors of this outcome with the same specified pathways, (3) found these predictors to have the same explanatory power (effect size), and (4) been reproduced in an independent sample (Roberts, 2005). Despite this the presence of SEM models in journal articles is a predictive factor in how frequently work gets cited (Hegarty & Walton, 2012). The continued failure to adequately consider the serious problems about the validity of this technique has repercussions for the credibility of scientific psychology and begs more questions about the aims of those who set the agenda within the discipline. What exactly is being sought – methodological fashion, power or truth?

Problems with replication are not confined to the multivariate arena. Following an attempted replication by Chris French, Richard Wiseman and Stuart Ritchie (see French, 2012; Ritchie, Wiseman & French, 2012) of an apparent demonstration of precognition by Bem (2011), French and colleagues found that almost nobody would review their paper let alone publish it – an experience similar to my own when attempting to get my discussion of replication in the multivariate arena into print. In French's words:

> This whole saga raises important questions. Although we are always being told that 'replication is the cornerstone of science', the truth is that the 'top' journals are simply not interested in straight replications – especially failed replications. They only want to report findings that are new and positive. (French, 2012)

Only when French took his concerns to the popular press (i.e. *The Guardian* newspaper), was an interest in replication awakened within the BPS. French's move prompted a hastily summoned 'stellar cast of contributors' (*The Psychologist*, 2012, *25*(5), 349) to comment, once again illustrating how the professional psychological agenda (circus?) appears to be driven more by publicity and celebrity than scientific substance. Ritchie, Wiseman and French (2012: 346) admitted that the affair raised questions about our 'current statistical paradigm', the very same questions which had been raised seven years previously when the editors of *The Psychologist* pronounced that another article on methodology would not be welcome. Clearly then the mistake may have been to try and initiate discussion in the professional literature rather than seeking out the nearest amenable journalist from a national newspaper. What next, authors reclining in suggestive poses to boost circulation figures (and impact factors)?

Being aware of the limitations inherent in psychology's addiction to scientific status and its frequently suspect methodology led Chomsky to consider it likely that we will 'learn more about human life and human personality from novels than from scientific psychology' (Chomsky, 1988: 159). The novel speaks to what we do as well as what we think and situates people at the mercy of the forces of culture, place and time. Academic psychology has forsworn such wisdom as well as that proffered by the physical disciplines of art, movement and action (e.g. dance, martial arts, political protest) to nail its own allegiance firmly to a wholly disincarnate unemotional cognate-linguistic form of knowledge – so that what we get in the end is science as PR and as a result an opportunity is missed to acknowledge, within the psychological curriculum, the moral and political maze that permeates our existence.

Such an opportunity lies buried in the experiments of Stanley Milgram (Milgram, 1974). As mentioned, Milgram's studies of obedience are now routine fodder for students to dissect the moral shortcomings of pretending to electrocute people in the name of science. When actually told, most are surprised to learn that in these studies Milgram not only introduced the principle of debriefing – to a degree rarely followed even today – but also provided the means to inspire people to resist the demands of illegitimate authority.

A particularly interesting example is provided by Ron Ridenhour, a participant in one of the subsequent successful replications (Rosenhan, 1969) of Milgram's findings, in which obedience rates of 85 per cent were obtained at the maximum shock level. In the course of the study Ridenhour refused to administer a single shock, the only person to do so. By a somewhat incredible coincidence, Ridenhour's name is associated with one of the whistle-blowers on the infamous massacre at My Lai during the Vietnam war, in which US soldiers on a search and destroy mission massacred hundreds of innocent civilians.

Though this was actually a different individual[13] these two men with the same name[14] are fine examples of what we could be teaching as well. The usual consideration of the obedience studies centres on the two-thirds of participants who were willing to inflict potentially lethal levels of shock on others. But it is precisely here that the principal moral aspects of the study are passed over. What about those participants who, like Ridenhour, despite the intimidating research environment, refused to administer what they believed were potentially lethal levels of shock? Isn't this the place where the most useful practical knowledge can be found? What factors enabled so many people to desist from the experimenter's exhortations that 'the experiment must continue?' Isn't this a wonderful opportunity to teach generations of students to think for themselves, to challenge the imperatives of authority? Of course this would necessitate a change in direction, from teaching 'value free' knowledge to teaching valuable knowledge, a move which might enable us to 'rediscover the vision, ambition and epic sense of scale' (Reicher & Haslam, 2011: 652) that is sorely needed.

As someone born in the aftermath of World War Two, growing up in Liverpool, for many years afterwards I saw first-hand the considerable physical destruction which had been wrought on the city by the Luftwaffe. I heard numerous wartime stories from my parents and learnt, through film and literature, of the unimaginable horrors perpetrated by the Nazis. We were told 'never again', but the question I put to myself concerned what I would have done had I been growing up in the midst of Nazi indoctrination in pre-war Germany. This I could not answer – but what I could address myself to was the present environment, which by common agreement was several orders of magnitude more benign. If I couldn't resist the unfair machinations of authority given these more favourable circumstances, then there would be scant hope of pursuing an ethical course of action should I have found myself passing the time in the dark days of the Reich.

A further aspect to the Milgram studies, pertinent to the present discussion, is that a singular focus on their dark side operates de facto as 'realist' instruction in pessimism about the human condition, as if our propensity for brutality is simply an inescapable fact of life about which we can do nothing. An alternative vision, as suggested could make equal 'capital' from disobedience as a facet of our 'positive psychology', thereby proffering hope that humanity is not to be written off as intrinsically savage, a proposition that Pinker (2011) challenges in his recent foray into the history of human violence. To do that however would not only risk contaminating the intrinsically apolitical vision of positive psychology[15] offered in the midst of our collapsing civilisation (see Ahmed, 2010) but would also question the implicit 'elevation of conformity and obedience to praiseworthy virtues' (Pinker, 2011: 559) which lies behind our slavish cultural celebration of celebrity and authority.

The Milgram experiments, as more thoughtful commentators have remarked (e.g. Blass, 2000) are a morality play. Milgram, like Reich, had the audacity to suggest that the fascist propensity toward unthinking obedience and cruelty could be found anywhere – even, God forbid, the US! In challenging the complacent status quo and venturing beyond the cosy political confines of psychological neutrality, he duly paid with his career. Post Cambodia, Rwanda, Bosnia, Darfur, Iraq, Afghanistan, accelerating climate change and the financial crisis, the cost for us of failing to heed the lessons may be incomparably greater. In the present era the body of Milgram's great work needs to be resuscitated and reenergised. The unquestioning conformity to military, political and financial power has moved human civilisation to the edge of a precipice and placed the planetary ecosystem on life support. Why its lessons have still not been learnt should occupy the minds of all in the discipline. Ridenhour's original letter to the US Congress quoted Churchill's maxim that 'a country without a conscience is a country without a soul'.[16] In the simultaneous incompatible pursuit of scientific neutrality and behavioural control, psychology in the twenty-first century, under state and corporate sponsorship, has become an enterprise lacking in both conscience and soul. Within the numerous books and journals which occupy the minds of the contemporary psychologist there is technical and material eloquence in abundance but such eloquence, as Confucius (2000: 169) knew well, does not automatically entail the possession of 'moral power'.

No discussion of the obedience studies or the ideological stain on psychology would be complete without mention of Milgram's repressed intellectual twin, the infamous Ewen Cameron. Cameron served as President of the Canadian, American and World Psychiatric Associations, the American Psychopathological Association and the Society of Biological Psychiatry during the 1950s and enjoyed status and privilege in his day way in excess of anything that Milgram could claim. Now however he is a largely forgotten figure, another outcast from the squeaky clean official histories of the behavioural sciences. Cameron's CIA-sponsored work on mind control (see Harper, 2007), formed part of the US Government's covert MK-ULTRA project, an electroshock, drug induced, sensory deprivation nightmare for his 'participants', who unbeknown to them had embarked on a Cold War journey toward the eradication and rebuilding of human memory and personality. Cameron's project ended in failure both morally and pragmatically for his paymasters, yet it formed the methodological backbone for subsequent forays into the slipstreams of torture and interrogation (Klein, 2007).

So, we find Milgram, positioned as bête noir of the discipline, a figure whose career went into a steep decline for administering simulated shock to his participants in order to alert us to the dangers of illegitimate authority. In contrast Cameron, at the summit of his profession, acting on behalf of such malign authority inflicted real shocks and much worse yet has managed to stay out of the firing line; a telling and contrasting set of fortunes if ever there was. When this significant comparison was offered to the readers of *The Psychologist* I was 'assured' by its well-intentioned editors that the more than 48,000 subscribers to the publication would have no interest in the comparison, which to the educated consumers of its celebrity-psychologist-packed pages would remain as an unknown and forgotten 'simple twist of fate'.[17] Students I have taught have always been astounded by the Milgram–Cameron comparison; not so their professional overseers. That it provoked such apathy at the BPS tells us a considerable amount about where its heart lies; a tell-tale heart oblivious to the professional debasement involved in lending moral support to the triumvirate of capitalism, nationalism and corporatism – the cornerstones of our 'modern' corrupt decaying society. Commenting on the BBC's subservience to political power in the Middle East, Robert Fisk (2009) remarked that 'If you allow yourself to bow down before those who wish you to deviate from the truth, you will stay on your knees forever'. If the BPS's current disdain for any lofty principles[18] is anything to go by, the discipline is destined to remain on its knees for quite some time.

Cinematic flashbacks of Cameron's flirtation with the dark side regularly adorn the big screen, as in *The Manchurian Candidate*, *The Bourne Ultimatum* and *Total Recall*. As science fiction writer Philip K. Dick realised somewhat presciently, we live in an age in which fiction is absolutely necessary in order to understand the quixotic, the duplicitous and the cognitive and emotional dimensions of human reality. But the necessity for us to fully engage with fiction in order to get to the core of the real goes beyond Dick's and for that matter Chomsky's championing of the novel and highlights further the inability of positivist psychology to get to the heart of the human project. The intertwining, indeed inseparability, of the real and the fictional in terms of both their construction and interpretation form the essence of the seductive and elusive post-modern world. In his numerous works Jean Baudrillard (e.g. 1994, 1996, 2010) mapped the psycho-geography of this slippery world. It is no accident that post-modernism has been described as a philosophy of consumerism, for almost the entire world is now online and deliverable to us à la simulacra as consumable product; this incorporates not only our interpretive forays as agent, witness and junkie to war, celebrity, and technology but, as suggested earlier, also our relationship to ourselves and others. Our obsession with image is technologically and market driven and in an act of corporate deception cognitively outsourced back to us courtesy of the 'science' of mind and behaviour. We wander perpetually through the hall of mirrors which reflects this world back to us and in orgies of longing, guilt and self-gratification endlessly police the body which is simultaneously starved of what we need and fed to excess with what we don't. Caught in a compulsive snare to refashion our own imaginable 'real' self as desirable object for both 'self' and 'other' our lives are a never-ending search for a way out.

Less depressing, our very hopes and dreams have always had their origins in the internal fictional worlds we create in order to propel us into action. At their best our lives owe everything to these. Too often the language of experimental psychology, philosophy and psychoanalysis has depicted a void at the centre of our experience. For Lacan and those who follow in his wake this void is the impenetrability of the 'Real', but this is a mistake. It is Lacan who is impenetrable.[19] The void at the centre of much of our experience is not the commoditised, sexualised, passionate hunger yearning to find solace from the deficits of one's life but simply love, 'the secret left untold' (Hobart, 2003: 141), the beauty and truth at the centre of existence which animates friendship, justice, compassion, laughter, tolerance, joy, music, wisdom and seamless movement through the winds of circumstance. To know when to advance, when to retreat and when to be still – in Fromm's (1995: 6) eyes, 'the answer to the problem of human existence' and as an 'attitude, an orientation of character' (ibid: 36), the 'ultimate consequence of psychology' (ibid: 25). The examination of love in psychology however is largely out of bounds, a dangerous, wild animal to the science hunter to be tranquillised, caged and tamed within the safe bounds of 'attraction'. In contrast it forms the cornerstone of much eastern lore – the centrepiece of the philosophy underpinning many Asian martial arts which are concerned as much with the cultivation of character as the effective application of defensive techniques (e.g. Hobart, 2003; Kit, 1981). The founder of Aikido, Morihei Uyeshiba, expressed this as follows; 'If the heart is open and pure, there is no place for harm to enter; and at the deepest level love and will are one' (cited in Payne, 1981: 36).

The wholeness of the person was emphasised by Kelly (1955), for whom the human being, as in the martial arts, was an integral form of motion – a psycho-biomechanical poem – that is sadly beyond the 'investigative competence of the natural sciences' (Laing, 1982: 18). To bring all such issues practically within the realm of our psychology would necessitate a revolution in practice that would make much of what we currently do seem pointless. Psychology would have to renounce the fiction that it can adopt the same investigative model as the natural sciences. Forty years ago Ornstein (1972: 7–8) lamented the fact that all too often 'the method of psychology has become the goal'. This remains the case, although arguably the malaise has grown deeper. Ornstein's postscript (p. 229) warned that a more complete science of psychology would be unattainable unless 'people make the effort to train those aspects of themselves which are usually uncultivated in Western education'. In our system of education in general and our pursuit of psychological knowledge in particular, love, the most important thing in the world, has been cultured out. Of it one might ask 'was it ever there?' or has it all but 'vanished in the wind'?[20] We must therefore recognise that *useful* knowledge is not exclusively rational. The primacy of the 'view from nowhere' must give way, not to another cognitive perspective, but to the primacy of the act and the manner of its execution. Any hopes that contemporary mainstream academic psychology[21] can achieve this must be considered slim. Trapped within the icy grip of state interests, strangled by the narrow mindedness and procedural inflexibility of official 'research assessment', hindered by a moribund[22] curriculum and shackled by physics envy, we should look elsewhere if we truly seek enlightenment about our place in the world. *The Glass Bead Game*, Hesse's (1972) great novel, lays bare the utter sterility of pursuing a purely intellectual aesthetic. It is time we learned the lesson. In Christopher Nolan's reinvention of the Dark Knight, Christian Bale's Batman, suitably trained in the Eastern martial arts and the harsh realities of city life understands very well the limitations of eschewing action as wisdom. What ultimately counts is what is realised in the world. This too, is what is ultimately desired – reality above its representation. 'The only way in which the world can be grasped ultimately lies, not in thought, but in the act' (Fromm, 1995: 61). To which we might add, thinking and action are one, and as spontaneous expressions of our being require nothing. They are to be experienced not kick-started into life. They can only remain that way with a certain discipline. The task before us, as it has always been, is how to live. 'Freedom and justice', Chesler (2005: 44) noted, 'does wonders for one's mental health'. Corporate, organised, big science psychology it must be said, does not. It is academic life in a spiritual death zone. For all of us in this discipline who long for a passionate understanding of our condition, and who are not 'ruled by deference to authority' or 'seduced by make-believe and the deregulation of pleasure' (Smail, 2005: 101) it is time to let go, and move on. The future is undecided – with a river of infinite possibilities in which to swim.

Endnotes

1. A joint 'International Benchmarking Review of Social Psychology' in the UK undertaken by the British Psychological Society and ESRC dismissed the impact of qualitative/critical/discursive approaches in the discipline despite the fact that the most highly cited UK social psychologists work within the discursive tradition and that the most highly cited publications in UK social psychology are also to be found within it (Billig et al., 2011).

2. Schekman, a Nobel prize winner, also suggested that the pursuit of impact factors has 'become an end in itself ... as damaging to science as the bonus culture is to banking'.

3. Some of these students will of course be studying psychology and will carry the fruits of their experience into their later careers. How this might influence the discipline is anybody's guess. They will of course already have learned how to present a front for the pleasure of others – not a great basis for challenging the status quo in the discipline.

4. And has long animated the discipline. Thus we can find one of the most celebrated members of the discipline – Hans Eysenck – effectively working in his latter days on behalf of the tobacco industry (see Buchanan, 2010).

5. A disorder in which a person holds a belief that a friend, spouse, parent, or close family member has been replaced by an impostor, physically indistinguishable from the real person.

6. *Zersetzung der Seele* [Decomposition of the Soul] edited By Klaus Behnke and Jürgen Fuchs (2010) examines the practice of psychology and psychiatry in the service of the Stasi.

7. A term used by Dimitrijevic (2011) to describe a state engaging in mass crime supported from its civilian base. Whilst Dimitrijevic had the Nazi and Serbian regimes in mind, the huge death toll perpetrated by the Anglo-American alliance since World War Two both independently and together in numerous illegal ventures (e.g. Vietnam, Nicaragua, Iraq, Suez) and supported by the citizenry of those countries makes the description here apt (see Curtis, 2003, 2004).

8. Myths, Szasz (1997: 120) informs us 'function as justificatory imagery and rhetoric for both the group' (e.g. the professional psychological community), 'and the individual' (e.g. individual psychologist as 'scientist').

9. Such concern is really an expression of the fear of litigation – the truth that dare not speak its name – yet another indication of the primacy of business in academic life.

10. Laying the foundations for the paradox of the wounded healer. There is data suggesting that a large proportion of psychology students have a history of serious emotional issues to contend with (Nikcevic, Kramolisova-Advani & Spada, 2007; Roberts, Bergström & Le Rooy, 2007b).

11. See Irvine, Miles & Evans (1979) for an interesting discussion of the social and historical roles of statistics.

12. 'Today its representation not only exists but thrives, autonomous and self

determining, unconnected and distinct from anything that may have preceded it' (White, 2010: 32–3).

13. See the letter by Gordon Bear. http://groups.google.com/group/spsp-discuss/msg/b7f9cebb868fd187 Last accessed May 2012.

14. One wonders what Jung would have made of this.

15. In 'positive psychology' sin has gone full circle. From being transformed to unhappiness, unhappiness has now once again become a sin. This lays bare the aim of its parent discipline – to accommodate to a damaging reality rather than to change it.

16. The full letter can be found at http://law2.umkc.edu/faculty/projects/ftrials/mylai/ridenhour_ltr.html Last accessed May 2012.

17. Song by Bob Dylan.

18. Ørner (2011: 797) described the BPS's in-house publication *The Psychologist* as promoting 'parochialism' in a profession now 'bound by proscriptions, suspicious of debate and intolerant of diversity'.

19. Rycroft was similarly unimpressed by Lacan. In a review of one of Rycroft's books, Laing (1985b) recalls Rycroft's view that 'apart from the single fact that he [Lacan] would like psychoanalysis to be rewritten from the point of view of linguistics, I found his writing a real load of rubbish'.

20. A fragment from Brecht's (1947) *In Memory of Marie A.* The poem was used in the film *The Lives of Others* to allude to the fact that something necessary to our existence – something central to our humanity – can so easily fade to almost nothing – living only on the fringes of memory, and barely reachable through the fog of state-sponsored everyday inhumanity.

21. If there is any hope within the discipline it will lie with the humanistic psychology and radical psychology movements.

22. Literally bound to death, which if things continue on their present course, may be the fate of all of us.

Chapter 11

The new politics of experience

> The only satisfaction that can give ... real happiness [is] the experience of the activity of the present moment.
>
> (Fromm, 1942/2004: 226)

The genesis of *The New Politics of Experience* lies in using subjective truth as a map to negotiate the growth of knowledge. As Fromm (1942/2004) argued in *The Fear of Freedom* this path must cultivate self-expression, thinking and willing as unalienated facets of our total being, rooted in our social relatedness with others. How we have decided to go about it here is to leave you, our readers, with a testimonial in human passion and compassion, a calculated stimulus to evoke reaction and experience 'out there'. The value of some experiences can be known only by undergoing them, by being at the centre of the truths revealed by a given subjectivity. This means that they may forever evade the naming grasp of language. Composers throughout the ages have known this well.[1] Some truths however we would rather not know – not only those where we have fallen from grace but also where we have borne witness to the misdeeds of others. Some things it has long been said are better not known. By this we certainly do not mean knowledge and experience as forbidden fruit, merely that some of what life throws at us leaves the bitterest of tastes. Yet for good or ill, touched by the muse or by the devil these experiences shape our humanity and our choices. No matter how intangible our experiences may seem, to say nothing of the choices we make which lead us to them, there is a universal longing for validation within each one of us, a deeply held desire to be linked with the rest of humanity.

The quest for the universal in human affairs is usually accompanied by trouble. Imperialism in the political sphere is one means of trying to stamp one's social, political, economic and psychological comforts everywhere. This must necessarily destroy the comforts and the histories of others. Religion is another sphere in which this is enacted. One is reminded of how Dostoevsky portrayed the experience of Jesus' second coming in his novel *The Brothers Karamazov*. On a walk with the Grand Inquisitor, Jesus remains silent, while the shamefully excited and worried grand inquisitor is bewildered, unable to accommodate this new experience. He tells Jesus that they rule in his name, that they follow him and conduct those holy rituals of obedience, all in reference to his first presence on earth. Chastising Christ who is now seen as an obstacle to the workings of the Church the Inquisitor warns him, 'we shall deceive them again, for we will not let Thee come to us again. That deception will be our suffering, for we shall be forced to lie' (Dostoevsky, 2003: 278). What makes the Grand Inquisitor such a stark and appallingly truthful figure in our earthly politics of experience? The former Archbishop of Canterbury concludes as follows:

> He is both the manager of a universal market in guaranteed security and comfort for a diminished human soul and the violent enforcer of a system beyond dialogue and change. (Williams, 2008: 237)

Organised religion and politics have always dined at the same table. Since we both desire and strive for independence (to a degree at least we may have achieved some) we hope to resist the structural lies of the totalising institutions which service our disciplines and utter public pronouncements of their beneficence. To the extent that we too may have succumbed, our writings must be interrogated. We play the game of knowledge, based on experience, interconnected to an unavoidably examined life and affirm that contemporary critical psychology and psychotherapy require honest courage and courageous honesty. One cannot do this and expect institutional rewards. The history of psychotherapy (and counselling) also tells us that one must take care with setting up one's own 'alternative' institutions. 'Serve no master' was the lead from Jet Li's encounters with Bob Hoskins in *Unleashed*. Do not serve but always be open to learning.

When, back in 1967, R.D. Laing published *The Politics of Experience*, he drew our attention to forms of human alienation omnipresent in the arts and sciences, an invitation to us all to address and undo the experiential knots which bind us.[2] The display of what can devastate experience through manipulation, repression, oppression, suppression, constriction, splitting, mystification and confusion is still very much with us, nearly half a century later. Marx described several varieties of alienation – from oneself, from others, from work and in the economic sphere. Contemporary psychology, far from addressing these fundamental modes of dislocation from authentic being in the world, actively furthers our malaise. For example, whereas Marx considered the effects of the capitalist mode of production on workers' ability to determine their own lives and destinies (i.e. capitalism deprives them of the right to think of themselves as the authors of their own actions), mainstream reductionist psychology posits free will as a delusion and assumes human agency disappears under an analysis of hypothetical cause and effect relationships at the biological level. Not surprisingly psychology has shed little light on the perennial problems of human existence – the 'sins' of dread, angst, terror, isolation and despair, to mention but a few of the everlasting sources of misery which humans inflict on one another in the name of love, righteousness, honour, progress and knowledge. Ian Parker elaborates:

> Alienation is not merely the separation of ourselves from others but a kind of separation from ourselves in which we experience ourselves as inhabited and driven by forces which are mysterious to us. These mysterious forces include economic forces that structure our lives as beings who must sell our labour power to others; however psychologisation of the different dimensions of oppression that have made capitalism possible also condenses 'race' and 'sex' into highly charged, sometimes exciting and sometimes frightening, forces out of our control. (Parker, 2007: 5)

Parker follows a long line of thought in psychoanalysis, from Reich and Fromm through to Laing and Žižek which has made the alienation at the centre of our experience one of its primary concerns. For example, over seventy years ago Fromm wrote that we believe ourselves 'to be motivated by self-interest and yet' our lives are 'actually ... devoted to aims which are not ... [our] own' (Fromm, 1942/2004: 101), sentiments which have retained their capacity to disturb. Psychoanalysis has always had more to say about this because of its fundamental concern with subjectivity – rejected as unscientific by those who inhabit the world of experimental psychology. One day may we awaken from their mad dreams of reason and acknowledge our role in the creation of monsters. When we were little they chased us in our dreams, now they stalk our waking world.

In *Dead Poets Society,* Robin Williams challenges us to 'seize the day' lest the cold wind of regret courses through our veins in the hours and minutes of our twilight. The bitter taste of the unfulfilled past can only be banished in the present with our hands firmly on the reins of experience, cultivating the arts of experiential resistance and revolutionary joy, combining our species' enchanting peculiarities into visible illuminating individual and social transformations – to finally put paid to civilisation's reverberating discontents. In *The Politics of Experience and the Bird of Paradise,* Laing (1967) deepened his analysis of ontological security/insecurity, a treatise for us readers (both then and now) on 'how the straightjacket of conformity imposed on us all leads to intense feelings of alienation and a tragic waste of human potential' (jacket from a Penguin reprint circa 1990). In his introduction Laing wrote:

> Humanity is estranged from its authentic possibilities. The basic vision prevents us from taking any unequivocal view of the sanity of common sense, or of the madness of the so called madman. However, what is required is more than a passionate outcry of outraged humanity. Our alienation goes to the roots. The realisation of this is the essential springboard for any serious reflection on any aspect of present inter-human life. (Laing, 1967: 11–12)

Laing assembled in his *Politics of Experience* various talks (six in all) that he had been invited to give during the three years between 1962 and 1965. They cover the topics of experience – psychotherapeutic, 'schizophrenic' and transcendental, as well as considering the mystification of experience and the role of experience in the relationship between persons. Of the latter he had this to say:

> Social phenomenology is the science of my own and of the other's experience. It is concerned with the relation between my experience of you and your experience of me. That is, with inter-experience. It is concerned with your behaviour and my behaviour as I experience it, and your and my behaviour as you experience it. Since your and their experience is invisible to me as mine is to you and them, I seek to make evident to the others, through their experience of my behaviour, what I infer from your experience, through my experience of your behaviour. This is the crux of social phenomenology. (Laing, 1967: 16–17)

He also wrote (Laing, 1967: 19): 'My psyche is my experience, my experience is my psyche', a charming operational definition, since experience is the basis of any theory making, the source of all our practice – and from the source to its end and back again.

> From the point of view of a man alienated from his source creation arises from despair and ends in failure, but such a man has not trodden the path to the end of time, the end of space, the end of darkness and the end of light. He does not know that where it all ends, there it all begins. (Laing, 1967: 38)

This statement is maddeningly simple, for its poetic flair assumes there never will be a knower. Where Laing ends, we begin, to reconstitute the embodied and socially constructed soul in our world. Our *New Politics of Experience* builds upon Laing's and others' reflections. We see this as vital. Just as the Talmud tells us that to save one life is to save the world, so to save our experience is to save our lives too. Here we have taken stock half a century on. We caution against the simplification and easy reductionism of complex issues.

For example, the British Psychological Society, according to its recent Annual Report (2012), sports, besides us two authors, another 49,678 society members and subscribers. The 18,342 chartered members are enmeshed into 62 member networks. This is quite an astonishing professional group to reckon with. Imagine that each one of these members is consciously aware and alert to the dangers of uncritically accepting stated facts at face value. All are charged with the task of coping with the ambiguous games of psychology and psychotherapy. How do they do it? How do their actions produce the current state of play? We seldom think of human systems of relationship of this magnitude, yet society is inordinately more complex still. How does all this revelatory professional experience, in relation to persons and events in our working lives, spread out over countless years, actually gel? Can it? Does it have to? Must a unitary self-consistent view of the world be the most fruitful? We have endeavoured, in these pages, to provide an account, a synthesis of our 40-odd years of practice, which gives credence to our desire to be authentically present in our work with other human beings, and to express what comes to mind freely, without censorship of will, thought or emotion. We cannot expect there to be no problems or internal contradictions in what we have written.

Is there another place of pilgrimage in the human potential movement than Esalen, in Big Sur, California? In their report of conference proceedings,[3] Kripal and Shuck (2005) present a rich discussion of the topos of research which has come out of Esalen and consider its place in the histories of American religion, psychology and culture. The founding members, Murphy and Price, had made two cardinal rules, which worked for a long time: 'No one can capture the flag; we hold our dogmas lightly'. 'Fuck history' was another mantra, which, given that the place was there because of history, is curious indeed. But then again we ignore history at our peril and our disciplines do this with disconcerting regularity. Esalen, like other teaching institutes, looks forward, in an old, odd ecumenical way, to reach a higher self, a true self, a core self etc. Any healthy scepticism, rooted in the basic assumptions of Hindu and Buddhist discipline and practice, cradled and shepherded in a community of like-minded folks, would lead one to suggest that the Esalen model could lead to a cornucopia of unfulfilled promises. I was once made aware that a devotee of George W. Bush revelled in the US mode of spirituality to be found there. That alone ought to invite some reflection. It brings to mind the 'golden' olden days of the new Kingdom of Heaven – God help psychology if this is where we are at. What do New Age visions enable us to do? A new business plan, of how do I get into the purse of other people, become rich and famous, influential in transcendental idealism – an executive plan for redemption in this world?

The film maker Adam Curtis (2002) bemoaned 'the Century of the Self' which saw how the politicisation of the personal, which began in the 1960s, was transformed into culture-wide navel gazing, accompanied by a studied neglect of the material and economic basis of much human suffering. The consequences of that are with us to this day. Esalen and its like, after all is said and done, look similar to a cop out. The longing is still there, an addictive searching for a Shangri-La, the trap of reaching for enlightenment in the future. This is a captivating message, not so easily avoided, even by seasoned academic psychologists and psychotherapists of our own day and age. The simple Guru test goes as follows: see for yourself if one of the three totems – money, power, sex – is involved. Begin with money, the greatest lure, which enables one to 'suffer in comfort'. When your answer is yes, forget her or him as a worthy leader on the path to enlightenment. In homage to Hegel's master–slave dialectic one must be ready at the appointed hour to kill the Buddha. Usually they show flawed vision, think bombastically in megalomaniac autocratic terms and cover up their emotional stupidity. Sexual excess is often to be found there. So what? One person's madness is another's sanity. The

Esalen project began in a blaze of glory to pursue and sustain an open-ended agenda. In the words of co-founder Michael Murphy, the vision was 'to create a space for everything that was excluded from academy' (Kripal & Shuck, 2005: 183). But what did he mean by 'everything'? Was it intended as a garden of love for oneself and others, somewhere with no holds barred and all up for grabs? Sounds attractive? But please, in the myriad of intellectual verbosity, don't get fooled.

It was the visual anthropologist and research director of the Birmingham Institute of Art and design Nick Stanley (1998), who for once not only looked at the experience of tourists (and Esalen and other sites of spiritual interest have attracted a few), but also 'the other part of the equation', the providers of experience. In Stanley's work he considers the 'strategies that performers adopt to make themselves the content of tourists' experience' (Stanley, 1998: 12). The study of experiences usually leads one to anthropological knowing, the opening up of a comparative way to see the world and one's own stance within it. Similarly as psychotherapists we accompany persons on their journey inwards,[4] making and remaking their experience and expanding their own knowledge of the soul. Music, meditation and martial arts all open one's eyes and widen the horizons of experience, to let in the sunshine of alternative takes on reality. These make our darkness visible and encourage us to be in touch with our self. In our psychophobic culture the refusal of grief means we are denied a chance to mourn all the past 'here and nows' which were not lived in a responsive presence. To live fully in the present means a space must be left for the contingencies of the past to be felt and expressed. Oliver Sacks (2007) has another three m's on offer – music, madness and melancholia. A piece of music can evoke such a particular affect, often but not always unanticipated, in a specific time and place, opening up a free space for passionately felt emotions and profoundly fresh experience of who we are and become. 'Music can pierce the heart directly; it needs no meditation' (Sacks, 2007: 329).

A few days after Loren R. Mosher died (10 July 2004), friends of his called up Judy Schreiber, his widow, in Berlin. I (TI) was with her when the call came in on her mobile. They wanted to organise a memorial congress at Hamburg University, which took place in the University Hospital Hamburg (UKE) over the 6th and 7th November 2004, under the title: 'Das Soteria Prinzip – Kontextualisierung der Schizophrenie'.[5] Before I gave my talk on 'Models of madness', I played the first four minutes of *Allegro ma non troppo* from Franz

Schubert's String Quintet in C Major, D.956.[6] This music was written by Schubert three months before he himself died. For the Hamburg audience this was a novel experience and moved a few, besides me, to tears. Then I began with a dream from Doris Lessing, who created many a healing work of fiction, to stabilise and balance out our vivid life coloured between the myriad shades of black and white. Music may prise one open and stir the nerves which link heart to brain, traverse the body from tip to toe and back again, releasing the grip of muscles held in tension for too long. The body too is an instrument – as Reich knew, and we too can learn to play it to reconnect with the music of the spheres.

Of course psychotherapy can make things worse, since it creates options to choose another path as well as take a rest in the middle of the piazza of our life, the hope to sense more clearly where we, as adults, want to go from now on in. Once we, as patients or users of the mental health system, become freer and less psychically determined by the scripts laid down in our primary family home movie, (and later institutional scripts rewritten from these) we can not only liberate ourselves from these bondages of behaving, experiencing and thinking (sentences of faith) but also dissociate from who we once were. Melanie Shepherd and her colleagues (2012) from the University of Nottingham have analysed case data from the 43 persons (out of a total of 1,416 clients seen over five years) whose wellbeing deteriorated over the course of psychotherapy. Their conclusion was that most of these declines happened with persons who were low to begin with and that to prevent such adverse outcomes, systemic rather than merely personal change was needed and furthermore that an attendant increase in the allocation of significant resources would have been required to achieve this.

Still it is vital, for our professional experience, that we practise what we preach, and preach in line with what we practise in order not to contribute to the ubiquitous misrepresentation of the professions of psychotherapy and psychology. This way, we, as attendants to the soul, can be aware of psychological difficulties entering our daily working life. We are challenged to cope with the stories of suffering we encounter day in and day out, and are impelled to find resourceful ways to cope with them so that we do not mistake or confuse our own difficulties with those we hear. The risk of becoming impaired in our work is a perennial one and the trapdoors to an ineffectual stance almost without limit. That is why we suggest maintaining a practice of discipline – music, meditation, martial arts, peer listening and support – to sustain our wellbeing.

As psychologists we can become blind to our own suffering, easily misled by the multitude of certificates accrued and workshops attended, the litany of publications both written and read. Nevertheless our good-enough mental wellbeing is our foundation to practice. Patrick Larsson (2012) offers some food for thought on this issue – focusing on psychologist suicide, which is painful and shows our own vulnerability as people. Opening up and sharing our experience, reflections, dreams and worries in supervision and groups will most certainly be a good preventive habit and a salutogenesis[7] for us and the mental health consumer movement. Who knows, we may eventually merge as one. It is time to open up the tribal boundaries.

Bentall (2009) argues that by recognising how we persist with dogmatic professional structures and contents, in full view of substantial research evidence which shows they are no longer relevant to healing, we are shooting ourselves in the foot, as well as our clients in the head. Much about the contemporary scene is a hindrance and makes life worse for people who seek help for their mental disturbances and temporarily silenced selves. Outspoken women who have suffered a second harm due to this disgraceful practice and have survived to write about their experience are Clare Shaw[8] on self-harm and decolonising language and Jacqui Dillon[9] on hearing voices, self-help and post-psychiatric models of madness.

Another reminder to 'please take care of yourself', to 'mind the gap' between what one professes (in one's profession) and what one preaches, is Yvonne Bates' (2006) collection of clients' views and experiences of psychotherapy. Entitled *Shouldn't I Be Feeling Better By Now?*, Bates focuses on the seldom discussed shadow of psychotherapy. The client's experience must always lie at the centre of attention in any psychotherapy, whatever modality is preferred by both client/patient and psychotherapist. It is ideally an equal partnership, practised level headedly at eye level, between equals who differ – with one person – the one sought out as aid – attuned to the rhythms of an absent ego – and the other – the one who presently is deep in trouble and mired in dire straits aware of that aliveness or at least believing in the striving to achieve it. It is a partnership, a social practice geared to the reconstitution of 'self' on both sides. If this is not practised, then God knows how quickly those who come to us for help can be seduced 'by the ego-boosting allure of being a facilitator in the field of human emotions' (Bates, 2006: ix). Our professions are a dangerous magnet for those who wish to enhance their view of their own status through the exercise of power over vulnerable people. The chance to play medicine and don the symbolic white coat is rarely discussed.

There was a song once, which I (TI) listened to in my early days in London. The lyrics ran as follows: 'I feel bad, I feel bad, but I haven't done anything wrong today, but I feel bad'. Troubles and the blues belong to living like rays belong to the sun. Troubles ask to be lived through, and to be sometimes endured, so that we can learn to live through them, take the appropriate lessons from them, pass these on to others who may need them and free ourselves from their effects. As psychotherapists and psychologists, not to mention citizens, we can ill afford the clichéd habits of thought and import that clutter up all manner of relationships in the world. Difficulties and troubles ask for something new to happen. Prospective solutions to life's uncertainties and difficulties are not arrived at through the anchored and rule-bound symbolic computations of mathematics. Instead we must master intuition and play as well as logic to look beyond the present impasse of mood(s) which more often than is ever said, is (are) contextually (and historically) bound – the contexts sometimes maddeningly unclear.

A desire for certainty in this quest for constructive change is not an ally. Seldom do we like to admit this, either to ourselves or to others. The language which circulates about and through our cherished social institutions promises eternal truth, proof, perfection, cure, justice and restoration. Marion Milner has explored a number of perspectives on how we fall into the certainty trap and how the suppressed longings of sane men and women to stick themselves fast to it are their undoing – to eliminate doubt, presumed visual 'imperfection', evidence of ageing, the negative 'self', conflict and not least, the use of perfection to deny the one certainty – the inevitability of death – the greatest 'imperfection' in all the human armoury, psychological or physical. After all is said and suffered, the desire for certainty and perfection can be seen through (diagnosed) as an ineffective defence strategy. But this must be on both sides. One must also renounce the dream of the 'perfect' therapeutic encounter along with an ultimate theory of psychotherapy. All our encounters are simply human and necessarily so, for once 'I am perfect' enters one's belief system, no one can criticise me, then as I cease to learn from those around me there is no more progression – and hence there is no more struggle – as there is no longer anything at issue. Only stagnation then awaits one and from there it is existential death. It is as simple as that. One's efforts to avoid the greatest dread lead directly to it. The chaotic nature of existence glances eternally in our direction. 'Life is what happens to you when you are busy making other plans,' John Lennon remarked.[10] True, it is not a rehearsal and one cannot rehearse for it; life is always the opening night. Milner concludes:

> Conflict is essential to human life, whether between different aspects of oneself, between oneself and the environment, between different individuals or between different groups. It follows that the aim of healthy living is not the direct elimination of conflict which is possible only by forcible suppression of one or other of its antagonistic components, but the toleration of it – the capacity to bear the tension of doubt and of unsatisfied need and the willingness to hold judgement in suspense until finer and finer solutions can be discovered which integrate more and more the claims of both sides. This is the psychologist's job to make possible the acceptance of such an idea so that the richness of the varieties of experience whether within the unit of the single personality or in the wider unit of the group, can come to expression. (Milner, 1987: 10, our emphasis)

Of these varieties of experience few appeal more to our curiosity and fear than what we customarily bracket under the rubric of madness. Two national conferences have been convened in recent years (in Nottingham, UK, 2008 and 2012) which have been at the forefront of efforts to remove conceptual straightjackets of old. More will undoubtedly follow. Steven Coles, Sarah Keenan and Bob Diamond (2013) have edited a grand selection of contributions to this debate, 'committed to seeking and supporting much-needed development and change in the way we currently understand and respond to madness' (ibid: viii). Cromby, Harper and Reavey's (2013) *Psychology, Mental Health and Distress* similarly is a game changer in the reappraisal of 'mad' experience. In both these volumes the voice of service users is central. Their own valuable researches based on personal testimony, history and experiential narrative are coming together to yield a new picture of the 'other'. This other is of course us. As this data grows new patterns will emerge from within it – a groundswell of new opinion will form and a new science of the person will perhaps emerge, which will permit social scientific statements to be made which will not obliterate the person as subject. The questions are always the same.

What is good for me? What helps me? Who decides with me about what is to be done and when, and in whose name, interests or theory? Who respects my experience and who does not? Who clings to past dogmas and who is well-informed concerning patients' or service users' needs and demands? Who will pay in future?

Let's leave behind the toxic settings of bygone psychiatric centres and venture forth into a collaborative, cooperative working environment, where service users, patients and clients are supported by mental health professionals, who ideally have undergone not only their training analysis or psychotherapy, but their own resourceful recovery experiences which they can pass on to fellow travellers (both old and new) through the experiential and semantic cosmos of the mind.

'Inevitable humans in a lonely universe' is the charming subtitle of a grand study on *Life's Solution* (Morris, 2003). Our pressing questions about the randomness of evolution and the unending mysteries of the universe (of which astrophysics claims to know only 4 per cent) points to complexity on a grand scale – its very existence and our place within it invite viewpoints from across both the natural and social sciences. In one sense we are the universe observing and reflecting upon itself, our 'evolutionary inevitability' opening the doors of perception on an unfolding creative enterprise which is existence itself. As in Hesse's *Steppenwolf* (and Hilbert's imaginary hotel[11]) there are an infinity of such doors – and doors upon doors, and through these doors pathways to other worlds of experience and there mirrors reflecting back to us, a light on our own preferred and feared modes of living – how we structure this reality, both conceptually and experientially. What we find when we cast our gaze 'out there' – whether toward deep space or the shifting subatomic world – always tells us something about who we are. Our systems of reasoning, both mathematical and non-mathematical, which are employed to comprehend and shape the world, produce the very cleavages in reality which we take to be independent of us. In truth they reveal to us the nature of mind – our mind – and the interconnectedness of all 'things' (Hagen, 2012). Wherever we go, there we are,[12] this peculiar cognate species, increasingly and perhaps dangerously populous on this island earth. Home sweet home. What we choose to see and experience there, and what we are permitted to experience both individually and collectively are most definitely a matter of politics.

Endnotes

1. Philosophy has already been served by Susanne K. Langer's work back in 1942, *Philosophy in a New Key*. She revealed a take on reality which serves to give new meanings to experience.

2. His family research collaborator and previous co-author (Laing & Cooper, 1964), David Cooper, published *Psychiatry and Anti-Psychiatry* in the same year.

3. The conference took place from 30 March to 5 April 2003.

4. Jesse Watkins' 'A ten day voyage' in Laing's *The Politics of Experience*, Chapter 7, is one useful example. Elyn R Saks (2007) with her report *The Center Cannot Hold: My journey through madness* is another.

5. Volkmar Aderhold organised it with Evelyne Gottwalz and Michael Krausz.

6. Played by Yo-Yo Ma and Isaac Stern.

7. Salutogenesis describes an approach which focuses on factors that support health and wellbeing.

8. See Baker, Shaw & Biley (2013).

9. See Dillon, Bullimore, Lampshire & Chamberlin: The work of experience-based experts, in Read & Dillon, 2013: 305-18.

10. Taken from John Lennon song 'Beautiful Boy' from the 1980 album *Double Fantasy*.

11. This is a reference to the mathematician Hilbert in his conceptualisation of the meaning of infinity.

12. With due homage to Kabat-Zinn (2004).

Chapter 12

Where do we go from here?

> The privatisation of stress has been part of a project that has aimed at an almost total destruction of the concept of the public – the very thing upon which psychic well-being fundamentally depends.
>
> (Fisher, 2011)

> Another world is not only possible, she is on her way. On a quiet day I can hear her breathing.
>
> (Arundhati Roy, cited in Gee, 2011: 156)

It is obvious from the preceding sections of this book that the disciplines of psychology and psychotherapy are becoming increasingly estranged from the values and aspirations of the general public[1] who for the most part remain oblivious as to its actual nature and its contribution to systems of social control. A number of critics (e.g. David Smail, 2005; Ian Parker, 2007; Jerome Kagan, 2012) have in recent years launched wholesale critiques of the assumptions, methods, practices and promises which emanate from the field. While Kagan's dissection of the crisis in the discipline is impassioned and well made, it fails to connect the poverty of contemporary psychology with the political environment within which it operates or the political nature of the subject itself.

By way of contrast both Smail and in particular Parker warn of the urgent necessity for the political left to put psychology on the agenda before the pathologising of both the victims and collective opponents of the capitalist system goes into overdrive. We are already far enough down the path on which political problems become reframed as ostensibly psychological ones to see that this warning is credible. Fisher (2011) connects this 'privatisation of stress' to the depoliticising of the wider world, seeing it as central to understanding the ascendency of neoliberal economics – the invisible reason behind contemporary psychology – and people's hopelessness in the face of it. Similarly, Smail sees the unmasking of psychology's approaches to 'mental health' as central to developing not only a coherent critique but also a coherent and viable alternative. In this analysis the construction of 'mental health' and the practices which develop around it become psychology's key point of resistance to capitalist realism. The current widespread uncritical acceptance of the concepts of mental health and illness and the legitimacy of medical and other authorities to intervene on these grounds simply illustrates what Cooper and Hardy (2012: 4) refer to as the 'basic problematic of politics' by which they mean the 'gap between where we are and where we want to be'.

If we are to make headway from our present position, unmasking the fraudulence of the mental health system is a good place to start. Fortunately abundant evidence exists that the clock is running down on the current hegemony of biological psychiatry. The publication of the new *DSM-5* has provoked a storm of criticism with acknowledgement even from the lead editor of the previous edition, Allen Francis, that attempts to define mental disorder are in fact 'bullshit' (Greenberg, 2011). The National Institute of Mental Health (NIMH) followed suit, announcing that it will no longer support the manual because 'it lacks validity' and is 'unscientific' (Piesing, 2013). As the *DSM* was being roundly condemned as 'unscientific' 'bullshit' from within the higher echelons of psychiatry, the British Psychological Society's Division of Clinical Psychology (DCP)[2] threw its hat into the ring, releasing a statement in May 2013 that marks a radical break from past practice. The DCP, in calling for 'a paradigm shift away from outdated disease models, towards one which gives much more weight to service user experience and psychosocial approaches', has set a clear direction for the future.

Not surprisingly reactionary elements from within the Society were quick to respond, with Viding and Frith (2013: 382–3) for example accusing the DCP of 'muddying mental health issues by ignoring their biology' and making 'unsubstantiated and alarmist pronouncements about child abuse and schizophrenia'. 'Their present stance', they wrote, 'will fail to deliver help for those who suffer from mental health problems.' Contributions from a good many psychologists in the following issue suggested Viding and Frith's ill-judged attack could mark them out as yesterday's people. Joffe (2013:

467) for example placed Viding and Frith's ideas in 'wonderland', while in my own response (Roberts, 2013a: 468) I pointed to the well-known, though seldom discussed, 'outright failure of behaviour genetic research over several decades to benefit service users in any way whatsoever', something which Viding and Frith in their expressed concern for those with 'mental health problems' appeared not to notice – another instance of memory failure amongst the supporters of biological psychiatry. There is only so long one can dine out on a systemic lie, and in so far as the psy professions have revelled in the pretension that they can usefully tell us how to live well or in a way which is 'mentally healthy', they have been dining out for some considerable time.

The only technical solutions which the psychology/psychiatry bandwagon can provide are those which serve the surveillance and control needs/demands of an authoritarian if not totalitarian industrial society. This has not happened overnight – though we might like to kid ourselves that it has. Several decades ago, Laing had already complained that:

> the possibility of being able to function efficiently and competently in our society without actually being a prisoner is something that quite a few people that I meet regard as rather a remote possibility. (Laing, in Cohen, 1977: 208)

A generation later Popper's 'open society' is no more. We inhabit a closed remodelled replacement, one which our parents and grandparents would scarcely recognise. Under the perpetual gaze of the 'Big Other', who can doubt that we have all become de facto prisoners?[3] Thus, revealing the nature of the mental health system, though a good place to start, can only take us so far. The growth of qualitative research within psychology, with its emphases on subjectivity, context, language, knowledge and power is also to be welcomed, but unless the products of this are put to good use in the form of a serious and coordinated challenge to the professional, socio-economic and political role of behavioural 'science' in enslaving us, they will remain a sideshow to the disastrous and dangerous mainstream. At the heart of the matter is the question of the aims, forms, limitations and emancipatory possibilities – if they exist – of psychological knowledge.

Kierkegaard (2004: 43) wrote that 'a human being is a synthesis of the infinite and the finite, of the temporal and the eternal, of freedom and necessity', a view which does not sit easily with any branch of psychology save perhaps Kelly's Personal Construct Theory. Kelly saw human existence as a form of action in and of itself – a reworking of Heidegger's notion of being-in-the-world. Currently however, psychologists of all persuasions have allowed themselves to be seduced by the notion that verbal intellectual knowledge of the human condition, rather than knowledge gained through action and engagement in the world, is of overriding importance – is all that truly counts – indeed in a hymn to the mass production of league tables, is all that can be counted. This is an error which not only isolates psychologists from other practical forms of knowledge but also contributes to their social and political isolation, one which mirrors the isolation of their subject matter from the totality of relationships through which life unfolds (Barrett-Lennard, 2013).

It is ironic given that a good proportion of psychology students begin their careers with the intention of improving other people's lives, as well as their own. They are misled into thinking that psychology is the best way to do it. Having heard nothing of Marx, they become, like the philosophers he criticised, only interested in interpreting the world in various ways, rather than seeking to change it. The psychological stance that pretends we can unproblematically stand above and apart from the world we study while simultaneously positing that we are a mere subset in the universal material flow of cause and effect is an intellectual hoax, a breathtakingly absurd and contradictory one at that. It not only negates the possibility of free will but along with it the possibility of ideas (including ideas of truth) operating at a conceptual level to shape the course of events. If all cause and effect really did operate only from the lowest common denominator of physical reality – as proposed by reductionists – and free will were as they suppose an illusion, their own arguments in favour of this proposition involve a fundamental contradiction. Why is this? Because the very beliefs which form the basis for the reductionist view, though seemingly derived from a combination of empirical evidence and logic, must have arisen, in the eyes of reductionists, not because of the diktats of reason but purely as the consequence of material physicochemical processes, which constitute the underlying brain state associated with the belief, unfolding in conformity to the laws of nature. Logic, reason and inference therefore, from this perspective would have to join the long list of illusory phenomena or epiphenomena. The activity of science and any understanding derived from it then also becomes epiphenomenal. It is not then just God who is dead,[4] as Nietzsche proclaimed, but meaning itself. With meaning irrelevant, values and morals disappear along with it. This is not a recipe for Nietzsche's 'transvaluation of all values' or a 'Gay Science' for the twenty-first century. This is the science of the extermination camps[5] and we may already be in its grip.

In *The Science Delusion* Rupert Sheldrake (2012) examines the rigid intellectual structures which maintain contemporary scientific habits. 'The science delusion', he writes, 'is the belief that science already understands the nature of reality. The fundamental questions are answered, leaving only the details to be filled in' (inside sleeve). Sheldrake's aim is to free the spirit of open and enthusiastic scientific enquiry. He no longer adheres to the materialistic scientific creed, dominated by big business and power structures in university enterprises. Materialistic science behaves like the medieval church – espousing uncritical dogma to the masses, and its high priests, the likes of Dawkins and Dennett, grace their habitat with a 'know it all' authority. Like us, Sheldrake has worked to keep the window and doors of the house of science (natural and human) wide open, to cultivate critical thinking and scepticism, taking on board the fruits of empirical research findings. Sheldrake supports his arguments with empirical findings and asks his materialistic colleagues, who reduce minds, for example, to objects, 'what if all self-organising systems are subjects?' (Sheldrake, 2012: 334).

If our open approach to all things psychological will bring new insights, they may well come from within, through the neglected art of introspection, practised with the virtuosity of a fine musician. Professional training in such competencies in our field is seldom taught to younger colleagues. The corporate adrenalin rush is for establishing open research centres, where we can study the effects of mental constructs of human beings (theories are not facts, but merely fanciful imaginations) on human beings. 'No one can claim absolute primacy. Everything is interlinked. Nothing is permanent and isolated from everything else. There is an interdependence of all things and all levels of organisation' (Sheldrake, 2012: 324).

Worldwide, we have by now over 25,000 scientific journals, getting more and more specialised, the knowledge they contain fuelling an ever greater divorce from reality. How good to know that when William Whewell[6] suggested the term 'scientist' in 1833, he and his fellow members of the British Association for the Advancement of

Science longed for an umbrella term to give shade to all their various and diverse activities. Unfortunately over the last 50 years this charming term has been pirated by people involved in the physical and biological sciences. It is somewhat ironic then that the people engaged in these fields of enquiry seldom use blind tests methodologies, to safeguard against experimenter expectancy effects.[7] At present only about 22 per cent of current research in psychology utilises controls against experimenter expectancy effects. Keeping this in mind we take the view that much of 'the scientific knowledge' which is on offer in our field of enquiry is mere opinionated, commercially infected ideology and is politically biased. We appeal for dropping the pretence that all is rosy. The screen wipers of peer review cannot hide the fact that something is rotten in the state of psychology. We agree with Sheldrake's summary, that:

> Scepticism is a healthy part of normal science but is often used as a weapon in defence of politically or ideologically motivated points of view, or to stave off the regulation of toxic chemicals. Product-defence companies emphasise uncertainty on behalf of big business, influencing policy decisions in favour of their clients. The separation of facts and values is usually impossible in practice, and many scientists have to exaggerate the value of their research to get funded. Although the objectivity of science is a noble ideal, there is more hope of achieving it by recognising the humanity of scientists and their limitations than by pretending that science has a unique access to truth. (Sheldrake, 2012: 317)

Kierkegaard of course, besides engaging with the paradox of freedom and necessity in the human realm, also wrote about the 'sickness unto death', the anxiety and dread of inauthentic existence. Here, we are concerned with an inauthentic discipline of whose drab subservience to an unjust status quo we are heartily sick to death! This brings us back to the question which lies at the head of this chapter; where do we go from here? Or to put it another way – what is to be done? In order to answer this effectively, to produce proposals for a different future we must first of all be able to imagine that future, and secondly be willing to believe in it.

We can begin by imagining the far future and follow it by beginning work in the near future to connect with it. Pablo Larrain's 2012 film *No*, the story of the campaign which unseated Chilean dictator Augustus Pinochet after years of state-sponsored repression, fear, brutality, torture, sudden 'disappearances' and mass murder, provides an instructive lesson. The most potent weapon in the hands of the opposition was not their force of arms but their ability to disseminate a credible vision of a brighter future combined with their own collaborative resistance in the face of the government's terror tactics. Rene Saavedra's inspired campaign against Pinochet was not rooted in some individualistic version of positive psychology – the pursuit of happiness by singular means – but a direct orchestrated mass mobilisation of people's hopes and dreams for an alternative future, one built on joy, humour, music, freedom from tyranny, corruption, and social unrest. Many of those involved also stuck to a well-thought-out strategy for dealing with the fear which the regime stirred in them. It was not science but principally art and entertainment, lived out on the streets and viewed in the homes of Chile's citizens, which were employed to liberate these positive visions and combat the dread of Pinochet. In the face of this, even his own generals deserted him.

A new higher education: Economic, academic and social futures

Our own preferences for a life of learning would unite something of the spirit of Tom Baker's incarnation of *Doctor Who* with the sensibilities of Joseph Knecht, Hesse's (1972) Magister Ludi from his novel *The Glass Bead Game* and the wisdom, not to say the skills of Bruce Lee. This would mean: irreverence for authority, absence of competition between scholars, abolition of peer review,[8] delight in creative thinking, a love and devotion to justice and an appreciation of the deep interconnections between all forms and cultures of knowledge, both mental and physical. Hesse's novel questioned the right and utility of isolating intellectual elites from life's and society's enduring problems – our "'real', brutal world history' (ibid: 340). In the places of learning yet to come to fruition, multidisciplinary knowledge, including all manner of practical and intellectual learning, could be encouraged – self-development and devotion to the common good going hand in hand. No doubt this is some way off, but even though there are urgent and pressing problems in the academy and the world beyond it we must not forget to have fun. Laughter is a great liberator of fixed conceptual schemes and is an essential ingredient for any recipe for creative thought. Every serious scholar should learn at least two jokes. I have found that one can go a long way.[9]

There is one about a famous nun and abbess, who upon entering heaven asked Peter, who let her in, if she could please have a meeting with the Virgin Mary. Oh yes, he said, he could arrange this, after all she was very devout and faithful. The abbess was introduced to the Virgin Mary in due course. She was praised for her dutiful work for the church and asked why she wanted to see her. Well, so she said, you my dear mother of God, on all the paintings and sculptures in praise of you, as a young mother, you really don't look thrillingly happy and joyous. Well, said Virgin Mary, leaning forwards so as not to be overheard, between us two women, I would have preferred a girl.

Before we move on to addressing issues of contemporary significance, elaborating as we do on our aspirations for the empires of learning in the present epoch, MacLeod provides a few sobering words:

> The post-war settlement and what it achieved has been hacked back and edited out of our common memory, to the extent that some aspects of the society I grew up in, [during] the 1960s and early 1970s sound today like utopian dreams. If we're going to imagine better futures we have first to recover the real past, including the recent past for ourselves. (MacLeod, 2013: 19–20)

In the past year a student of mine asked me in all seriousness whether it was true, as she had heard, that once upon a time, students had not only paid no fees but had been given a grant (by the UK Government) to live on whilst they studied. I replied that this was not some Sci-Fi phantasy or fairy tale but was indeed true, with an added allowance for trips home at the end of each term and the possibility of claiming unemployment benefit out of term time. She stood visibly stunned. It was not the answer she had expected. The rebuilding of Europe following World War Two had furnished such opportunities – but these were opportunities won on the back of a collective and organised will.[10] They have been denounced as unaffordable by all political parties and the bodies representing students (NUS) and staff (UCU) despite the fact that the UK debt as a proportion of GDP was much greater in the 1940s, 50s, 60s and 70s than in recent years.[11]

As has been discussed elsewhere in this book, a good deal of the current malaise stems from the market initiatives rolled out since the 1980s – the Research Assesment Exercise (RAE), replaced by the Research Excellence Framework (REF) in 2014, the Teaching Quality Assurance (TQA) and National Student Survey (NSS). It is not a pipe dream that these can be rejected and consigned to the dustbin of history. The need to decouple/challenge the imposition of state bureaucracy[12] on the discipline has never been greater. It is the job of academics and those who represent them to educate those around them as to the damage wrought by these instruments and to the gains which can follow from their abandonment. This will not necessarily be easy, not least because the current union bureaucracies (of both staff and students) have been largely tied into the system. In this regard the challenge of reclaiming higher education for students and workers is no different than that which faces workers right across the labour movement. However, psychologists and psychotherapists also have their scientific and professional credentials as cards to play and it is time for radical demands to be made.

The performance indicators which flow from the likes of the REF and NSS need to be shown for the scientific twaddle that they are. They are certainly not valid metrics as most academics well know. Pressure needs to be brought on the BPS and other relevant professional bodies such as UKCP, and MIND to adopt hostile policies towards these instruments not least because they threaten the wellbeing of the discipline. If the BPS chooses non-engagement with such political issues they will likely render themselves increasingly irrelevant as market forces – capitalist demands for increased student numbers, fewer academic staff, and greater corporate profits – push them out of the picture. Such a process would benefit from coordinated action with professional interest groups representing a wide variety of disciplines (e.g. the British Medical Association). Before one discounts the possibility of this, one should consider Haslam and Reicher's (2012: 166) observation that 'there is no part of the known universe ... in which resistance is either unthinkable or completely absent'.

A promising development which might just kick start academics into action is the increasing attacks on the use of the National Student Survey by current students. Ratcliffe (2013) for example reports that the LSE's (London School of Economics) students' union 'was among those calling on the NUS to organise a national boycott of the survey at the organisation's annual conference this April'. UK students have also been stepping up their opposition to the corporate control of their education.[13] Such efforts must go hand in hand with efforts to reclaim academic freedom, about which the unions have so far shown little interest despite the fact that almost 80 per cent of academics surveyed believed it 'was being sacrificed to a culture of "bully and blame"' (Baty, 2006). The current state of play as regards academic freedom is that we are free to research anything that either furthers cooperation with business and government or promotes entrepreneurship. Of course Orwell (1977) had it about right when in *Nineteen Eighty-Four* he had the party declare 'freedom is slavery'. The freedom to promote a corporate agenda certainly constitutes a form of slavery while its opposite – old-fashioned liberal independent thinking – is now considered 'thoughtcrime'. Taking the 'decisive step', sat at his table, Orwell's protagonist, Winston Smith, pulled out his secret diary and wrote 'Thoughtcrime IS death' (Orwell, 1977: 26). In academia in the twenty-first century, it is career suicide! Readers need to be aware – as very few are – what the actual legal climate for freedom of speech, expression and publication now is in the Ivory Towers. Those of a faint disposition should skip the following section.

The academy and freedom of speech

Concerns about the legal basis for academic freedom – said to be protected by Section 202 of the Education Reform Act 2008[14] and Article 10 of the European Convention on Human Rights[15] – have arisen following two cases in the UK. In the first of these a recent (2012) Employment Appeal Tribunal case[16] involving a school dinner lady raised the issue of the balance between public authority employees' duties of confidentiality and their right to freedom of expression. Greatorex (2013a) explains the background:

> ... in Hill v Great Tey Primary School UKEAT/0237/12/SM, a dinner lady told a child's parents that their daughter had been tied to a fence and whipped with a skipping rope by some other pupils, and subsequently repeated that to the press. These allegations were true, but the dinner lady was dismissed for breach of confidentiality and acting in a manner likely to bring the school into disrepute. Lawyers for the dinner lady argued that this represented an unjustified interference with her right to freedom of speech under Art 10 of the ECHR. The EAT[17] (Langstaff J presiding) rejected this argument, holding that a school had a reputation to protect, and that it was entitled to take steps to manage the flow of information from a school in the interests of all pupils and staff ... 'Though we consider that the disciplinary proceedings constituted a restriction upon the claimant's freedom of speech, it was open to the school to seek to justify the interference by reference to the legitimate aims of protecting the reputation'. (Greatorex, 2013a)

In the second case, Duke v University of Salford (2013) EWHC 196 (QB) the High Court[18] recently confirmed that a university is also

When this information reached the pages of *The Independent* (Brown, 2013) I was later informed that Universities UK, 'who describe themselves as "the representative organisation for the UK's universities" had tried to get them to drop the story' (Roberts, 2013b).

Counterpower

> It is through disobedience that progress has been made, through disobedience and through rebellion. (Oscar Wilde, cited in Gee, 2011: 9)

On one hand then we have the vision of a community of students and scholars engaged in the vibrant, shared, exciting, fun and free pursuit of intellectual and personal challenges aiming to build a world for the common good, unfettered by competition, time pressure, elitism, bureaucracy, organisational threats and state-sanctioned surveillance of both academic output and students' learning experiences; on the other hand the current dystopian reality of teaching, learning and research packaged to suit corporate demand and led by intellectual narrow-mindedness, fear, apathy and boredom. In the light of this tragic contrast, our principal hope for maintaining, our 'stubborn, self-willed exile' (Orwell, 1977: 239) from the love of 'Big Brother'[21] and advancing outward from the trenches will depend on the extent to which various forms of 'counter power' (Gee, 2011) can effectively be brought to bear to loosen things up.

In analyses of behaviour, psychologists, more often than not, have been accustomed to analysing failure rather than success – interpreting depression or withdrawal for example as learned responses to helplessness and repeated social invalidation. Secondly, such analyses are customarily made of individuals, not groups, as they invariably must be when the sine qua non of contemporary psychological investigation is to divorce people from their social context. Thirdly, even when group behaviour has been the subject of interest, the concern has been with understanding how existing power is reproduced, for example through conformity or obedience to authority (see Chapter 10). In considering available avenues of resistance, Gee's notion of counterpower therefore is of particular importance. It is certainly true that few have cared to reflect on what the critical ingredients are, in terms of tactics and strategies, of successful social movements. Gee considers the cultivation of three forms of counterpower to explain the dynamics of social change; these are idea counterpower (consciousness raising and coordination), economic counterpower and physical counterpower. Though Wilde considered disobedience humanity's 'original virtue', these forms of counterpower must be cultivated. As forms of social action they are predicated on the existence or development of a sufficient level of group cohesiveness. This is where some degree of social psychological analysis can be useful.

The default option in social psychology as Haslam and Reicher (2012: 154) have argued has all too often been to preclude 'the possibility of resistance' and to 'put the topic beyond the realm of scientific imagination'. These authors, the driving force behind 'The Experiment', the prime time BBC[22] aired replication of the Stanford Prison Experiment, see their aim as the promotion of a psychology of resistance. Like Gee they direct attention to the collective basis of resistance and social change. Whilst Gee does make use of autobiographical material from leaders of social movements, his approach can be better characterised as social, historical and pragmatic, rather than explicitly psychological. Nonetheless there are important areas of overlap in their ideas.

Haslam and Reicher's social identity model of resistance involves a number of stages; the first two of these, 'unity around an oppositional social identity' and 'development of organisation and leadership', can be subsumed under Gee's notion of idea counterpower. A key aspect of this, consciousness raising, is commonly understood to be an identity project involving the recognition of the shared experiences and practical struggles of an identified group of people. This is also the place where individual memories and expectations become conjoined to social and collective memory. A necessary condition for identity to progress to protest and confrontation, that is, 'challenge to the current system', the third stage in Haslam and Reicher's model, is that the system of oppression is seen as illegitimate. At this point they also note that securing external support can be a crucial factor in shaping the overall balance of forces, which ultimately can determine whether social change is effective or not. The comparable stage in Gee's schema describes the practical use of economic and physical counterpower.

Concluding comments

If one applies the above schemata to the dire state of play in the knowledge economy and psychology's place within it, an immediate obstacle to mounting effective counter action is the lack of a common professional identity rooted in an understanding of the exploitation and co-option of psychology and psychologists to oppressive system goals. This is not unique to the Anglo-American axis of psychology.

Decomposition of the Soul (Behnke & Fuchs, 2010) is a collection of voices from the former DDR,[23] detailing how psychology and psychiatry were exploited by the Stasi (Ministerium für Staatssicherheit, MfS). One of the editors, the critical spirit and writer Jürgen Fuchs, finally died from plasmacytoma, a rare form of leukaemia, reinforcing the long-held suspicion, that, as a prisoner of the Stasi, he was wilfully exposed to gamma rays.[24] Every student of psychology knows by now – or at least ought to know – that dictators the world over, with the aid of their secret services use psychological knowledge and social psychological techniques against their political opponents. The former DDR, as a so-called socialist dictatorship, was no exception to this and used psychologists, psychotherapists, psychiatrists and general practitioners to staff their psychological operations programmes. The principal purposes of these were on the one hand, to assess, control and manipulate the cadres of the political class and their informal collaborators, and on the other, to train interrogators in psychological torture. All this was of course pivotal to maintaining the existing totalitarian order. We ask our readers not to dismiss the possibility of something similar in our so-called democratic states. Psychiatry all over the world has been a willing accomplice to those in power to silence voices of freedom, equality and justice. One of the voices in Behnke and Fuchs' collection is Herbert Loos. Loos notes how an entire generation of German psychiatrists moved from the Nazi system into the DDR's contributing to the production of a gigantic paranoid security system.

With complicity in abuse comes the denigration of the self and the loss of scientific and professional independence. The assault on one's own humanity that comes from practising this debased form of psychology, one must not forget, is 'rewarded' with feelings of omnipotence and professional power (over those upon whom one practises). Loos reminds us that we have to remember (that is what we do here) and guard against these professional crimes against humanity. The time has come, he writes, to go beyond mere individual finger pointing. Now we must face up to the total structural institutional system of the modern state (Loos, 2010: 241). Whether the current generation of practitioners can follow Loos' call will depend on whether those who identify professionally as psychologists can realise that their professional survival and reputation may actually be enhanced by calling into question the existing neoliberally orientated higher education system, with its devaluation of knowledge (and qualifications), use of pseudo-scientific measuring instruments, mass production of narrow disciplinary interests, restrictions on academic freedom, and last but not least, the escalating inhuman bureaucracy that threatens the generation of any meaningful work at all. Given the tentacles which the military have long had in the subject – particularly in cognitive psychology – this will not be easy. But it is not impossible. Some feasible future steps, to simultaneously de-legitimise the status quo, encourage belief in the possibility of change, and foster/rediscover a greater sense of purpose in what we do, (perhaps) encouraged and led by those from the social side of the discipline are suggested below.

1. Begin widespread open debate throughout the ranks of the discipline involving (a) an honest appraisal of the future strength and direction of the discipline if current trends continue, and (b) serious consideration of the political nature of *all* psychology and its inherent potential to cause harm.

2. Following from the above, the subject matter of psychology needs to heal the rift between its applied and theoretical cousins. This might involve a critical examination of and re-engagement with, not only the history and purpose of psychotherapy within the discipline, but a reconsideration of the centrality of experience to understanding and respecting human life. Such an examination is essential if the drift toward psychology as an instrument of state/corporate behavioural control is to be halted and for students of the discipline to reconnect the content of their lives with what they study. This would necessitate a humanistic rather than mechanistic stance at the heart of our endeavours and a rejection of the enduring 'cult of the fact' which is antagonistic to 'the elusive shifting world of everyday meanings' (Hudson, 1976: 39). At present psychology has lured its students into a honey trap – with the false promise of personal development and recovery from personal and social ills through its study. In my own experience, by the time their three-year study period is over many students have come to realise the nature of the deception. In relation to this, we need a fuller understanding of what changes an education in psychology brings to people's outlook on the world – both in regard to themselves and to what they understand of the human condition – in particular the root causes of human and social misery.

It follows that greater understanding of the social consequences of the 'mass psychology' of studying psychology will follow. Contrary to the routine indoctrination in psychology curricula one should not expect the outcomes of such study to be rosy.

3. We need a coherent and sustained critique of, and ultimately non-cooperation with, systems such as journal impact factors, the RAE (REF), NSS and peer review which purport to measure quality of academic output. As discussed, this is likely to be more successful if alliances are sought not only with academics and professionals from a wide range of other disciplines but also with the general public. As ever, unity is a necessary rallying cry.

4. The non-capitalist function and purpose of the 'university' needs to be extended beyond the campus and onto the streets. History provides a number of examples which illustrate the possibilities which such action can afford. It was for good reason that Robben Island, where the leading opponents of the apartheid system were held prisoner, became known as 'the University'. Mandela (1994: 454) describes how 'we became our own faculty, with our own professors, our own curriculum, our own courses'. Employing a Socratic style of teaching, the courses taught included a systematic examination of the Black liberation struggle in South Africa as well as liberation struggles elsewhere. Mandela himself taught political economy. As he remarks, 'we learned from each other'.

Closer to home the Anti-University of London was an experimental project in communal living and self-organised education[25] set up in Shoreditch, East London in February 1968, following the Dialectics of Liberation conference the preceding year. Promoting an ideology of counter-culture knowledge and free expression, the Anti-University, as Alan Krebs one of the founders commented, shunned the notion of 'education as a licence to practise in the establishment', a far cry from the university as factory (Alibhai-Brown, 2013) we see today. The courses offered there covered a variety of aspects of contemporary arts, politics and existential psychiatry, including specific offerings on black power, the future of capitalism, counter-culture and revolution. Laing, David Cooper, Francis Huxley, Jeff Nuttall, Juliet Mitchell and Yoko Ono were amongst the luminaries who gave lectures there. Though the project lasted a year before the premises were reclaimed by landlords, one of its longer lasting legacies was the renowned

Compendium Bookshop. A further less radical, though successful example of an alternative to the neoliberal model of higher education can be gleaned from the history and purpose of the Worker's Education Association, set up in 1903 (and still in operation) to offer 'social purpose education' to those who are socially and economically disadvantaged. The courses offered cover health and wellbeing, employability, community engagement, and cultural education. They can be considered to offer, in small measure, a degree of resistance to the prevailing utilitarian motif which permeates, so sadly at the present moment, the higher education experience.

One thing is certain, the current system, now in permanent crisis, cannot and will not go on forever. Change is the stuff of life. Resistance is ever present and even if the tiniest of resistance may seem to constitute nothing more than making the dog of the colossal system scratch, it remains essential and vital – the need to scratch may after all prevent the dog from exercising its bite in more dangerous territory. We are still as Capra (1985) argued at a turning point. His closing words in 1985 are if anything even more relevant today.

> ... our academic institutions are now part of the declining culture. They are in a process of disintegration. The social movements of the 1960s and 1970s represent the rising culture ... While the transformation is taking place, the declining culture refuses to change, clinging ever more rigidly to outdated ideas; nor will the dominant social institutions hand over their leading roles to the new cultural forces. But they will inevitably go on to decline and disintegrate while the rising culture will continue to rise, and will eventually assume its leading role. As the turning point approaches, the realisation that evolutionary changes of this magnitude cannot be prevented by short-term political activities provides our strongest hope for the future. (Capra, 1985: 466)

Thus, must we remain optimistic, though continuously alert, like Guanshiyin, Goddess of Mercy, to observing and acting on the cries of the world. The new politics of experience open up the celebration of experience as a conscious unifying awareness in the everlasting present moment.

> To see a world in a grain of sand,
> And a heaven in a wild flower,
> Hold infinity in the palm of your hand,
> And eternity in an hour.
> (William Blake, 1917: 105)

Endnotes

1. Perhaps psychology students also.

2. The full press release can be found here http://dxrevisionwatch.files. wordpress.com/2013/05/position-statement-on-diagnosis-master-doc.pdf Last accessed August 2014.

3. When Dürrenmatt gave his laudation to Vaclav Havel (22 November 1990), then president of Czechoslovakia, he compared Switzerland with a self-chosen and self-produced prison. With state surveillance and self-regulation now ubiquitous we are all now simultaneously guard and prisoner. Friedrich Dürrenmatt http://www.litart.ch/fd/fdrede.htm Last accessed December 2012.

4. Of course since 9/11 all manner of believers proclaim the deity lives – and use this 'truth' to justify just about anything. So the absence of meaning and its absolute certainty – whether in religion or science (see Sheldrake, 2012) produces more or less the same boundaryless inhumanity.

5. In Dostoevksy's The Brothers Karamazov Ivan remarks that 'if God is dead, then everything is permissible' (Laing, 1967: 114). The point is similar but not identical. Our point is that a materialist reductionist approach to the scientific study of being human is incompatible with a truly *ethical* science.

6. Whewell was a mathematical astronomer. See Sheldrake (2012: 321).

7. Watt, C & Nagtegall, M (2004) Reporting of blind methods: An interdisciplinary survey. *Journal of the Society for Psychical Research, 68*, 105–14. Sheldrake, R (1999) How widely is blind assessment used in scientific research? *Alternative Therapies*, 5, 88–91.

8. The current anonymous peer review system dates from the eighteenth century. It has been lambasted by sociologists as a process susceptible to control by elites and personal jealousy. The editor of *The Lancet*, Richard Horton (2000) commented, 'We portray peer review to the public as a quasi-sacred process that helps to make science our most objective truth teller but we know that the system of peer review is biased, unjust, unaccountable, incomplete, easily fixed, often insulting, usually ignorant, occasionally foolish, and frequently wrong'. In addition to Horton's criticisms, evidence suggests it is also a poor method for detecting errors in a paper (Baxt, Waeckerle, Berlin & Callaham, 1998).

9. My personal favourite: there was a fight in the chip shop the other night – fish got battered!

10. See Ken Loach (2013) The Spirit of 45. Fly Film, Sixteen Films, Film4, BFI Film Fund.

11. See http://www.ukpublicspending.co.uk/uk_national_debt_chart.html Last accessed August 2013.

12. Aided and abetted by the media via the use of spurious league tables.

13. See http://revolution-news.com/brutal-repression-students-uk-amid-mainstream-media-blackout/ Last accessed December 2013.

14. Previously also contained in the 1988 Education Reform Act, Section 202 holds that University Commissioners for certain institutions have an obligation in exercising their functions 'to ensure that academic staff have freedom within the law to question and test received wisdom, and to put forward new ideas and controversial or unpopular opinions, without placing themselves in jeopardy of losing their jobs or privileges they may have at their institutions'.

15. This *provides the right to* freedom of expression.

16. http://www.bailii.org/uk/cases/UKEAT/2013/0237_12_2901.html   Last accessed April 2013.

17. EAT – Employment Appeals Tribunal.

18. http://www.bailii.org/ew/cases/EWHC/QB/2013/196.html Last accessed April 2013.

19. Winters was discussing the nature of oligarchy. Our present system of rule (an alliance between government and those of extreme wealth) is considered, in Winters' schema, an example of a 'civil' oligarchy. See Tombs (2012) for further discussion of the State–corporate 'symbiosis'.

20. At the time of the study these fees were £3,290 for home students. Since then average fees are now closer to £9,000 per annum.

21. And his relative 'Big Science'.

22. See http://www.bbcprisonstudy.org/ Last accessed April 2014.

23. *Deutsche Demokratische Republik* (East Germany).

24. This form of radiation was used in Gera Stasi prison with the intention of damaging the bodies of prisoners. Thus the shocking revelation, that decomposition operative psychology was used for body and soul.

25. See http://antihistory.org/ and http://greatwen.com/2010/12/15/the-london-anti-university/ for a collection of articles, press cuttings, videos and texts. Last accessed 10 April 2014.

The Bitter Herbs

Healing experience, healing knowledge, healing wisdom, with warm and attentive empathy; the compassion of healing. Sustaining wellbeing and grounding innovations on the curve of habits, thus we chew the bitter herbs. Franz Kafka, in his novel *The Castle* (written in 1922), had his main character K mention to Hans, whose mother was curiously ill – nobody could make sense of it nor understand the meaning of her malaise – that he, K, had acquired some healing knowledge of the bitter herbs. In such cases, where a slight shining ailment is neglected for its inner message – illness as a communication from the unconscious – a more serious harmful development can take its place. Communication we say is at the heart of the matrix of experience, as well as the healing arts. K continues, what is more valuable than his medical knowledge is the fact of having some experience in treating and attending the suffering of one's fellow human beings. Often he, K, was lucky to be tending so-called helpless cases, those people given up by their doctors, bringing them through, what we might imagine to be the darkest nights of the soul, to the threshold of an open field of healing and renewed health. This is the reason those people call him, for his healing presence and effects, by the name *the bitter herb* (Kafka, 2000: 130). If we do not listen to the soul, it will find ways and embodied means to make us know.

There are illnesses of course that just will not yield, even with the engaging support of dedicated and respecting therapists. Death as well as life must be respected. Kafka knew this, his own life taken by the ravages of tuberculosis. Once we are ill, health is hidden in the midst of illness, and when we seem well underlying illness may be similarly camouflaged. The paraphrased passage from *The Castle* has given us our subtitle for the book in your hands. Before K briefed the character Hans Brunswick with the knowledge of his healing he was pondering a plan of how he might slip into the mysterious castle. Hans' ill mother was serving as a housewife in that magic, yet for strangers, closed place. K felt the strong and compelling impulse to be at her bedside that he might give her reason to live that he might permit her health to arise from within. At the same time K was aware that Hans' father didn't want him anywhere near his wife, thus he artfully employed his craft of *the bitter herb* to achieve his aim.

The visual fragrance and clutter of the Chinese tourist shop – ornamental gifts of jewel-encrusted tigers and junk boats for the perusal of the casual Western nocturnal visitor – abruptly gave way to a sensory bombardment instigated from the confines of the waking world by Alexander Graham Bell's infernal invention. It was Sunday morning, Alfonso Alonso, university lecturer, aficionado of solitary slumber, collector of books antiquarian and modern, psychologist and a martial arts devotee (a mixture of the Northern and Southern Shaolin styles) had been brought to his senses immediately, unhappily and with little choice by a telephone call that became so strongly embedded within the confines of his memory that it appeared capable of warding off the ravages of Alzheimer's disease. Moments before his insertion into the sensory surround of the oriental, his mind had been occupied with the thought of snipers on the roof targeting people with wet hair, whose lives could only be saved by the prior application of the correct conditioning treatment. An antidote guaranteed by the guardians of sleep to ward off any incoming high velocity projectile.

Stefano was a student of Alfonso Alonso. He was a tall, lean, moustached, mean and moody figure who had secured himself a reputation for frightening cleaning ladies, some of whom swore he was really a werewolf – nobody dared mention the moon. The local ensemble of pigeons, sparrows and rooks foreswore any likelihood that they would alight on the window ledge assigned to the office in which he worked. The neighbourhood avian life were both abundant and fastidious in their habits, taking their siestas and mealtimes with an honourable regularity. A member of staff, Franscisco Matrimonio Iglesias, an Irishman by temperament though self-proclaimed Mexican by birth, who was well versed in the nuances of statistical theory, had taken the trouble to calculate the probability that Stefano's window ledge alone would remain vacant to the charms of our winged brethren, based on a census of the local bird population, the regularity of their feeding breaks and the number of faculty privileged with a window view. He had been unable to publish the results in any reputable parapsychological journal but had assured all who were willing to listen that they were significant both spiritually and statistically. All who would drink from the cup of life and chew the bitter herb would see this.

Isabella's body, minus her now departed soul, the policeman informed Alfonso Alonso, in a voice entirely lacking even the trace elements of irony, had been found in the forensic psychology laboratory, along the lonely corridor from his office, adjacent to the technician's tea room, which Isabella whilst alive had frequented, being renowned for her passion for the jasmine infusions to be imbibed there. Outside the room hung a reproduction of Vermeer's *Girl with the Pearl Earring*. In the days which followed some would imagine that the once alluring innocent expression radiating from the half turned face of the seventeenth century Dutch maiden had been replaced through a delicate transfiguration of light and colour by a haunted accusing admonition of the dangers of immorality, jealousy and the research assessment exercise.

Inside the laboratory, minus her earrings and her life lay Isabella. In the years to come, when actual details of her murder had long been forgotten, and all social remembrance of the events reconfigured – the guilty names, faces and places, as well as the innocent, Isabella's presence could once again be found there, delivering evening lectures to part-time international students, bewitched by the floating scent of jasmine, her transparent attire, invisible feet and incorporeal knowledge of algebra. By then any importance which might have been attached to the distinction between the real and the unreal, between truth and invention or the living and the dead had vanished under the incessant forward (and backward) march of the post-modern philosophy which had enchanted the academy – along with a cornucopia of intellectual phantasms supported by an ever imaginative press and full time police state.

The Bitter Herbs are a further reference to the bitter herbs one eats at the Passover meal[1] in the Jewish religion. *Bitter herbs* (maror) make reminding of their bitter experience as enslaved people more bearable (the ancient Jewish people endured this for 400 years at the hands of the Egyptians) and rekindles the joy of liberation by metanoia (change of mind) and movement away from bondage. It is generally agreed among scholars that the original bitter herbs were chicory, coriander, dandelion, sow thistle, and wild lettuce. Other herbs that were probably part of this group include: hawkweed, horehound, horseradish, mint, sorrel, watercress, and wormword.[2]

Marga Minco was a Jewish schoolgirl in the Holland of 1940, and her book, *The Bitter Herbs* (1991) tells how she experienced life in the country of her birth. She, alone of her family, escaped arrest and death in a concentration camp, yet, like the diary of Anne Frank, this book appears not so much as an accusation as a comfort. Minco likens ancient Egyptian slavery (a slave is someone who cannot speak his or her mind) to what the Jewish people once again endured at the hands of the Nazis – the earthbound hell of the Holocaust.

Eating bitter herbs makes one listen to the inner voice of the soul, respecting one's own autonomy to think freely and act independently. To understand the desire and need for change, from the 'know it all' stance of megalomania, to the tender yet subtle offering to take another path. The other day I (TI) called a taxi centre as one of his clients needed a lift to the central station.

Theodor: Can you please send a car to Magniberg 10?

Switchboard operator: This address doesn't exist.

T: Oh, I am calling you from this address in Sankt Gallen. Can you please send a car?

SO: This street, as I told you before, does not exist.

T: OK, you are annoying me slightly. I will explain to you how you can find it.

Of course a taxi was there three-quarters of an hour later. A 'know it all' attempts to overcome low self-esteem, vis à vis a person who experiences the here and now, from here. This fits with the story of a research presentation by John Read (2013), about childhood adversity and psychosis. Having presented a considerable amount of research information to an assembly of psychiatrists in the UK pertaining to the causal role childhood adversity plays in most mental health problems and childhood disorders, the first respondent, after his talk said, 'This does not exist', just like Theodor's switchboard operator. The denial of sound social scientific evidence by those (slaves of the pharmaceutical industries) who can't even produce a shred of independent thinking shows just how widespread stupidity and ignorance are among medically trained organically fixated psychiatrists. Let them have a wee dose of the bitter herbs, while listening to Jan Dismas Zelenka's *Lamentations* (1679–1775),[3] a sure fire bet to melt the ice within. After all, it is the ancient task of healers of the soul to re-warm and rekindle the frozen heart of fellow human beings.

References

Kafka, F (2000) *The Castle*. London: Penguin Classics.

Minco, M (1991) *Bitter Herbs: The vivid memories of a fugitive Jewish girl in Nazi-occupied Holland*. London: Penguin.

Read, J (2013) Childhood adversity and psychosis. From heresy to certainty. In J Read & J Dillon (Eds.) *Models of Madness* (pp. 249–57). London: Routledge.

Endnotes

1. The Israelites were instructed to mark the doorposts of their homes with the blood of a slaughtered spring lamb and, upon seeing this, the spirit of the Lord knew to *pass over* the first-born in these homes, hence the name of the holiday. There is some debate over where the term is actually derived from. When the Pharaoh freed the Israelites, it is said that they left in such a hurry that they could not wait for bread dough to rise (leaven). In commemoration, for the duration of Passover no leavened bread is eaten, for which reason it is called 'The Festival of the Unleavened Bread'. Thus Matzo (flat unleavened bread) is eaten during Passover and it is a symbol of the holiday. http://en.wikipedia.org/wiki/Passover

2. http://voices.yahoo.com/what-bitter-herbs-bible-6693824.html; http://www.heraldmag.org/2008/08ma_5.htm. Last accessed 28 April 2014.

3. http://www.hyperion-records.co.uk/al.asp?al=CDH55106 Last accessed 10 April 2014.

References

Abric, JC (Ed.) (1994) *Pratiques Sociales et Représentations*. Paris: Presses Universitaires de France.

Adams, F (Trans) (1994) *Of the Epidemics, Book I, The Hippocratic Corpus*. MIT Classics Archive. Online at classics.mit.edu/ Last accessed 13 August 2014.

Aderhold, V & Gottwalz-Itten, E (2013) Family therapy and psychosis – Replacing ideology with openness. In J Read & J Dillon (Eds.) *Models of Madness* (2nd ed) (pp. 378–91). London: Routledge.

Aderhold, V, Gottwalz-Itten, E & Haßlöwer, H (2010) Die Behandlungskonferenz – Dialog, Reflexion und Transparenz. *Psych Pflege, 16*, 142–52.

Ahmed, NF (2010) *A User's Guide to the Crisis of Civilisation*. London: Pluto Press.

Alibhai-Brown, Y (2013) When did university become a factory? *The Independent*. 18 August 2013. Last accessed August 2013. http://www.independent. co.uk/voices/comment/when-did-university-become-a-factory-8773207. html?origin=internalSearch

Amantea, C (1989) *The Lourdes of Arizona*. San Diego, CA: Mho & Mho Works.

American Psychiatric Association (2013) *Diagnostic and Statistical Manual of Mental Disorders* (5th ed). Washington, DC: American Psychiatric Association.

Amering, M & Schmolke, M (2009) *Recovery in Mental Health*. Chichester: Wiley-Blackwell.

Anshen, RN (2013) World perspectives. In E Fromm *To Have or to Be* (pp. viii– xvi). London: Bloomsbury.

Appignanesi, L (2009) *Mad, Bad and Sad. A history of women and the mind doctors from 1800 to the present*. London: Virago Press.

Applebaum, S (2005) Review of J Bakan (2004) *The Corporation*. London: Constable. In *The Sunday Herald*.

Arnold, M (1939) The Hymn of Empedocles. In A Quiller-Couch (Ed.) *The Oxford Book of English Verse, 1250–1918* (2nd ed) (p. 763). Oxford: Oxford University Press.

Arnold, M (1979) *Culture and Anarchy*. London: Cambridge University Press. (First published 1869).

Assay, TP & Lambert, MJ (1999) The empirical case for the common factors in therapy: Quantitative findings. In MA Hubble, BL Duncan & SD Miller (Eds.) *The Heart and the Soul of Change: What works in therapy?* (pp. 33–56). Washington, DC: American Psychological Association.

Bair, D (2003) *Jung. A biography*. London: Little Brown & Co.

Bakan, J (2005) *The Corporation. The pathological pursuit of power and profit.* London: Constable & Robinson.

Baker, C, Shaw, C & Biley, F (Eds.) (2013) *Our Encounters with Self-Harm.* Ross-on-Wye: PCCS Books.

Balint, M (1968) *The Basic Fault: Therapeutic aspects of regression.* London: Tavistock.

Bannister, D & Fransella, F (1971) *Inquiring Man.* Harmondsworth: Penguin.

Barnes, M & Berke, J (2002) *Mary Barnes – Two Accounts of a Journey through Madness.* New York: Other Press.

Barrett, M (1991) *The Politics of Truth: From Marx to Foucault.* Cambridge: Polity Press.

Barrett-Lennard, GT (2013) *The Relationship Paradigm.* New York: Palgrave MacMillan.

Bates, Y (Ed.) (2006) *Shouldn't I Be Feeling Better by Now? Client views on therapy.* London: Palgrave.

Baty, P (2006) Academia has sold out. 72% believe. *The Times Higher Education Supplement, 1766.* 27 October.

Baudrillard, J (1994) *Simulacra and Simulation.* Ann Arbor, MI University of Michigan Press.

Baudrillard, J (1996) *The Perfect Crime.* London: Verso.

Baudrillard, J (2010) *America.* London: Verso.

Baxt, WG, Waeckerle, JF, Berlin, JA & Callaham, ML (1998) Who reviews the reviewers? Feasibility of using a fictitious manuscript to evaluate peer reviewer performance. *Annals of Emergency Medicine, 32,* (3 Pt 1), 310–17.

BBC (2008) *Amy: My body for bucks.* BBC 3, April 20. http://www.bbc.co.uk/programmes/b00b0x35 Last accessed May 2008.

BBC News Online (2007) Fees 'pushing up student debts'. http://news.bbc.co.uk/1/hi/education/6945975.stm Last accessed 14 August 2007.

BBC News Online (2012) Srebrenica 'not genocide' – Serbia's President Nikolic. http://www.bbc.co.uk/news/world-europe-18301196 Last accessed June 2012.

Behnke, K & Fuchs, J (2010) *Zersetzung der Seele – Psychologie und Psychiatrie im Dienste der Stasi.* Hamburg: Rotbuch Verlag.

Bellah, RN (2011) *Religion in Human Evolution.* Cambridge: The Belknap Press.

Bem, DJ (2011) Feeling the future: Experimental evidence for anomalous retroactive influences on cognition and affect. *Journal of Personality and Social Psychology.* Advance online publication. doi: 10.1037/a0021524.

Bentall, RP (2004) *Madness Explained: Psychosis and human nature.* London: Allen Lane.

Bentall, RP (2009) *Doctoring the Mind.* London: Allen Lane.

Berger, J (1972) *Ways of Seeing.* London: BBC and Penguin Books.

Bertoluzza, E, Gitzl, M & Ralser, M (Eds.) (1994) *Pathos, Psychose, Pathologie:*

der weibliche Wahnsinn zwischen Ästhetisierung und Verleugnung. Wiener: Frauenverlag.

Beveridge, A (2011) *Portrait of the Psychiatrist as a Young Man: The early writing and work of RD Laing, 1927–1960.* Oxford: Oxford University Press.

Biko, S (1987) *I Write What I Like.* London: Heinemann.

Billig, M et al. (2011) Benchmarking and social psychology. Letters. *The Psychologist, 24*(10), 710–11.

Blake, W (1917) Auguries of innocence. In DHS Nicolson & AHE Lee (Eds.) *The Oxford Book of English Mystical Verse* (p. 105). London: Oxford University Press.

Blass, T (Ed.) (2000) *Obedience to Authority: Current perspectives on the Milgram paradigm.* London: Lawrence Erlbaum.

Boyle, M (2002) *Schizophrenia: A scientific delusion?* (2nd ed). London: Routledge.

Bracken, P & Thomas, P (1999) Let's scrap schizophrenia. *Open Mind, 99.* September/October.

Bracken, P & Thomas, P (2001) Postpsychiatry: A new direction for mental health. *British Medical Journal, 322,* 724–7.

Brecht, B (1947) *Selected Poems.* New York: Harcourt Brace Jovanovich, Inc.

Brendel, A (2002) *Me of All People: Alfred Brendel in conversation.* Ithaca, NY: Cornell University Press.

Brinkworth, L (2007) Students who sell sex. *Cosmopolitan.* July, 60–2.

British Psychological Society (2004) *Annual Report 2012.* http://www.bps.org.uk/ system/files/documents/annual_report_web.pdf Last accessed August 2014

Brockmeier, J (2002) Remembering and forgetting: Narrative as cultural memory. *Culture & Psychology, 8*(1), 15–43.

Brook, D (1976) *Naturebirth: You, your body, and your baby.* New York: Pantheon.

Brown, J (2013) Sex for tuition fees: Are universities just refusing to face up to the facts? *The Independent,* 20 June 2013. http://www.independent.co.uk/ student/news/sex-for-tuition-fees-are-universities-just-refusing-to-face-up-to-the-facts-8667648.html Last accessed June 2013.

Brunton, P (2009) *The Quest of the Overself.* Varanasi: Pilgrims Publishing. (First published 1937).

Brunton, P (2011) *The Secret Path.* York Beach, ME: Samuel Weiser Inc. (First published 1935).

Brysbaert, M & Rastle, R (2013) *Historical and Conceptual Issues in Psychology.* London: Pearson.

Buchanan, RD (2010) *Playing With Fire: The controversial career of Hans J Eysenck.* Oxford: Oxford University Press.

Burgoyne, B (Ed.) (2000) *Drawing the Soul: Schemas and models in psychoanalysis.* London: Karnac.

Burgoyne, B (2013) *Neighbourhood of Love: Technique and science in psychoanalysis.* London: Karnac.

Burgoyne, B & Sullivan, M (Eds.) (1996) *The Klein-Lacan Dialogues*. London: Karnac.

Burston, D (1996) *The Wing of Madness*. Cambridge: Harvard University Press.

Burston, D (2000) *The Crucible of Experience: RD Laing and the crisis of psychotherapy*. Cambridge: Harvard University Press.

Cage, J (1973) *Silence: Lectures and writings*. Middletown, CT: Wesleyan University Press.

Capra, F (1985) *The Turning Point. Science, society and the rising culture*. London: Fontana.

Castro, F (2007) *My Life*. London: Penguin.

Chapman, M (2001) Red light finds its way onto campus. *Times Higher Educational Supplement, 1486*. 5 November 2001.

Charlton, BG (1990) A critique of biological psychiatry. *Psychological Medicine, 20*, 3–6.

Chesler, P (2005) *Women and Madness*. New York: Palgrave Macmillan.

Chesler, P & Laing, RD (2012) A conversation in two beds. In T Itten & C Young (Eds.) *RD Laing: 50 years since The Divided Self* (pp. 11–30). Ross-on-Wye: PCCS Books.

Chomsky, N (1988) *Language and Problems of Knowledge: The Managua lectures*. Cambridge, MA: The MIT Press.

Clare, A (1989) A divided view of madness. *The Guardian*, 25 August.

Clare, A (1993) *In The Psychiatrist's Chair*. London: Mandarin.

Cleary, T (Trans) (1993) *The Essential Tao*. New York: HarperCollins.

Cobain, I (2012) *Cruel Britannia: A secret history of torture*. London: Portobello Books.

Cohen, D (1977) *Psychologists on Psychology*. London & Henley: Routledge and Kegan Paul (2nd ed, 2004 Routledge).

Cohen, S (2001) *States of Denial*. Cambridge: Polity.

Coles, S, Keenan, S & Diamond, B (Eds.) (2013) *Madness Contested: Power and practice*. Ross-on-Wye: PCCS Books.

Collier, A (1977) *RD Laing: The philosophy and politics of psychotherapy*. Hassocks: The Harvester Press.

Collier, G, Minton, HL & Reynolds, G (1991) *Currents of Thought in American Social Psychology*. Oxford: Oxford University Press.

Collins, HM & Pinch, T (2012) *The Golem: What you should know about science*. New York: Cambridge University Press.

Collins, K (2008) Joseph Schorstein: RD Laing's 'rabbi'. *History of Psychiatry, 74*(2), 185–201.

Confucious (2000) *The Analects* (A Waley, Trans). London: Everyman.

Connerton, P (2008) Seven types of forgetting. *Memory studies, 1*, 59–71.

Connerton, P (2009) *How Modernity Forgets*. Cambridge: Cambridge University Press.

Cooper, D (1967) *Psychiatry and Anti-psychiatry*. New York: Ballantine Books.

Cooper, D (1971) *The Death of the Family*. Harmondsworth: Penguin.

Cooper, D (1978) *The Language of Madness*. London: Allen Lane.

Cooper, L & Hardy, H (2012) *Beyond Capitalism? The future of radical politics*. Winchester: Zero Books.

Cooper, M & McLeod, J (2011) *Pluralistic Counselling and Psychotherapy*. London: Sage.

Cromby, J, Harper, D & Reavey, P (2013) *Psychology, Mental Health and Distress*. New York: Palgrave MacMillan.

Cross, M (2013) Demonised, impoverished and now forced into isolation: The fate of disabled people under austerity. *Disability & Society, 28*(5), 719–23.

Curtis, A (1995) *The Living Dead*. London: BBC.

Curtis, A (2002) *A Century of the Self*. London: BBC.

Curtis, M (2003) *Web of Deceit. Britain's real role in the world*. London: Random House.

Curtis, M (2004) *Unpeople. Britain's secret human rights abuses*. London: Random House.

Deem, R, Hillyard, S & Reed, M (2007) *Knowledge, Higher Education and the New Managerialism: The changing management of UK universities*. Oxford: Oxford University Press.

Dennett, D (1992) *Consciousness Explained*. London: Allen Lane.

Deutsch, M (1968) *Field Theory in Social Psychology*. New York: Basic Books.

Dillon, M (2013) *Hunger and Hoarders*. A review of Yang Jisheng's *Tombstone*. *TLS, 5747*, 27.

Dimitrijevic, N (2011) *Duty to Respond: Mass crime, denial and collective responsibility*. Budapest: CEU Press.

Dimond, SJ & Beaumont, JG (1974) *Hemisphere Function in the Human Brain*. London: Elek.

Dobson, R (2011) Conditionality and homelessness services; 'Practice realities' in a drop-in centre. *Social Policy and Society, 10*(4), 547–57.

Dolman, K (2008) Selling sex to study. http://www.timesonline.co.uk/tol/life_and_style/education/student/article3396280.ece Last accessed 19 February 2008.

Dostoevsky, F (2003) *The Brothers Karamazov*. London. Penguin.

Doyal, L & Harris, R (1986) *Empiricism, Explanation and Rationality*. London: Routledge & Kegan Paul.

Doyal, L & Pennell, I (1979) *The Political Economy of Health*. London: Pluto.

Dunaway, DK (1990) *Huxley in Hollywood*. London: Bloomsbury.

Dunaway, DK (1999) *Aldous Huxley Recollected*. London: Altamira Press.

Duvall Smith, A (2006) Thousands of students 'join sex trade to fund degrees' http://www.independent.co.uk/news/europe/thousands-of-students-join-sex-trade-to-fund-degrees-422287.html Last accessed 31 October 2006.

Edwards, D, Ashmore, M & Potter, J (1995) Death and furniture: The rhetoric, politics and theology of bottom line arguments against relativism. *History of the Human Sciences, 8,* 25–49.

Eliot, TS (2004) *The Hollow Men.* London: Faber & Faber. (First published 1925).

Ellenson, G (1985) Detecting a history of incest. *Social Casework,* November, 525–32.

Ensink, B (1992) *Confusing Realities.* Amsterdam: Vu University Press.

Ensink, B (1993) Trauma: A study of child abuse and hallucinations. In M Romme & S Escher (Eds.) *Accepting Voices* (pp. 165–71). London: Mind Publications.

Ernst, S & Maguire, M (1987) *Living with the Sphinx: Papers from the Women's Therapy Centre.* London: The Women's Press.

Esterson, A (1972) *The Leaves of Spring: Schizophrenia, family and sacrifice.* Harmondsworth: Penguin.

Evans, B (2012) The impact of the ideas of RD Laing on UK psychology students. In T Itten & C Young (Eds.) *RD Laing: 50 years since The Divided Self* (pp. 218–25). Ross-on-Wye: PCCS Books.

Evans, B & Waites, B (1980) *IQ and Mental Testing: An unnatural science and its social history.* London: Macmillan.

Evans, J (2000) *Adults' Mathematical Thinking and Emotions.* London: Routledge.

Evans, RI (1976) *RD Laing: The man and his ideas.* New York: EP Dutton.

Faggen, R (2002) Introduction. In K Kessey, *One Flew Over the Cuckoo's Nest.* London: Penguin.

Fallowfield, LJ & Roberts, R (1992) Cancer counselling in the United Kingdom. *Psychology and Health, 6,* 107–17.

Figal, G (2009) *The Heidegger Reader.* Bloomington & Indianapolis, IN: Indiana University Press.

Filz, A & Young, C (2009) The core principles of psychotherapy. *International Journal of Psychotherapy, 13*(3), 5–10.

Fisher, M (2009) *Capitalist Realism. Is there no alternative?* Winchester: Zero Books.

Fisher, M (2011) The privatisation of stress. http://www.newleftproject.org/index. php/site/article_comments/the_privatisation_of stress Last accessed July 2013.

Fisk, R (2009) How can you trust the cowardly BBC? *The Independent,* 16 April 2009. http://www.independent.co.uk/opinion/commentators/fisk/robert-fisk-how-can-you-trust-the-cowardly-bbc-1669281.html Last accessed May 2012.

Foucault, M (1979) *The History of Sexuality: Volume I: An Introduction.* London: Allen Lane.

French, C (2012) Precognition studies and the curse of the failed replications. *The Guardian,* 15 March 2012. http://www.guardian.co.uk/science/2012/ mar/15/precognition-studies-curse-failed-replications Last accessed March 2012.

Freud, S (1972) *Das Unbewusste*. Zürich: Exlibris. (First published 1915).

Friedenberg, EZ (1973) *Laing*. Fontana Modern Masters. London: William Collins Sons & Co Ltd.

Fromm, E (1973) *The Crisis of Psychoanalysis*. Harmondsworth: Penguin.

Fromm, E (1995) *The Art of Loving*. London: HarperCollins.

Fromm, E (2004) *The Fear of Freedom*. London: Routledge. (First published 1942).

Fromm, E (2011) *Marx's Conception of Man*. Mansfield Center, CT: Martino Publishing.

Fromm, E (2013) *To Have Or To Be?* London: Bloomsbury. (First published 1976).

Gee, T (2011) *Counter Power: Making change happen*. Oxford: New Internationalist Publications.

Geller, JD, Norcross, JC & Orlinsky, DE (Eds.) (2005) *The Psychotherapist's Own Psychotherapy*. Oxford: Oxford University Press.

Gergen, K (1973) Social psychology as history. *Journal of Personality and Social Psychology, 26*(2), 309–20.

Gerrard, E & Roberts, R (2006) Student parents, hardship and debt: A qualitative study. *Journal of Further and Higher Education, 30*(4), 393–403.

Glaurdić, J (2011) *The Hour of Europe. Western powers and the breakup of Yugoslavia.* New Haven, CT: Yale University Press.

Greatorex, P (2013a) Telling tales out of school. *Local Government Lawyer.* 27 February 2013. http://www.localgovernmentlawyer.co.uk/index.php?option=com_content&view=article&id=13410%3Atelling-tales-out-of-school&catid=49%3Acomment-a-analysis-articles&Itemid=9 Last accessed March 2013.

Greatorex, P (2013b) Protecting the reputation of schools and universities. *Education Law Blog.* 22 February 2013. http://www.education11kbw.com/2013/02/22/protecting-the-reputation-of-schools-and-universities/ Last accessed March 2013.

Green, J (1998) *Days in the Life: Voices from the English underground 1961–1971.* London: Pimlico.

Greenberg, G (2011) Inside the battle to define mental illness. *Wired Magazine* http://www.wired.com/magazine/2010/12/ff_dsmv Last accessed January 2011.

Greenwood, JD (2004) *The Disappearance of the Social in American Social Psychology.* Cambridge: Cambridge University Press.

Gregory, RL (Ed.) (1987) *The Oxford Companion to the Mind.* Oxford: Oxford University Press.

Gregory, RL (1997) *Eye and Brain.* Oxford: Oxford University Press.

Griffin, S (2012) Possibilities of reprieve. In T Itten & C Young (Eds.) *RD Laing: 50 years since* The Divided Self (pp. 160–3). Ross-on-Wye: PCCS Books.

Gruen, A (1987) *Der Wahnsinn der Normalität-Realismus als Krankheit.* München: Kösel Verlag.

Guze, SB (1989) Biological psychiatry: Is there any other kind? *Psychological*

Medicine, 19, 315–23.

Hagen, S (1999) *Buddhism Plain and Simple.* London: Penguin.

Hagen, S (2012) *Why the World Doesn't Seem to Make Sense. An inquiry into science, philosophy and perception.* Boulder, CO: Sentient Publications.

Halbwachs, M (1992) *On Collective Memory.* Chicago & London: University of Chicago Press.

Haldane, JBS (1977) *Possible Worlds and Other Papers.* North Stratford, NH: Ayer Company Publishers Inc. (First published 1927).

Halilovich, H (2011) Beyond the sadness: Memories and homecomings among survivors of 'ethnic cleansing' in a Bosnian village. *Memory Studies, 4*(1), 42–52.

Hall, B (1994) *The Impossible Country.* Harmondsworth: Penguin.

Hammersley, P, Dias, A, Todd, G, Bowen-Jones, K, Reilly, B & Bentall, RP (2003) Childhood trauma and hallucinations in bipolar affective disorder: Preliminary investigation. *British Journal of Psychiatry, 182,* 543–7.

Harper, D (2007) The complicity of psychology in the corporate state. In R Roberts (Ed.) *Just War: Psychology and terrorism* (pp. 15–45). Ross-on-Wye: PCCS Books.

Harper, D, Roberts, R & Sloboda, J (2007) A psychology for peace? In R Roberts (Ed.) *Just War: Psychology and terrorism* (pp. 213–34). Ross-on-Wye: PCCS Books.

Hartley, D (1995) The 'McDonaldization' of higher education: Food for thought? *Oxford Review of Education, 21(4),* 409–23.

Hartley, J (2012) We can't take impact factors as read. Letters. *The Psychologist, 25*(5), 330–31.

Haslam, SA & Reicher, SD (2012) When prisoners take over the prison: A social psychology of resistance. *Personality & Social Psychology Review, 16*(2), 154–79.

Hawkes, D (2013) Renounce! *TLS,* 12 July 2013, 5754. London.

Heather, N (1976) *Radical Perspectives in Psychology.* London: Methuen.

Heaton, J (1968) *The Eye.* London: Tavistock.

Hedges, C (2009) *Empire of Illusion.* New York: Nation Books.

Hegarty, P & Walton, Z (2012) The consequences of predicting scientific impact in psychology using journal impact factors. *Perspectives on Psychological Science, 7*(1), 72–8.

Heidegger, M (2005) *Being and Time.* Oxford: Blackwell. (First published in 1927).

Heins, T, Gray, A & Tennant, M (1990) Persisting hallucinations following childhood sexual abuse. *Australian and New Zealand Journal of Psychiatry, 24,* 561–5.

Heller, J (1961) *Catch-22.* New York: Simon & Schuster.

Hepburn, A (2003) *An introduction to Critical Social Psychology.* London: Sage.

Hesse, H (1972) *The Glass Bead Game.* Harmondsworth: Penguin.

Hewer, C & Kut, M (2010) Historical legacy, social memory and representations of the past within a Polish community. *Memory Studies, 3*(1), 18–32.

Hewer, C & Roberts, R (2012) Towards a dynamic model of social memory. *Culture & Psychology, 18*(2), 167–83.

Heydt, V von der (1976) *Prospects for the Soul. Soundings in Jungian psychology and religion.* London: Darton, Longman and Todd.

Heydt, V von der (1983) A session with Jung. In M Tuby (Ed.) *In the Wake of Jung* (pp. 24–5). London: Coventure.

Heydt, V von der (1988) How I do it. In JM Spiegelmann (Ed.) *Jungian Analysts: Their visions & vulnerabilities* (pp. 5–10). Las Vegas, NV: New Falcon Publications.

Heydt, V von der (1994) Jung and religion: Its place in analytical psychology. In J Ryce-Menuhin (Ed.) *Jung and the Monotheisms* (pp. 7–19). London: Routledge.

Hillman, J (1996) *The Soul's Code.* New York: Random House.

Hillman, J (1997a) *Dream Animals.* San Francisco: Chronicle Books.

Hillman, J (1997b) *Suicide and the Soul* (2nd ed). Woodstock, CT: Spring Publications.

Hillman, J (1998) *Healing Fiction.* Putnam, CT: Spring Publications.

Hillman, J & Shamdasani, S (2013) *Lament of the Dead. Psychology after Jung's Red Book.* London: WW Norton & Co.

Hillman, J & Ventura, M (1993) *We've Had a Hundred Years of Psychotherapy and the World's Getting Worse.* San Francisco: HarperCollins.

Hobart, P (2003) *Kishido: The way of the Western warrior.* Arizona: Hohm Press.

Holl, A (1985) *Mitleid im Winter.* Reinbek bei Hamburg: Rowohlt.

Honig, A, Romme, MAJ, Ensink, BJ, et al. (1998) Auditory hallucinations: A comparison between patients and nonpatients. *Journal of Nervous and Mental Disease, 186,* 646–51.

Hopkins, L (2006) *False Self: The life of Masud Khan.* New York: Other Press.

Horton, R (2000) Genetically modified food: Consternation, confusion, and crack-up. *The Medical Journal of Australia, 172*(4), 148–9.

Howarth-Williams, M (1977) *RD Laing. His work and its relevance for sociology.* London: Routledge & Kegan Paul.

Hudson, L (1976) *The Cult of the Fact.* London: Jonathan Cape.

Hunter-Brown, I (2008) *RD Laing and Psychodynamic Psychiatry in 1950s Glasgow: A reappraisal.* London: Free Association Books.

Huxley, A (1977) *The Human Situation.* New York: Harper & Row.

Huxley, F (1956) *Affable Savages: An anthropologist among the Urubu Indians of Brazil.* London: Rupert Hart-Davis.

Huxley, F (1961) Marginal lands of the mind. In J Huxley (Ed.) *The Humanist Frame* (pp. 169–79). London: George Allen & Unwin.

Huxley, F (1962a) Who and why? In N Mitchinson (Ed.) *What Is the Human Race Up To?* (pp. 273–88). London: Victor Gollancz.

Huxley, F (1962b) Which may never have existed. *The Kenyon Review. Vol. XXIV* (1). Also published (1970) in EN Hayes (Ed.) *Claude Lévi-Strauss – The Anthropologist as Hero* (pp. 6–19). Cambridge, MA: MIT Press.

Huxley, F (1966a) *The Invisibles.* London: Rupert Hart-Davis.

Huxley, F (1966b) The ritual of voodoo and the symbolism of the body. *Philosophical Transactions of the Royal Society London, 251*(772), 423–7.

Huxley, F (1966c) 'The Body and the Mind' *RD Laing Collection*, Special Collections Department, University Glasgow Library, MS Laing L 226 (17 February).

Huxley, F (1974) *The Way of the Sacred.* London: Aldous Books.

Huxley, F (1976) *The Raven and the Writing Desk.* London: Thames and Hudson.

Huxley, F (1982) Anti-psychiatry and other disorders. *The Guardian*, 28 January.

Huxley, F (1990) *The Eye: The seer and the seen.* London: Thames and Hudson.

Huxley, F (1997) Foreword. In A Getty *A Sense of the Sacred* (pp vi–viii). Dallas, TX: Taylor Publishing.

Huxley, F (1999) 'Aldous'. In DK Dunaway (Ed.) *Aldous Huxley Recollected* (pp. v–xiv). London: Altamira Press.

Huxley, F (2005) Shamanism, healing and RD Laing. In S Raschid (Ed.) *RD Laing: Contemporary perspectives* (pp. 186–203). London: Free Association Books.

Illner, E (Hrg.) (2013) *Eduard von der Heydt – Kunstsammler, Bankier, Mäzen.* München: Prestel.

Inman, P (2013) Economics students aim to tear up free-market syllabus. *The Independent.* 24 October 2013. http://www.theguardian.com/business/2013/oct/24/students-post-crash-economics Last accessed October 2013.

Irvine, J, Miles, I & Evans, J (Eds.) (1979) *Demystifying Social Statistics.* London: Pluto Press.

Itten, T (1977) Standing and understanding living in a therapeutic community. Medard Boss, RD Laing and the Archway Community of the Philadelphia Association. BA (Hons) Dissertation. Unpublished. Enfield College.

Itten, T (1979) Myth of madness: A report of a PA network event and a study of Francis Huxley's work. (Manuscript p. 58).

Itten, T (1993) In der Villa Therapeutica. In A Holl (Hrg.) *MONSTREN. 'manuskripte'*, Graz, Jg.33, Heft 121a, S.5-15 (R Martin, English Trans).

Itten, T (1997) RD Laing: Fair well. In B Mullan (Ed.) *RD Laing: Creative destroyer*, (pp. 144–77). London: Cassel.

Itten, T (2001) Laing in Austria. Special issue: The Legacy of RD Laing (*Janus Head* 4(1), 69–89).

Itten, T (2002) From RD Laing to Jack Lee Rosenberg. In T Itten & M Fischer *Jack Lee Rosenberg: Celebrating a master psychotherapist* (pp. 52–70). St Gallen, Switzerland: IBP Books.

Itten, T (2007) Psychotherapy instead of psychiatry? A no-brainer. In P Stastny & P Lehmann (Eds.) *Alternatives Beyond Psychiatry* (pp. 240–51). Eugene, OR: Peter Lehmann Publication.

Itten, T (Ed) (2009) Different approaches to depression. Special issue: *International Journal of Psychotherapy, 13*(2), 3–74.

Itten, T (2011a) Intuition und Wissenschaft in der Psychotherapie. In G Fischer & C Eichenberg (Hrsg.) *Zeitschrift für Psychotraumatologie, Psychotherapiewissenschaft und Psychologische Medizin* (pp. 31–42). Heft 4. Asanger Verlag: Kröning S.

Itten, T (2011b) *Rage – Managing an Explosive Emotion* (R Martin, Trans) from *Jähzorn, 2007,* Springer-Verlag. Faringdon: Libri Publishing.

Itten, T & Fisher, M (2002) *Jack Lee Rosenberg: Celebrating a master psychotherapist.* St Gallen, Switzerland: IBP Books.

Itten, T, Barwinski, R, Schmidt, V, Schulthess, P, Stutz, E, Weibel, U & Van Gisteren, L (2010) *Psychotherapie-Wissenschaft (PTW) – Bericht über die Entwicklungsmöglichkeiten eines eigenständigen PTW-Studiums und eines integralen Konzeptes für die wissenschaftliche Berufsausbildung.* Zürich: ASP.

Itten, T & Young, C (Eds.) (2012) *RD Laing: 50 years since* The Divided Self. Ross-on-Wye: PCCS Books.

Jahoda, M (1966) Foreword. In RD Laing, H Phillipson, & AR Lee *Interpersonal Perception.* London: Tavistock.

Joffe, J (2013) Distortions and maps of wonderland. *The Psychologist, 26*(7), 466–7.

Jones, T & Gilliam, T (1983) *The Meaning of Life* [film] Universal Pictures.

Jung, CG (1962) *Erinnerungen, Träume und Gedanken.* Zürich: Exlibris.

Jung, CG (1968) *Man and His Symbols.* New York: Dell Publishing.

Kabat-Zinn, J (2004) *Wherever You Go, There You Are.* London: Piatkus.

Kafka, F (1946) *The Trial [Der Prozess].* New York: Schocken Verlag.

Kafka, F (1976) *Das Schloss [The Castle].* Frankfurt aM: Fischer Taschenbuch Verlag.

Kafka, F (2000) *The Castle.* London: Penguin Classics.

Kagan, J (2012) *Psychology's Ghosts.* New Haven & London: Yale University Press.

Kahn, M (1974) *The Privacy of the Self.* London: Hogarth Press.

Kansteiner, W (2002) Finding meaning in memory: A methodological critique of collective memory studies. *History and Theory, 41,* 179–97.

Keats, J (2009) *Poems of John Keats.* London: Penguin.

Kelly, GA (1955) *The Psychology of Personal Constructs.* New York: WW Norton & Co.

Kierkegaard, S (1969) *Concluding Unscientific Postscript.* Princeton, NJ: Princeton University Press.

Kierkegaard, S (1991) *Practice in Christianity.* Princeton, NJ: Princeton University Press. (First published 1850).

Kierkegaard, S (2004) *The Sickness unto Death*. London: Penguin.

King, L & Randall, R (Ed.) (2003) *The Future of Psychoanalytic Psychotherapy*. London: Whurr.

Kirk, RE (1996) Practical significance: A concept whose time has come. *Educational and Psychological Measurement, 56,* 746–59.

Kit, WK (1981) *Shaolin Kung Fu*. London: Paul H Compton Ltd.

Klein, N (2007) *The Shock Doctrine*. London: Allen Lane.

Kotowicz, Z (1997) *RD Laing and the Paths of Anti-psychiatry*. London: Routledge.

Kottler, JA (2010) *The Assassin and the Therapist*. London: Routledge.

Kripal, JJ & Shuck, GW (Ed.) (2005) *On the Edge of the Future: Esalen and the evolution of American culture (religion in North America)* Bloomington, IN: Indiana University Press.

Kuhn, T (1970) *The Structure of Scientific Revolutions* (2nd ed). Chicago: University of Chicago.

Kvale, S (1992) *Psychology and Postmodernism*. London: Sage.

Laing, RD (1960) *The Divided Self*. London: Tavistock.

Laing, RD (1965a) *The Divided Self*. Harmondsworth: Penguin.

Laing, RD (1965b) Mystification, confusion and conflict. In I Boszormenyinagi & JL Framo (Eds.) *Intensive Family Therapy: Theoretical and practical aspects*. New York: Harper and Row.

Laing, RD (1966) Ritualization and abnormal behaviour. Philosophical transactions of the Royal Society of London. Series B, *Biological Sciences, 251*(772), 331–5.

Laing, RD (1967) *The Politics of Experience and the Bird of Paradise*. Harmondsworth: Penguin.

Laing, RD (1968) The obvious. In D Cooper (Ed.) *The Dialectics of Liberation* (pp. 13–33). Harmondsworth: Penguin.

Laing, RD (1970) *Knots*. London: Tavistock.

Laing, RD (1971) *The Politics of the Family and Other Essays*. London: Tavistock.

Laing, RD (1972) Metanoia: some experiences at Kingsley Hall, London 1968. In HW Ruitenbeek (Ed.) *Going Crazy: The radical therapy of RD Laing and others* (pp. 11–21). New York: Bantam Books.

Laing, RD (1975) What is the Philadelphia Association? Lecture 11 December 1975. Special Collections department. University Glasgow Library, MS Laing, A78. Glasgow.

Laing, RD (1976) *The Facts of Life*. London: Allen Lane.

Laing, RD (1977) *Asylum*. London: Leaflet of the Philadelphia Association.

Laing, RD (1982) What's the matter with mind? In S Kumar (Ed.) *The Schumacher Lectures* (pp. 1–27). London: Abacus.

Laing, RD (1983) *The Voice of Experience*. Harmondsworth: Penguin.

Laing, RD (1984a) The Tao of Therapy, RD Laing Collection, Special Collections

Department. University Glasgow Library, MS Laing, A338. Soul-making. Psyche as a leading figure in his vision of health.

Laing, RD (1984b) CHIOS interview, RD Laing Collection, Special Collections Department. University Glasgow Library, MS Laing, L 157.

Laing, RD (1985a) *Wisdom, Madness & Folly.* London: Macmillan.

Laing, RD (1985b) The innocence of vision – review of 'Psychoanalysis and Beyond' C Rycroft. *New Scientist,* 28 November, *108*(1484), 56.

Laing, RD (1985c) What is asylum? In R Terrington (Ed.) *Towards a Whole Society: Collected papers on aspects of mental health* (pp. 35–8). London: Richmond Fellowship Press.

Laing, RD (1987a) The use of existential phenomenology in psychotherapy. In J Zeig (Ed.) *The Evolution of Psychotherapy.* (pp. 203–9) New York: Brunner/ Mazel. Also available at http://laingsociety.org/colloquia/psychotherapy/ evolofpsych.htm#cit Last accessed September 2013.

Laing, RD (1987b) Laing's understanding of interpersonal experience. In RL Gregory (Ed.) *The Oxford Companion to the Mind* (pp. 417–18). Oxford: Oxford University Press.

Laing, RD (1987c) Hatred of health. *Journal of Contemplative Psychotherapy, IV,* 77–86.

Laing, RD (1989) *Lies of Love.* Unpublished manuscript. Special Collections Department, Glasgow University Library, RD Laing Collection, A 326 – Lies of Love and Love of Lies, Version 8/1988.

Laing, RD (1990) Foreword. In RW Firestone, *Compassionate Child-Rearing.* New York: Insight Books.

Laing, RD & Cooper, D (1964) *Reason and Violence.* London: Tavistock.

Laing, RD & Esterson, A (1964) *Sanity, Madness and the Family.* London: Tavistock.

Laing, RD & Esterson, A (1970) *Sanity, Madness and the Family* (2nd ed). Harmondsworth: Penguin.

Laing, RD, Phillipson, H & Lee, AR (1966) *Interpersonal Perception.* London: Tavistock.

Lambert, MJ & Ogles, BM (2004) The efficacy and effectiveness of psychotherapy. In MJ Lambert (Ed.) *Bergin and Garfield's Handbook of Psychotherapy and Behavior Change* (5th ed). New York: John Wiley & Sons.

Langer, SK (1942) *Philosophy in a New Key.* London: Harvard University Press.

Lantz, S (2004) Sex work and study: The new demands facing young people and their implications for health and well being. *Traffic, 3.*

Larsson, P (2012) Psychologist suicide: Practising what we preach. *The Psychologist 25*(7), 550–2.

Lehmann, P (Ed.) (2002) *Coming Off Psychiatric Drugs. Successful withdrawal from neuroleptics, antidepressants, lithium, carbamazepine and tranquillizers.* Berlin: Peter Lehman Publishing.

Lem, S (2003) *Solaris.* London: Faber and Faber.

Levi, P (1989) *The Drowned and the Saved*. London: Abacus.

Lévi-Strauss, C (2011) *L'Anthropologie Face aux Problèmes du Monde Moderne*. Paris: Seuil.

Li, T & Fung, LL (2013) How negative interactions affect relationship satisfaction: The paradoxical short-term and long-term effects of commitment. *Social Psychological and Personality Science, 4,* 274–81.

Linney, YM & Peters, ER (2007) The psychological processes underlying symptoms of thought interference in psychosis. *Behaviour Research and Therapy,* 45(11), 2726–41.

Littlewood, R & Lipsedge, M (1997) *Aliens and Alienists. Ethnic minorities and psychiatry*. London: Routledge.

Liu, JH & Hilton, DJ (2005) How the past weighs on the present: Social representations of history and their role in identity politics. *British Journal of Social Psychology, 44,* 537–56.

Lodge, D (1996) *Therapy*. London: Penguin Books.

Lomas, P (2003) Telling it like it is. In L King & R Randall (Eds.) *The Future of Psychoanalytic Psychotherapy* (pp. 179–91). London: Whurr Publishers.

Loos, H (2010) Der Januskopf der Psychiatrie. In K Behnke & J Fuchs (Ed.) *Zersetzung der Seele* (pp. 228–41). Hamburg: Rotbuch Verlag.

Lovelock, J (2008) *Gaia. A new look at life on Earth*. Oxford: Oxford University Press.

MacLeod, K (2013) Other worlds are possible: Science fiction authors roundtable. *Red Pepper, 190,* 18–21.

Magolda, PM (2000) The campus tour ritual: Exploring community discourses in higher education. *Anthropology and Education Quarterly, 31*(1), 24–36.

Mahrer, AR (2004) *Theories of Truth, Models of Usefulness*. London: Whurr.

Malcolm, J (1997) *Psychoanalysis: The impossible profession*. London: Granta Books.

Malone, D (2010) *The Debt Generation*. Lancaster: Level Press.

Mandela, N (1994) *Long Walk to Freedom*. London: Little, Brown and Company.

Manning, K (2000) *Rituals, Ceremonies and Cultural Meaning in Higher Education*. Westport, CT: Bergin & Garvey.

Marks, DF, Murray, M, Evans, B & Estacio, EV (2011) *Health Psychology* (3rd ed). London: Sage. (First published 2000).

Marx, K (2006) *The 18th Brumaire of Louis Bonaparte*. Rockville, MD: Wildside Press. (First published 1852).

Marx, K & Engels, F (1975) *Manifesto of the Communist Party*. Beijing: Foreign Language Press. (First published 1888).

Masson, JM (2003) *The Assault on Truth. Freud's suppression of the seduction theory*. New York: Ballantine Books.

Mattanza, G, Meier, I & Schlegel, M (Hrg.) (2006) *Seele und Forschung – Ein Brückenschlag in der Psychotherapie*. Basel: Karger.

McNair, B (2002) *Striptease Culture: Sex, media and the democratization of desire*. London: Routledge.

Mendel, R, Hamann, J, Traut-Mattausch, E, Bühner, M, Kissling, W & Frey, D (2010) What would you do if you were me, doctor? Randomised trial of psychiatrists' personal v. professional perspectives on treatment recommendations. *The British Journal of Psychiatry, 197*, 441–7.

Menzies-Lyth, I (1960) Social systems as a defence against anxiety. An empirical study of the nursing service of a general hospital. *Human Relations, 13*, 95–121.

Merleau-Ponty, M (1964) *The Primacy of Perception*. Evanston, IL: Northwestern University Press.

Mezan, P (1972) After Freud and Jung, now comes RD Laing. *Esquire, 77*, 1 January 1972.

Miles, J & Shevlin, M (2003) Navigating spaghetti junction. *The Psychologist, 16*(12), 639–41.

Milgram, S (1974) *Obedience to Authority*. London: Tavistock.

Miller, IS (2013) *Beckett and Bion: The (im)patient voice in psychotherapy and literature*. London: Karnac.

Miller, GA (1973) *Psychology: The science of mental life*. Harmondsworth: Pelican Books.

Milner, M (1987) *The Suppressed Madness of Sane Men*. London: Tavistock.

Milner, M (1988) *The Hands of the Living God*. London: Virago.

Minco, M (1991) *Bitter Herbs: The vivid memories of a fugitive Jewish girl in Nazi-occupied Holland*. London: Penguin.

Mitchell, J (2000) *Psychoanalysis and Feminism*. New York: Basic Books.

Molvaer, J, Hantzi, A & Papadatos, Y (1992) Psychotic patients' attributions for mental illness. *British Journal of Clinical Psychology, 31*, 210–12.

Morris, SC (2003) *Life's Solution*. Cambridge: Cambridge University Press.

Morrison, D & Henkel, R (Eds.) (1970) *The Significance Test Controversy*. Chicago: Aldine Publishing Company.

Moscovici, S & Duveen, G (Eds.) (2000) *Social Representations: Explorations in social psychology*. Cambridge: Polity.

Moscovici, S & Markova, I (2006) *The Making of Modern Social Psychology: The hidden story of how an international social science was created*. Cambridge: Polity.

Mosher, LR & Burti, L (1989) *Community Mental Health: Principles and practice*. New York: WW Norton & Co.

Mosher, LR, Hendrix, V & Fort, DC (2004) *Soteria: Through madness to deliverance*. Bloomington, IN: Xlibris.

Mullan, B (1988) *Are Mothers Really Necessary?* London: Boxtree Ltd.

Mullan, B (1995) *Mad to be Normal: Conversations with RD Laing*. London: Free Association Books.

Mullan, B (Ed.) (1996) *Therapists on Therapy*. London: Free Association Books.

Mullan, B (Ed.) (1997) *RD Laing: Creative destroyer*. London: Cassel.

Narby, J & Huxley, F (2004) *Shamans Through Time*. New York: Penguin.

National Committee of Inquiry into Higher Education (1997) https://bei.leeds. ac.uk/Partners/NCIHE/ Last accessed 5 March 2009.

Neisser, U (1976) *Cognition and Reality: Principles and implication of cognitive psychology*. San Francisco: WH Freeman and Co.

Newman, A (1995) *Non-compliance in Winnicott's Words*. London: Free Association Books.

Newman, P (2012) Novak Djokovic: Patriot's game. *The Independent*, 25 May 2012. http://www.independent.co.uk/news/people/profiles/novak-djokovic-patriots-game-7786080.html Last accessed May 2012.

Nikcevic, AV, Kramolisova-Advani, J & Spada, MM (2007) Early childhood experiences and current emotional distress: What do they tell us about aspiring psychologists? *The Journal of Psychology, 141*(1), 25–34.

Nolan, C (2008) *The Dark Knight*. Warner Bros.

Oakley, C (2007) *Football Delirium*. London: Karnac.

Oakley, CA (1967) *The Second City*. Glasgow: Blackie & Son.

O'Brien, B (2011) *Operators and Things: The Inner life of a schizophrenic*. Los Angeles, CA: Silver Birch Press.

O'Brien, E (2012) *Country Girl: A memoir*. London: Faber and Faber.

Oring, E (1992) *Jokes and Their Relations*. Lexington, KT: The University Press of Kentucky.

Ørner, RJ (2011) Why no mention of Brevik? Letters. *The Psychologist, 24*(11), 797.

Ornstein, RE (1972) *The Psychology of Consciousness*. San Francisco: WH Freeman.

Orwell, G (1977) *Nineteen Eighty-Four*. Harmondsworth: Penguin. (First published 1954).

Parker, I (1989) *The Crisis in Modern Social Psychology – and How to End It*. London: Routledge.

Parker, I (2007) *Revolution in Psychology: Alienation to emancipation*. London: Pluto Press.

Parker, I (2013) Managing neoliberalism and the strong state in higher education: Psychology today. *Qualitative Research in Psychology*. DOI: 10.1080/14780887.2013.872214

Partridge, E (1966) *Origins*. London: Routledge & Kegan Paul.

Patel, N (2007) Torture, psychology and the 'war on terror': A human rights framework. In R Roberts (Ed.) *Just War: Psychology and terrorism* (pp. 74–108). Ross-on-Wye: PCCS Books.

Payne, P (1981) *Martial Arts: The spiritual dimension*. London: Thames and Hudson.

Pearson, J (Ed.) (2004) *The Analyst of the Imagination: The life and work of Charles Rycroft*. London: Karnac.

Piesing, M (2013) *The Diagnostic and Statistical Manual of Mental Disorders has been updated but should we beware this manual's diagnosis? The Independent.* 8 May 2013. http://www.independent.co.uk/life-style/health-and-families/features/the-diagnostic-and-statistical-manual-of-mental-disorders-has-been-updated-but-should-we-beware-this-manuals-diagnosis-8608342.html Last accessed May 2013.

Pinker, S (2011) *The Better Angels of Our Nature.* London: Allen Lane.

Plato (1978) *The Collected Dialogues, Including the Letters.* E Hamilton & H Cairns (Eds.) Princeton, NJ: Princeton University Press.

Poole, R (1972) *Towards Deep Subjectivity.* London: Allan Lane.

Poole, R (1982) *The Unknown Virginia Woolf.* Atlantic Highlands, NJ: Humanities Press.

Poole, R (1993) *Kierkegaard – The Indirect Communication.* Charlottesville: University Press of Virgina.

Poole, R (2005) RD Laing's reading of Kierkegaard. In S Raschid (Ed.) *RD Laing: Contemporary perspectives* (pp. 100–11). London: Free Association Books.

Rabinow, P (Ed.) (1991) *The Foucault Reader.* London: Penguin.

Ramet, SP (2002) Can a society be sick? The case of Serbia. *Journal of Human Rights, 1*(4), 615–20.

Ramet, SP (2007a) The denial syndrome and its consequences: Serbian political culture since 2000. *Communist and Post-Communist Studies, 40,* 41–58.

Ramet, SP (2007b) Martyr in his own mind: The trial and tribulations of Slobodan Milošević. *Totalitarian Movements and Political Religions, 5*(1), 112–38.

Ramet, SP (2012) The ICTY – controversies, successes, failures, lessons. *Southeastern Europe, 36,* 1–9.

Raschid, S (Ed.) (2005) *RD Laing: Contemporary Perspectives.* London: Free Association Books.

Ratcliffe, R (2013) Students: We can't get no satisfaction. *The Guardian.* http://www.guardian.co.uk/education/2013/jul/08/students-fees-consumer-power Last accessed July 2013.

Rayner, E (1991) *The Independent Mind in British Psychoanalysis.* London: Free Association Books.

Read, J (2013) Childhood adversity and psychosis. From heresy to certainty. In J Read & J Dillon (Eds.) *Models of Madness* (pp. 249–57). London: Routledge.

Read, J & Dillon, J (Eds.) (2013) *Models of Madness. Psychological, social and biological approaches to psychosis* (2nd ed). London: Routledge.

Reicher, SD & Haslam, SA (2011) The shock of the old. *The Psychologist, 24*(9), 650–2.

Richards, G (1994) The social contexts of psychology. *The Psychologist, 7*(10), 456–7.

Richards, G (2002) *Putting Psychology in its Place* (2nd ed). London: Routledge.

Rickman, HP (2004) *The Riddle of the Sphinx – Interpreting the human world.* Madison, NJ: Fairleigh Dickinson University Press.

Ritchie, SJ, Wiseman, R, & French, CC (2012) Replication, replication, replication. *The Psychologist, 25*(5), 346–7.

Robben, AC (2012) The politics of truth and emotion among victims and perpetrators of violence. In AC Robben & JA Sluka (Ed.) *Ethnographic Fieldwork* (pp. 175–90). Chichester: Wiley & Blackwell.

Robben, AC & Sluka, JA (Ed.) (2012) *Ethnographic Fieldwork: An anthropological reader.* Chichester: Wiley & Blackwell.

Roberts, R (1981) Personal constructs and dreaming. *New Forum: Journal of the Psychology and Psychotherapy Association, 7*(3), 60–2.

Roberts, R (1990) Psychiatry, science and mental health. *Critical Public Health, 4,* 15–21.

Roberts, R (2005) Problems in replicating multivariate models in quantitative research. *Health Psychology Update, 14*(3), 10–16.

Roberts, R (Ed.) (2007) *Just War: Psychology and terrorism.* Ross-on-Wye: PCCS Books.

Roberts, R (2007) Power illusion and control: Families, states and conflict. In R Roberts (Ed.) *Just War: Psychology and terrorism* (pp. 160–9). Ross-on-Wye: PCCS Books.

Roberts, R (2010) Researching students in sex work: Market values and academic freedom. *Journal of Critical Psychology, Counselling and Psychotherapy, 10*(1), 12–17.

Roberts, R (2011a) Liberation by illusion: Image and reality in the construction of security. *Democracy and Security in South-Eastern Europe, 2*(8/9), 46–9.

Roberts, R (2011b) *Real to Reel. Psychiatry at the cinema.* Ross-on-Wye: PCCS Books.

Roberts, R (2013a) Methodological shortcomings of biological research. *The Psychologist, 26*(7), 468.

Roberts, R (2013b) Student sex work project. Guest Blog 10 July 2013. http://www.thestudentsexworkproject.co.uk/?p=657 Last accessed July 2013.

Roberts, R, Bećirević, E & Paul, S (2011) Truth and denial: Psychological perspectives on reconciliation in Bosnia. In RJ Elford (Ed.) *Just Reconciliation: The practice and morality of making peace* (pp. 129–46). New International Studies in Applied Ethics, Vol. 6. Oxford: Peter Lang.

Roberts, R, Bergström, S & La Rooy, D (2007a) Commentary: UK students and sex work: Current knowledge and research issues. *Journal of Community and Applied Social Psychology, 17,* 141–6.

Roberts, R, Bergström, S & La Rooy, D (2007b) Sex work and students: An exploratory study. *Journal of Further and Higher Education 31*(4), 323–34.

Roberts, R & Fallowfield, LJ (1990a) Who are the cancer counsellors? *Nursing Times, 86*(36), 32–4.

Roberts, R & Fallowfield, LJ (1990b) The goals of cancer counsellors. *Counselling, 1*(3), 88–91.

Roberts, R, Golding, J, Towell, T, Reid, S, Woodford, S, Vetere, A & Weinreb, I (2000) Mental and physical health in students: The role of economic circumstances. *British Journal of Health Psychology, 5*(3), 289–97.

Roberts, R, Jones, A & Sanders, T (2013) The relationship between sex work and students in the UK: Providers and purchasers. *Sex Education: Sexuality, Society and Learning, 13*(3), 349–63.

Roberts, R, O'Connor, TG, Dunn, J, Golding, J and the ALSPAC study team (2004) The effects of child sexual abuse in later family life; mental health, parenting and adjustment of offspring. *Child Abuse & Neglect, 28*(5), 525–45.

Roberts, R, Sanders, T, Smith, D & Myers, E (2010) Participation in sex work: Students' views. *Sex Education, 10*(3), 145–56.

Roethke, T (2005) *Selected Poems.* New York: Library of America.

Rohde, D (1998) *Endgame. The betrayal and fall of Srebrenica, Europe's worst massacre since World War II.* New York: Farrar, Straus and Giroux.

Ronson, J (2011) *The Psychopath Test.* London: Picador.

Rose, H & Rose, S (2001) *Alas Poor Darwin. Arguments against evolutionary psychology.* London: Vintage.

Rose, S, Lewontin, RC & Kamin, LJ (1984) *Not in Our Genes.* Harmondsworth: Penguin.

Rosenberg, JL (1973) *Total Orgasm.* New York: Random House.

Rosenberg, JL & Kitaen-Morse, B (1996) *The Intimate Couple.* Atlanta, GA: Turner Publications.

Rosenberg, JL, Rand, M & Asay, D (1985) *Body, Self & Soul-sustaining Integration.* Atlanta, GA: Humanics Ltd.

Rosenhan, D (1969) Some origins of concern for others. In P Mussen, J Langer & M Covington (Eds.) *Trends and Issues in Developmental Psychology.* New York: Holt, Rinehart and Wintgon.

Rosenthal, R (1979) The file drawer problem and tolerance for null results. *Psychological Bulletin, 86*(3), 638–41.

Rushforth, W (1981) *Something Is Happening: Spiritual awareness and depth psychology in the new age.* London: Gateway Books.

Rushforth, W (1984) *Ten Decades of Happenings.* London: Gateway Books.

Russell, B (1967) *Why I Am Not a Christian.* London: George Allen & Unwin.

Russell, D (2013) *The Life and Ideas of James Hillman.* Vol. I. New York: Helios Press.

Rycroft, C (1972) *A Critical Dictionary of Psychoanalysis.* Harmondsworth: Penguin.

Rycroft, C (1991) *Viewpoints.* London: Hogarth Press.

Sacks, O (2007) *Musicophilia.* London: Picador.

Sagar, K (2000) *The Laughter of Foxes: A study of Ted Hughes.* Liverpool: Liverpool University Press.

Saks, ER (2007) *The Center Cannot Hold: My journey through madness.* New York: Hyperion.

Sartre, J-P (2009) *Critique of Dialectical Reason* (2nd ed). London: Verso.

Schacht, TE (1985) DSM-III and the politics of truth. *American Psychologist, 40*(5), 513–21.

Schekman, R (2013) How journals like *Nature, Cell* and *Science* are damaging science. *The Independent.* 9 December 2013. http://www.theguardian. com/commentisfree/2013/dec/09/how-journals-nature-science-cell-damage-science Last accessed December 2013.

Scheurer, H (1940) *Mit Eisernem Willen- Ein Missionsleben unter den Indianerstämmen Guyana.* Basel: Basler Missions Buchhandlung.

Scheurer, H (1941) *Lars Olsen Skrefsrud – Der Apostel des Santalvolkes.* Basel: Basler Missions Buchhandlung.

Scheurer, H (1942) *Ein Brand aus dem Feuer. Eine Erzählung aus China. Missionshefte, Nr. 18.* Basel: Basler Missions Buchhandlung.

Scheurer-Flückiger, R (1941) *Unsichtbare Mauern-Autobiographie.* Basel: Basler Missions Buchhandlung.

Scheurer-Flückiger, R (1944) Die Weihnachtsglocken von Sinfung. In *Freude aus aller Welt* (pp. 15–24). Basel: Basler Missions Buchhandlung.

Schorstein, J (1963) The metaphysics of the atom bomb. *The Philosophical Journal, 1*(1), 33–46.

Schulthess, P & Itten, T (2008) Radical changes in psychotherapy – The present Swiss scene. *International Journal of Psychotherapy, 12(3),* 62–6.

Schützenberger, AA (2004) *The Ancestor Syndrome: Transgenerational psychotherapy and the hidden links in the family tree.* London: Routledge.

Scruton, R (1985) *Thinkers of the New Left.* Harlow: Longman Group.

Seabrook, J (1990) *The Myth of the Market.* Hartland Bideford: Green Books.

Sedgwick, P (1982) *Psychopolitics.* London: Pluto Press.

Sedgman, J (2004) Sex work more attractive option for students. *The World Today,* 2 April 2004.

Seery, MD (2011) Resilience. A silver lining to experiencing adverse life events? *Current Directions in Psychological Science, 20,* 390–4.

Seery, MD, Leo, RJ, Lupien, SP, Kondrak, CL & Almonte, JL (2013) An upside to adversity? Moderate cumulative lifetime adversity is associated with resilient responses in the face of controlled stressors. *Psychological Science, 24*(7), 1181–9.

Segal, L (Ed.) (1983) *What Is to Be Done about the Family?* London: Penguin.

Segal, L (1999) *Why Feminism? Gender, psychology, politics.* London: Polity Press.

Segal, L (2007) *Making Trouble: Life and politics.* London: Serpent's Tale.

Semyon, M (1995) In B Mullan (Ed.) *RD Laing: Creative destroyer* (pp. 184–209). London: Cassell.

Sennett, R (2011) From 'disturbing memories'. In JK Olick, V Vinitzky-Seroussi & D Levy (Eds.) *The Collective Memory Reader* (pp. 283–6). New York: Oxford University Press.

Shakespeare, W (1992) *Hamlet.* Ware: Wordsworth Classics.

Sheldrake, R (1999) How widely is blind assessment used in scientific research? *Alternative Therapies, 5,* 88–91.

Sheldrake, R (2012) *The Science Delusion*. London: Coronet.

Shelley, PB & Shelley, MW (1839) *The Poetical Works of Percy Bysshe Shelley*. London: Edward Moxon.

Shepherd, M, Evans, C, Cobb, S & Ghossain, D (2012) Does therapy make things worse? *Clinical Psychology Forum, 233*, 8–12.

Shore, C & Wright, S (1999) Adult culture and anthropology: Neo-liberalism in British higher education. *Journal of the Royal Anthropological Institute (N-S), 5*, 557–75.

Showalter, E (1987) *The Female Malady*. London: Virago Press.

Siegler, M, Osmond, H & Mann, H (1972) Laing's models of madness. In R Boyers & R Orrill (Eds.) *Laing and Anti-psychiatry* (pp. 99–122). Harmondsworth: Penguin.

Smail, D (2005) *Power, Interest and Psychology*. Ross-on-Wye: PCCS Books.

Smith, S (2001) Is postpsychiatry so radical? *Electronic British Medical Journal*. (*bmj.com*) Rapid responses for Bracken and Thomas, 322(7288), 724–7.

Snyder, S (1976) *Medical World News*, 17 May, 24.

Sprenger, J & Kramer, H (1486) *Malleus Maleficarum* (M Summers, Trans. with introduction, bibliography, and notes also by M Summers). London: Pushkin Press, 1948.

Stanley, N (1988) *Being Ourselves for You: The global display of cultures*. London: Middlesex University Press.

Szasz, T (1988) *The Ethics of Psychoanalysis: The theory and method of autonomous psychotherapy*. Syracuse: Syracuse University Press. (First published 1965).

Szasz, T (1997) *The Manufacture of Madness*. New York: Syracuse University Press.

Szasz, T (2002) *The Meaning of Mind: Language, morality and neuroscience*. New York: Syracuse University Press.

Szasz, T (2006) *My Madness Saved Me: The madness and marriage of Virginia Woolf*. New Brunswick, NJ: Transaction Publishers.

Szasz, T (2007) *Coercion as Cure: A critical history of psychiatry*. London: Transaction Publishers.

Szasz, T (2009) *Anti-psychiatry Quackery Squared*. Syracuse, NY: Syracuse University Press.

Szasz, S. (2010) *Psychiatry: The science of lies*. Syracuse, NY: Syracuse University Press.

Thompson, MJ (2012) 'A road less travelled': The dark side of RD Laing's conception of authenticity. *Psychotherapy in Australia, 18*(2), 20–9.

Thropp, EA (2009) *Psychotherapy, American Culture, and Social Policy – Immoral Individualism*. New York: Palgrave Macmillan.

Tombs, S (2012) State–corporate symbiosis in the production of crime and harm. *State crime 1.2*, 170–95.

Totton, N (2012) *Not a Tame Lion: Writings on therapy in its social and political context*. Ross-on-Wye: PCCS Books.

Tschuschke, V, Crameri, A, Koemeda, M, Schultess, P, Von Wyl, A & Weber, R (2010) Fundamental reflections on psychotherapy research and initial results of the naturalistic psychotherapy study on outpatient treatment in Switzerland (PAP-S). *International Journal of Psychotherapy, 14*(3), 23–35.

Tucker, A (2012) Bully U. Central planning and higher education. *The Independent Review, 17*(1), 99–119.

UCU (2008) RAE 2008. http://www.ucu.org.uk/index.cfm?articleid=1442 Last accessed 7 March 2009.

Ussher, J (1991) *Women's Madness: Misogyny or mental illness?* London: Harvester.

Ussher, J (2011) *The Madness of Women.* London: Routledge.

Viding, E & Frith, U (2013) Debate on *DSM-5*: A false dichotomy? *The Psychologist, 26*(6), 382–3.

Vulliamy, E (2012) *The War is Dead, Long Live the War. Bosnia: The reckoning.* London: The Bodley Head.

Watt, C & Nagtegall, M (2004) Reporting of blind methods: An interdisciplinary survey. *Journal of the Society for Psychical Research, 68,* 105–14.

Weitzer, R (Ed.) (2000) *Sex for Sale: Prostitution, pornography and the sex industry.* London: Routledge.

Welzer, H (2005) Grandpa wasn't a Nazi: The Holocaust in German family remembrance. *International Perspectives, 54* (B Cooper, Trans.). New York: American Jewish Committee.

Whitaker, M (2001) Actuality at school. BBC Radio 4, 24 June 2001.

White, H (2010) Beneath statistical rhetoric: The social representations of statistics in psychology research. Unpublished dissertation. Kingston University.

Williams, R (2008) *Dostoevsky: Language, faith and fiction.* London: Continuum.

Wilson, RA (2001) *The Politics of Truth and Reconciliation in South Africa.* Cambridge: CUP.

Winnicott, DW (1980) *The Piggle.* Harmondsworth: Penguin Books.

Winters, JA (2011) *Oligarchy.* New York: Cambridge University Press.

Wittgenstein, L (1976) *Tractatus Logico-Philosophicus [Logisch-philosophische Abhandlung].* Frankfurt aM: Suhrkamp.

Young, C (2012) (Body) Psychotherapy is a 'Craft', not a 'Science'. In C Young (Ed.) *About the Science of Body Psychotherapy* (pp. 185–227). Stow: Body Psychotherapy Publications.

Young, C, Szyszkowitz, T, Oudijk, R, Schulthess, P & Stabingis, A (2013) The EAP Project to establish the professional competencies of a European psychotherapist. *International Journal of Psychotherapy, 17*(2), 39–57.

Name Index

CPSIA information can be obtained at www.ICGtesting.com
Printed in the USA
LVOW04s1808260415

436102LV00007B/12/P